FIXING THE IMAGE

FIXING THE IMAGE

ULTRASOUND AND THE VISUALITY OF
CARE IN PHNOM PENH

Jenna Grant

UNIVERSITY OF WASHINGTON PRESS

Seattle

Fixing the Image was made possible in part by a grant from the Association for Asian Studies First Book Subvention Program.

Additional support was provided by the McLellan Endowment, established through the generosity of Martha McCleary McLellan and Mary McLellan Williams.

Composed in Warnock Pro, typeface designed by Robert Slimbach

UNIVERSITY OF WASHINGTON PRESS
uwapress.uw.edu

LIBRARY OF CONGRESS CATALOGING-IN-PUBLICATION DATA
Names: Grant, Jenna, author.
Title: Fixing the image : ultrasound and the visuality of care in Phnom Penh / Jenna Grant.
Description: Seattle : University of Washington Press, [2022] | Includes bibliographical references and index.
Identifiers: LCCN 2021058925 (print) | LCCN 2021058926 (ebook) | ISBN 9780295750606 (hardcover) | ISBN 9780295750613 (paperback) | ISBN 9780295750620 (ebook)
Subjects: LCSH: Medical anthropology—Cambodia—Phnom Penh. | Ultrasonic imaging—Social aspects—Cambodia—Phnom Penh. | Medical personnel and patient—Social aspects—Cambodia—Phnom Penh. | Medical technology—Cambodia—Phnom Penh—Philosophy.
Classification: LCC GN296.5.C16 G73 2022 (print) | LCC GN296.5.C16 (ebook) | DDC 306.4/61—dc23/eng/20211210
LC record available at https://lccn.loc.gov/2021058925
LC ebook record available at https://lccn.loc.gov/2021058926

Contents

Acknowledgments

My mother's death in November 2019 greatly affected me and thus this book. How does one finish a manuscript when one's core source of love and support is suddenly, bewilderingly gone? In mourning and struggle. My mom, JoAnn, inspired me and many others through her work as a nurse, her generosity and loyalty to friends, her straight talk, her cooking, her love of family, and the dignity with which she faced the inevitable advance of multiple sclerosis in the later years of her life. I dedicate this book to her and to my father, Igor, in deep gratitude for everything. For everything.

At the other end of this project was the birth of my son, Boris, in 2009, during fieldwork in Phnom Penh. He is the light of my life. I marvel at his creative and kind spirit and openness to the world. This book is also dedicated to you, sweet thing; thank you for showing me the wonder and pleasure of *moel knong*, seeing inside.

The research and writing for this book took a long period of time, almost ten years, and spanned three continents. So these acknowledgments will also be long and yet still not comprehensive. I am sorry to those whom I left out, but you know you matter.

My research in Cambodia depended upon the thinking, goodwill, and efforts of many people. I thank the doctors, nurses, midwives, secretaries, orderlies, and students with whom I interacted on a regular basis at Russian and Maternal Hospitals and Sorphea VIP in Phnom Penh. I do not name you personally to preserve anonymity, but I thank you for ongoing conversations about imaging, health care, and historical experience and for tolerating my presence and questions under difficult working conditions. I thank the patients and family members whose openness and curiosity, even in the face of uncertainty, hardship, or pain, inspired and kept me accountable in this work. I thank Dr. Say Seng Ly, Dr. Chan Dara, Dr. Koum Kanal, and Dr. Pech Sothy for permitting me to conduct research at their institutions and the

Ministry of Health National Ethics Committee for Health Research for ethics approval.

After Neary Hean Sokhom came on board, the work really took off. I thank her for sticking with this rather strange project; for sharing ideas about medicine and education; and for translations linguistic, professional, and pop cultural. I am also grateful to Neary's father, mother, and husband for dinners and conversations about research, hospitals, parenting, and so many other things, including the loan of a white hospital coat. Loak kru Y Socheat's Khmer lessons opened up everyday life, and his wry humor and encouragement to study Buddhist healing was important to this project. I thank Loak kru Frank for teaching, support, and patience over the years. Thanks also to my other Khmer teachers in the United States and Cambodia: Pho Sophavy, Chhany Sak-Humphry, Khun Sokhary, Panh Hannah, Kheang Leang, and Bun Thet. Thank you, Ulvy, for research assistance, including patient scanning of documents.

During fieldwork, I looked forward to afternoons, when I would read documents at the National Archives of Cambodia (NAC) and watch films at the Bophana Audiovisual Resource Center. Staff at these remarkable institutions show great knowledge of and care for their materials, and I am grateful for their expertise and support. The death of Y Dari, director of NAC, in 2021, is a tremendous loss, especially for Cambodia studies. I am lucky to be able to continue to work with Sopheap Chea and the brilliant archivists at the Bophana Center. I am also thankful to the librarians at the Archives de l'institut de médecine tropicale du service de santé des armées (AIMTSSA) and librarians and staff at the Center for Khmer Studies for their assistance.

For their work in and about Cambodia, I am grateful to Anida Yoeu Ali, Anti-Archive, Sokhieng Au, Elizabeth Becker, Ruth Bottomley, Frédéric Bourdier, Alison Carter, Sopheap Chea, Rethy Chhem, Erik W. Davis, Sambath Eat, Penny Edwards, Lindsay French, Pascale Hancart-Petitet, Anne Hansen, Tracy Harachi, Lynn Heller, Tom Heller, Siti Keo, Viet Lê, Judy Ledgerwood, Khathaleeya Liamdee, Jim LoGerfo, Boreth Ly, John Marston, Sylvia Nam, Astrid Norén-Nilsson, Jonathan Padwe, Rithy Panh, Alberto Pérez Pereiro, Andy Roberts, Jenne Roberts, Amy Sanford, Sophearith Siyonn, Emiko Stock, Farrah Tek, Ashley Thompson, Kanitha Tith, Krisna Uk, Kheang Un, Leang Un, Hubert Vesselle, and Luoth Yin. Alice Smith's knowledge, connections, encouragement, and friendship have been invaluable to me. Thank you, Dr. Theavy, staff, and volunteers at Operation Smile Cambodia and Lep Ke, Sarath, Kimas, and Yusoh. I miss our visits.

This book draws on research and writing conducted while in graduate school at the University of Iowa. During that time and after, Erica Prussing has mentored me with intellectual sharpness, pragmatic wisdom, and kindness. I cannot thank her enough. I thank my dissertation committee for believing in this project through its ups and downs and asking hard questions in order to strengthen it: Laurie Graham, Virginia Dominguez, Ellen Lewin, David Depew, and Judy Ledgerwood. Intellectual communities in anthropology, cinema, and comparative literature and the local music and art scene sustained me during those years and beyond, especially Olga Balema, Sushmita Banerji, Alexis Bravos, Tomi Castle, Matthew Conn, Lauren Cook, Ofer Eliaz, Michele Hanks, Katy Hoffer, Lexi Matza, Orion Meyer, John Olson, Sarah Ono, Claudia Pummer, Shawn Reed, Louis-Georges Schwartz, and Andy Spore.

I lived in Amsterdam from 2011 to 2015 while writing my dissertation and holding a postdoc and was nourished by a vibrant intellectual community and dear friends. Amade M'charek and Janus Oomen kindly welcomed me as an affiliate to the Health, Care and the Body program at the University of Amsterdam, giving a wayward graduate student a home. I was lucky to be a "fluid member" of the Eating Bodies group, led by Annemarie Mol, which opened to me a rich scene of talks, workshops, and walking seminars. For their intellectual community, I thank Uli Beisel, Filippo Bertoni, René Gerrets, Tjitske Holtrop, Anna Mann, Julien McHardy, Amade M'charek, Annemarie Mol, Eileen Moyer, Vinh-Kim Nguyen, Jeanette Pols, Jeltsje Stobbe, Else Vogel, and Emily Yates-Doerr. Being part of the beginning of *Medicine Anthropology Theory*, with Eileen Moyer, Vinh-Kim Nguyen, and Erin Martineau, was a privilege (and a lot of work!). My postdoc at the International Institute for Asian Studies (IIAS) in Leiden was a golden time to write and expand my understanding of Asian studies; thanks to Philippe Peycam and all of the staff at IIAS. Friends in Amsterdam were crucial for my soul and my thinking: Sara Kendall, Wouter Kleppe, Rebecca Sakoun, Carolyn Strauss, and, also in Phnom Penh and Bangkok, Andy Ianuzzi.

One of the privileges of writing a book is that the meandering drafts and messy ideas you share are grounds for co-thinking. I am blessed to have been able to think with Vivian Choi, Leslie Grant, Doreen Lee, Angela Reginato, and Emily Yates-Doerr over many years. Super abrazos to Sara Gonzalez, Radhika Govindrajan, and Linh Nguyen for being the best colleagues and co-conspirators. And though we are scattered, Shadow Anthropology forever! I could not have done this without you ladies. John Marston generously read the entire manuscript, a true gift, as did Claudia Castañeda, in the role of skilled editor. I am grateful to the following people whose comments on drafts of chapters and related articles shaped this book: Sareeta Amrute, Julia Cassaniti, Megan Carney, Rethy Chhem, Vivian Choi, Catelijne Coopmans,

Jean Dennison, Sara Gonzalez, Radhika Govindrajan, Danny Hoffman, Tjitske Holtrop, Celia Lowe, Anna Mann, Sylvia Nam, Rima Praspaliauskiene, Priti Ramamurthy, Josh Reid, Emiko Stock, Lynn Thomas, Marieke van Eijk, Kathy Woodward, and Emily Yates-Doerr.

I only found the power of writing and working groups well after grad school. The Indigenous studies writing group at the University of Washington (UW) was formative for me in my early years here. The Walter Chapin Simpson Center for the Humanities is a shining light on campus that fosters interdisciplinary conversation. Thank you, Kathy Woodward, for ongoing support and for counsel at a key moment in the book process, and Rachel Arteaga, Caitlin Palo, and staff at the center, for the work you do. I received generative feedback on parts of this manuscript as part of the Simpson Center First Book Fellowship (2021) and the Society of Scholars (2019–2020). I learned a lot from being part of "Humanistic Perspectives on Global Health Partnerships" (2016–2017), convened by Lynn Thomas, Johanna Crane, and Nora Kenworthy, and the "Humanitarianisms: Migrations and Care through the Global South" Sawyer Seminar (2020–2022), convened by Arzoo Osanloo and Cabeiri Robinson.

At UW, I have been in community with incredible colleagues, staff, and students. In anthropology, they are Sareeta Amrute, Ann Anagnost, Holly Barker, Laada Bilaniuk, Chris Chan, Rachel Chapman, Tess Chen, Bettina Shell Duncan, Sasha Duttchoudury, Michael Esveldt, Sven Haakanson, Danny Hoffman, Kat Liamdee, Celia Lowe, Michael Pérez, James Pfeiffer, Raphaëlle Rabanes, Dimas Romadhon, Hope St. John, Janelle Taylor, and Marieke van Eijk. I want to thank my chairs, Diane Kendall, Patricia Kramer, and Janelle Taylor, and deans, Judy Howard and George Lovell, for their support. I especially thank Patricia for granting me a course release after my mother's death, when I really needed it, and for guiding me through tenure. I appreciate John Cady, Michael Caputi, Jay Flaming, Diane Guerra, Morgan Hale, Haley Lee, and Catherine Zeigler for all they do to sustain the department.

The Southeast Asia Studies program is my second home. It is a pleasure to work closely with colleagues and students from across campus: Adrian Alarilla, Rick Bonus, Sambath Eat, Christoph Geibel, Judith Henchy, Celia Lowe, Linh Nguyen, Vince Rafael, Pauli Sandjaja, Vanna Song, Christina Sunardi, Bich-Ngoc Turner, Michael Walstrom, and Luoth Yin. Special thanks to Southeast Asia Center (SEAC) directors, first Laurie Sears and now Celia Lowe, for supporting my research and teaching.

Across campus, I am grateful to colleagues and students for the work they do, their openness to conversation, and their keen insight: Rawan Arar, Katie Bunn-Marcuse, Megan Finn, Elias Greendorfer, Tracy Harachi, Babita Joy,

Jim LoGerfo, David Ribes, Daniela Rosner, Maya Smith, Lynn Thomas, Philip Thurtle, Hubert Veselle, Supasai Vongkulbhisal, and Sasha Su-Ling Welland. Teaching and working with students, artists, and organizers in the Cambodian American community is one of the things that keeps me going. For their collaboration, creativity, and commitment, I thank Bunthay Cheam, Sopheakvatey Chey, Kunteang Som Haskins, Sameth Mell, Tess Ros, Thyda Ros, Ammara Touch, and Stephanie Ung. I am in awe of the work of the Khmer Community of Seattle King County (KCSKC). And one more Seattle shout out: much of the book was revised in 2018 and 2019 at Lighthouse Coffee, where I could get my fix, where it smelled like heaven, and where the rhythm of the roaster was a low-level, machinic chant.

Conversations over the years about anthropology, science and technology studies, or Southeast Asia have made their way into the book, though you may not recognize it. Thank you, Patricia Alvarez Astacio, Casper Bruun-Jensen, Jia-Ching Chen, Mona Damluji, Eli Elinoff, Susan Erikson, Tine Gammeltoft, Sarah Grant, Kat Gutierrez, Anne Hansen, Biff Keyes, Christopher Kortright, Justin McDaniel, Juno Salazar Parreñas, Charles Pearson, Natalie Porter, Jeff Schonberg, Nick Shapiro, Michelle Stewart, Alice Street, Noah Tamarkin, Allen Tran, Ayo Wahlberg, Trent Walker, and Eve Zucker. Thanks to Doreen Lee, Jonathan Padwe, Juno Salazar Parreñas, and Noah Tamarkin for conversations about the book process at crucial moments.

I have presented portions of this work at different talks and workshops and thank the organizers and audiences who provided generative comments on the work at Oregon State University, Washington State University, University of Oregon, Thammasat University, the History of Medicine in Southeast Asia (HOMSEA) conferences in Singapore and Vientiane, and "Framing Technology and Care in Asian Contexts" at the Asia Research Institute, National University of Singapore. Thanks especially to Laurence Monnais, Hans Pols, and Michele Thompson (HOMSEA), who mentored me through my first publication (!), and Catelijne Coopmans and Karen McNamara (formerly at National University of Singapore) for also serving as editors on papers that came from these conferences.

Funding for research and writing came from the Center for Khmer Studies Senior Fellowship; the Wenner-Gren Foundation Dissertation Fieldwork Grant; the University of Iowa Presidential Fellowship, Center for Asian and Pacific Studies Graduate Student Fellowship, and T. Anne Cleary International Dissertation Research Fellowship; and the International Institute for Asian Studies (IIAS) Fellowship. At UW, the Department of Anthropology, SEAC, and the Simpson Center have supported work on this book.

Portions of this book have been previously published: parts of chapters 1 and 2 were published in "Cambodian Pathology" in *Translating the Body: Medical Education in Southeast Asia* and "How to Rename a Hospital" in *Anthropological Quarterly*; parts of chapter 5 will be published in "Portrait and Scan" in *Public Culture*. I thank the editors and anonymous reviewers for their comments on this work.

I thank the editors and team at UW Press for their steadfast work on this project: Larin McLaughlin, Neecole Bostick, Joeth Zucco, and Alja Kooistra. I also thank the anonymous readers, whose comments helped immensely to strengthen the manuscript.

Friends are important too! For their wisdom, mischief, meals, and emotional support, I thank Stephanie Shelton and Zack Thomas, Katrina Hoch and Hugh MacMillan, friends around the Jets and the Cheetahs. My therapist, Bonnie Wolkenstein, saved my life. I could count on the B.F. Day crew—teachers, staff, and parents—to take good care of Boris. Erik Hoversten, Tricia Johnson, Amanda Lasher, Maggie Manes, Andra Miller, Alicia Reginato, Katherine Webb-Martinez, and friends I have missed, thank you for tolerating the long silences as I completed this project. I am also thankful for La Jolla Nurses who took good care of my mother and Hamp and Peggy Atkinson, Bob and Holly Heaton, Pat Judd, Holly McCormick and Barney Rickett, and Jenny and Wes Mudge for being good friends to my family my entire life.

Thomas, you have been the most close to me and the joys and sorrows of this project the entire time. Thank you for taking me to Cambodia and for making a life with me in Phnom Penh, Amsterdam, Iowa City, and now Seattle, and for taking on more of the family care work during key periods of writing. Boris, I thank you for your patience when I am typing instead of paying full attention to you talking or goofing or playing ukulele. Hanging out with you is my favorite thing to do. My sister, Leslie, is my closest friend and a brilliant artist. Thank you for everything! Thanks to Alex Terzich, Uncle Ken, the Riess family, and, of course, Cookie for their support. Dad, you are a model of strength, optimism, creative pragmatism, and generosity. I love you all.

FIXING THE IMAGE

INTRODUCTION

THE OPEN-AIR WAITING AREA FOR THE IMAGING WARD WAS SEARING hot, as it got once the earth moved enough that the sun shone directly on us, above the trees and below the concrete louvers, melding yellow and gray tiles into one vibrating surface, slowing the sound and movement of the ward. People got up to move, but there were only a few shaded seats and most of us chose to stand. The sounds of the hospital moved in and out of focus: an announcement over the PA system, relatives chatting, a nurse calling the name of a patient to collect her ultrasound report, the janitor offering drinks for sale, the paperboy's flip-flops slapping the tiles, arms cradling an unwieldy stack of Khmer dailies. I stepped over a small pile of shoes at the threshold of Exam Room 2, closed the door behind me, and sat on a chair at the foot of the exam bed. It took a moment to adjust to the relative darkness, the relative coolness, the relative quiet of the ultrasound exam room.

Dr. Chhum, the director of the imaging ward, sat at the side of the exam bed, his right hand on the ultrasound sensor, talking to two young women. One woman lay on the bed, her red-and-white striped shirt pushed up around her ribs to expose her abdomen. The other woman, her friend, stood at her side. I gave a *sompeah*, upright palms joined together, in greeting. The standing woman smiled and ducked her head into a *sompeah*. Dr. Chhum told them that I am a researcher at the hospital and continued with his examination, moving the sensor over the curve of her abdomen, deliberately on the right, the left, the center, glancing over his shoulder at the monitor at particular moments and pressing a button to capture an image. After a minute or so of working in silence, he concluded with a brief declaration: "I see nothing. You are healthy." He handed the patient a roll of pink toilet paper to wipe the gel from her belly. She got off the bed, the two young women thanked

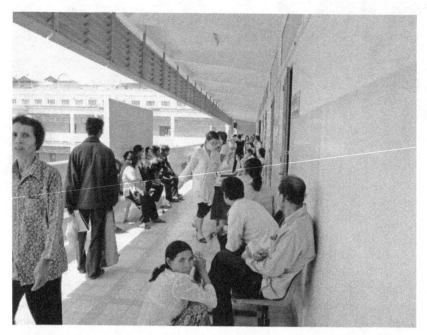

FIGURE I.1. The open-air waiting area of Russian Hospital's imaging ward is a long passageway of yellow and gray concrete tiles, lined on one side by exam rooms and on the other by a balcony overlooking lawns and parking at the entrance of the hospital. On a busy morning, as in this photo, the passageway is filled with people seated and people walking through. Patients sit on plastic chairs and stone benches, family members standing or sitting next to them. Some dress formally for the visit, as the woman in the foreground, wearing a white embroidered blouse and *sompot*, a long skirt made of patterned cloth, wrapped around and tied at the waist; others wear everyday clothes. Nurses in white coats move between exam rooms, taking turns at the intake desk, trying to keep the flow moving. Photo by author, 2009.

the doctor, and they left to wait for the report in the bright light of the waiting area.

Dr. Chhum wheeled his stool over to the computer, where he began typing the report.

"*Koat phey khmaoch, chång moel*" (She is afraid of ghosts, so she wants to look), he said to me, not turning from his typing.[1] This was not his typical impression. Being a general imaging ward, the doctors looked at abdomens, necks, breasts, uteruses, fetuses. They noted knots and shadows on the screen, measured tumors growing or shrinking with treatment, monitored babies approaching term, diagnosed cysts to be cut out. The ward did not specialize in ghosts (there are other experts for those beings), yet doctors and nurses understood that patients might connect pain or a dream with a supernatural intervention that could result in a malady of the flesh.[2] What was intriguing to me was that the ultrasound machine drew this woman and her friend to the hospital for a situation for which they could have gone to a monk or a *krou*, a traditional healer. Perhaps they visited them all.

Though the suspicion of physical and visible harm from a ghost may read as an exotic case (better or worse to open a book with?), the fact that people turn to a government hospital or private clinic because of its imaging technologies is not exotic at all. As one elderly woman explained, "The *krou*, he just treats you. Now, with *echo*, we can know what the illness is."

The desire for diagnostics in addition to therapeutics is important. The young women in the imaging ward knew that ultrasound, commonly called *echo*, might give answers, or at least hints. The body is permeable to ultrasound radiation and to spirits. The image made from sound might connect pain and suspicion to tissue. The elderly woman who traveled from the provinces did so because she wanted to know first and then treat rather than treat as a diagnostic, as a *krou* often does. This desire is also a vulnerability, one steeped in the need for better health care, mistrust of doctors and their institutions, and wanting something tangible for the dear cost, in terms of time and money, of a consultation.

Dr. Chhum did not believe that a ghost caused the girl's pain, though ghosts come to health professionals too.[3] He could have performed a physical exam instead of an ultrasound exam in order to communicate this conviction. But it would not have been enough. "Patients do not want to pay for consultation or advice on its own," he told me, after I asked him why he did the exam. "They want to receive *something*: medicine, usually, but now, an *echo*." He continued: "Of course, ultrasound is important. If you have symptoms—stomach pain, for example—ultrasound will help to see the soft tissue inside and perhaps permit knowledge of what is causing the pain. And yes, ultrasound can give valuable information in pregnancy: the sex, the organs, whether the pregnancy is ectopic or not, if there are neural tube defects."

Dr. Chhum finished typing the exam report and printed it on the small printer that sat on the desk next to the computer.

"But, as any doctor knows, you must give a lot, not a little."

On the opposite side of town from Russian Hospital, just north of Wat Phnom, is a cluster of clinics positioned to attract patients from Kantha Bopha IV and Preah Ket Mealea hospitals, or even Calmette Hospital up the road. Cruising on the back of a moto one morning, I was struck by the façade

FIGURE I.2. Diagnostic abundance. Signs and parked motos crowd the front of the private practice of Dr. Ngaet Sophy. A sign that runs the length of the roof carries the blue cross, symbol of medical practice, a color photograph of a mobile ultrasound machine, and a list of services: consultation, medical exams, gynecology, surgery, and general medicine. Dr. Ngaet offers color ultrasound imaging, X-ray, and ECG. A banner below it provides the same information and more: tests for blood, stool, liver; imaging of bones, abdomen, nose, lungs, stomach, and head. Two cabinets have signs announcing color ultrasound and X-ray services in Khmer and Vietnamese. On top of one, a small red and yellow sign, standard for money changers, states the day's exchange rates between US dollars and Cambodian riel. Two additional signs face drivers on the road: "color ultrasound" (in Khmer and Vietnamese) and "ultrasound" and "X-ray." Photo by author, 2010.

of the private practice of Dr. Ngaet Sophy (figure I.2). An abundance of signs (eight) and languages (three) told passersby that the doctor handles general illnesses, illnesses particular to women, and surgery. Dr. Ngaet offers diagnostic imaging: color ultrasound, X-ray, and electrocardiogram (ECG). Dr. Ngaet also exchanges dollars and riel, the Cambodian currency. Among these offerings of expertise, technology, and money, the emphasis on ultrasound is striking. "Color ultrasound" is listed six times—four in Khmer and twice in Vietnamese. What to make of this excess?

In this book, I argue that the force and appeal of ultrasound imaging—indeed, in some cases, its excess—have to do with the potential of repair and stability, offerings peculiar to the mechanized image. Repair and stability have resonance in Phnom Penh because of the ways that the content and form of its social and political economic history entangle with practices of care and neglect, with the authority of skilled vision in diagnosis, and with ontologies of beings and images that guide how viewers relate to ultrasound images and consequently how images relate to bodies. Set within long genealogies of vision and skilled diagnosis in Theravada Buddhist practice, the association of advanced medical technologies with white colonizers, and the new abundance of image-making technologies, ultrasound offers stabilizing authoritative knowledge, nudges unfolding beings toward desired futures, and elicits desire and pleasure, particularly for pregnant women.

My argument is drawn from what I have learned from people in Phnom Penh—the terms that doctors, pregnant women, bureaucrats, and patients use; the things they do and do not do; the jokes and stories they tell; the affect with which they engage with machines and mechanized images. The argument is also drawn from Phnom Penh, from my experience of living in and moving through the dynamic and image-saturated city. Through an analytic process of juxtaposition of ethnographic materials and film, development reports, scientific articles, and Khmer terms, I have come to think of the way that people relate to imaging technologies in terms of the polysemous metaphor of "fixing."

The English verb "to fix" has many senses:

> *to mend or repair*
> *to fasten in place or position*
> *to make permanent, as with a photograph, or a specimen prior to*
> *microscopy*
> *to influence the outcome of something, by underhand means*
> *to prepare or arrange something*

And then there is the noun, "the fix":

> *a dose of a drug to which one is addicted*
> *the experience of something from which one derives great pleasure*
> *or stimulation*

This is a gorgeous, dizzying array of meanings and concerns. The three senses that I use to frame the stories in this book are the sense of mending or repairing; the sense of stabilizing or making permanent, as when an image seems to stabilize uncertain bodily matter and knowledge of that matter; and the interaction with technology and images as experiences of pleasure, verging, for some, on compulsion. Repair, stabilization, and a dose of something to which one is addicted.

Fixing the Image is a study of a technology that is quite ordinary. Introduced in Phnom Penh around 1990, at the twilight of socialism and after two decades of conflict and upheaval, ultrasound took root in humanitarian and then privatized medicine. Relative to other imaging technologies, ultrasound machines are small, affordable, and easy to use, and the radiation is low-risk for patients and providers. Ultrasound works through sound waves emitted from a transducer that reflect off of internal structures and are received back again by the transducer. These differential reception data are used to create a visual representation on the ultrasound monitor. While looking back and forth between the transducer and the monitor, the user moves the transducer to get a desirable image and might "capture" or freeze the image and take certain measurements. Some of these captures are printed in the ultrasound report, one for the hospital file and, in most cases, one for the patient. At the time of my research, a black-and-white printout cost 13,000 riel (US$3.25), and color cost 20,000 riel (US$5.00) at a government hospital and 30,000 riel (US$7.50) at a private clinic. A scan using the endovaginal sensor cost 40,000 riel (US$10.00).

The ordinariness of ultrasound relates to its broad, frankly wondrous clinical utility. Ultrasound is used to screen healthy people, most notably, pregnant women. It is used to help diagnose a disease or condition in people who might be sick. It is used to monitor therapy in people who are sick. It *branches*, in Stuart Blume's (1992) term, meaning it is not confined to a narrow expertise or a single hospital ward. Ultrasound machines are in the imaging ward, alongside X-ray, CT, endoscopy, and mammography. Ultrasound is also in the ER, in radiology, in obstetrics and gynecology, in internal medicine.[4] This branching of ultrasound imaging means a wide range of specialists is familiar with ultrasound, even if they are not called upon to produce or read images. When specialists and general medicine doctors open private practices to supplement non-living wages in conditions of minimal regulation and a growing consumer culture, they install ultrasound there, even if they do not have training or regular experience performing and interpreting ultrasound exams. Ultrasound machines are in a general medicine private clinic, in a midwife's home practice. Overuse and the uncertain quality of services trouble doctors, officials, and patients alike, yet ultrasound has become routinized in general medicine and prenatal care.

FIGURE I.3. Simply echo. On the ground floor of shophouses behind O'Russei market in central Phnom Penh, private medical clinics abut clothing and handbag shops. In the photo, a sign hangs out from a pink-tiled clinic façade, stating merely: echo, "ultrasound," in blue. Next door is Always New, a shop that promises to take you "Toward your modern lifestyle." Two large color images of runway models adorn the walls on either side of the door, and a mannequin dressed in a blue collared shirt stares across the street. Ultrasound is part of everyday commerce in the city. Photo by author, 2009.

The ordinariness of ultrasound is accompanied by abundant public visibility. One of the reasons I was drawn to study ultrasound was this visibility. Private medical clinics in Phnom Penh and in provincial towns advertise their health care services with images of ultrasound machines, sometimes merely with *"echo,"* an economy of words that is significant for the project of this book (figure I.3). *Echo,* the short version of *echosâsrt,* pronounced *"echosaah,"* the Khmer term for ultrasonography, conjoins *echo* from the French *echographie* and *sâsrt,* the Khmer morpheme for "science of." How did the image of this technology, and the word for its medium, come to stand for medical services? The visibility relates to its wondrous utility and to something else. *Fixing the Image* is an attempt to think this something else.

In this book, I pursue the idea that representation in a medical technological image is a technique for *fixing* things, in multiple senses of the term.

Fixing involves technological images to improve circumstances material and spiritual, medical ("Now, with *echo*, we can know what the illness is") and economic ("As any doctor knows, you must give a lot, not a little"). Fixing also involves technological images to give some, if momentary, stability to ever-changing objects—bodily tissue or a gestating fetus. Ultrasound images offer the possibility of ontological stability to objects in process—not because there is one singular, predetermined, or essential truth to ontology, but because the mechanical image as an intervention can sometimes help to fix the bio-spiritual matters of concern.

I claim the generative senses of *fixing* with caution. In the pages that follow, I hope it is clear that my approach depends upon diverse genealogies of scholarship in which "fixing"—the term and its practices—is the object of critique. In the social sciences and humanities, a "technological fix" is one that does not address the root problem. Who and what are the problems that can be "fixed" by technology? As Ruha Benjamin (2019, 137) asks, "Do fixes fix us?" Scholars of feminist and queer technoscience, and critical race and disability studies, have shown how technologies are involved in the definition of particular people and particularly raced, gendered, and abled bodies as problems and thus deserving of surveillance, control, neglect, or injury. Critical public health scholars describe how technology that intended to make health care more accessible, standardized, efficient, or mobile can divert attention and resources from health infrastructures and basic primary care.[5] In other words, far from neutral or benevolent (Benjamin 2019), technological fixes are part of world-making practices that are narrow and patterned in their definition of problems and of the means to repair them. An ultrasound machine that substitutes for a general prenatal exam can be thought of as a technological fix, one that does not necessarily improve health outcomes for the pregnant woman or the fetus, costs money, diverts resources, and sidelines other ways of assessing health, such as taking blood pressure and weight or testing for diabetes.

The senses of fixing as fastening in place and making permanent, *as with a photograph, or a specimen prior to microscopy*, are also fraught.[6] Stabilizing categories of race, gender, or health shift attention from the practices of making these categories to these categories as natural facts in the world that are merely described by the appropriate medium, or modest witness. Critical scholarship in anthropology and across the humanities has documented how naturalization of categories of beings, in terms of biology or morality, is part of hierarchical ordering that justifies inequality and domination. The challenge, as Amade M'charek (2013, 424) writes, is to denaturalize without dematerializing, to attend to materiality without the body being "fixed"; biology is not determined or determining.

As an antidote to fixing and its harms, scholars have shown the instability of categories of race and gender, the material and semiotic instability of images, the malleability of the biological body. Work in postcolonial science studies and in critical visual studies shifts our understandings of what is foundational and unalterable in biological nature and what changes, or can be changed, through technology, representation, and intervention. As Emilia Sanabria (2016, 28) writes, "biology and nature may also supply notions of instability and changeability" and "how human action is often geared to fixing and stabilizing this flux." *Fixing the Image*, in the spirit of its title, calls attention to the ongoing, incomplete, and fragmentary work of improvement and stabilization. The twist in the plot is *not* that bodies are malleable and all is impermanent. The twist is, given malleability and impermanence, that people keep trying to fix things and selves, that technological images are central to this work, and that these fixings are variable in their politics and effects.

Thus, *Fixing the Image* asks for precision regarding the value of disruption and unsettling in social theory. Instability and concepts related though not reducible to instability—fluidity, improvisation, unsettling, plasticity, indeterminacy—are theoretical interventions into understandings of technology, knowledge, and the body and how they shape one another. These further feminist and critical race commitments to denaturalize categories that asymmetrically structure social and biological life. The challenge I take up in this book is how to think the relations of humans and technologies while holding these commitments and when instability is not a radical intervention; when instability is what people are trying to get away from, to move beyond; and when people crave the stability, even if temporary, of a diagnosis and the predictability of a machine yet do not have naive expectations that the machine has the one and only answer. If instability is a prevailing historical experience, and dominant in forms of economic, political, and spiritual life, the scholarly desire for "disruption" might not serve liberatory ends.

ETHNOGRAPHY OF AND AGAINST DISRUPTION

Fixing the Image locates Khmer idioms of care, of seeing, and of aesthetics in the imaging wards of public hospitals and private clinics and outside of clinical settings in the rapidly changing urban landscape of Phnom Penh.

Phnom Penh's dynamic present derives from a history characterized in the global imagination by exceptional and spectacular violence. This violence was its most extreme during the official regime of the Khmer Rouge, Democratic Kampuchea, from 17 April 1975 to 7 January 1979, though the chronology of violence and turmoil is variable across the country. The US bombing of the eastern half of Cambodia, from the mountains to the sea, from the Tonlé Sap to Viet Nam, was truly exceptional violence, causing terror, destruction, and mass movements of people to Phnom Penh between 1965 and 1973. In 1975, the Khmer Rouge forced these refugees, along with the entire population of the city, to leave. To where, people were not told. The Khmer Rouge operationalized uncertainty and suspicion to the extent that not-knowing and not-trusting became elements of both terror and survival. The objective of the Khmer Rouge was to obliterate the individual and the social in order to remake Cambodia from nothing. This required violent undoing of categories of thought and affect as well as the social institutions upon which they depend—the family, the wat, the hospital, the school, the market, the rice field. The violence and suffering were, are, unspeakable. A story about medical imaging is at once distant from this history and dependent upon it. How? One of the legacies of this history is that Cambodia as a whole is often depicted as a place in need of "fixing," a place that can be "fixed."

I have struggled with how to write in a way that conveys the importance of the past for what doctors, patients, family members, officials, and institutions are doing with imaging technologies yet does not reduce everything to the past. History is no more crucial to ultrasound imaging in Cambodia than it is to ultrasound imaging in the United States or the Netherlands. Yet in academic and popular discourse, Cambodia is a place that is particularly burdened by its history, and, as such, the (whichever) Cambodian situation must be explained through this violence. I address this issue here because, in my experience, people have violent expectations about Cambodia. Which histories do we hold up in our stories, which cultural practices?

I have thought deeply about which histories to hold up in this book, and how to write an ethnography of medical imaging that is generative for theorization and specific to Cambodia but does not assume violent history is the only story to tell. Ultrasound is a way to bring forward different histories, in addition to exceptionally violent ones, that broaden our understanding of Cold War and de–Cold War (Chen 2010) dynamics in postcolonial nations. These stories have their own violence. These are histories of technological aid to newly independent nations, of postcolonial prioritization of technology as an ideologically neutral form of modernity, of entanglements of public and private health care in postsocialist market speculations. A genealogy of medical technology makes connections to anthropology of postcolonial Africa and post-Soviet Europe, with the potential for insights about the way that medical technologies configure, and are configured by, forms of authoritarian elite capitalism that emerge after war, after socialism, after humanitarianism. A logic of speculation innervates different domains of practice in Phnom Penh like a mild electric field: buying and selling land, opening cafés, building wats and commercial and residential towers, or, in some cases, the unfulfilled promise of developing real estate.[7] The ongoing reorganization of health care is not immune to this speculative mood, and ultrasound machines and ultrasound images are investments that generate profit in the form of images and services.

Imaging technologies have a genealogy of multiple decades of building medicine, neglecting medicine, and repairing medicine as projects in which technology has been central. In my conversations with people about imaging technologies, *presence* and *absence* of technology and the *qualities* of technology—Is it old or new? Is it in need of repair?—are open to comparison with and speculation about the past. People evaluate the salience of imaging technologies for care—Is there now more trust? Is there now better care?—in relation to histories of bodily damage and neglect of the human. People relate to the *qualities* of a medical image—Is it color or black-and-white, is it clear?—in relation to histories of aesthetics. Prenatal ultrasound, in particular, can activate an aesthetics of portraiture, including a preference for color images.

Phnom Penh around 2010 was, and is still, a city in rapid change, a nexus of forces specific and general, local and global, the textures of which this book attempts to articulate. First, a brief description. Phnom Penh is expanding, in terms of its geography and its population. Lakes and wetlands have been filled with sand to support new suburbs, slums, clinics, factories, wats, and universities. Density has increased, often vertically, in the form of residential and commercial towers pressing down on the earth of a city at the confluence of three rivers: the Mekong, the Bassac, the Tonlé Sap. A saturation of new and projected images remakes the look and experience of moving through the city. Shop signs line narrow streets and boulevards, and intersections glow with LED billboards. Life is composed with images on screens large and small: on the phone or in the salon, the restaurant, the car, the tuk-tuk taxi.[8] Ultrasound participates in the material expansion of the city up and out, as income for and reason to travel to new clinics in city center high-rises or in suburban shophouses. Desire for affordable and hopefully skilled imaging services draws people from factory dormitories and newly peri-urban communities to government hospitals in the city center. People from the countryside and provincial towns undertake the long drive to Phnom Penh in search of diagnostic expertise and comprehensive health care. Ultrasound images participate in the visual economy of the city, rematerializing the interior of the body as a surface (Taylor 2005), offering new possibilities for intervention and for care.

My research was grounded in this vibrant city from January 2009 to February 2011, with additional research in 2015, 2017, and 2019. In 2009 and 2010, I spent mornings in the imaging wards of government hospitals, first Russian Hospital and later the National Center for Maternal and Child Health, which I will also refer to as "Maternal Hospital."[9] In the afternoons and early evening, I visited private clinics. My fieldwork in these spaces involved informal conversations about ultrasound services with patients, family members, and staff in the waiting areas and observation of ultrasound exams. I attended hospital events and ceremonies related to GE Healthcare's donation of medical technologies to government hospitals and health centers. From June 2010 to February 2011, I worked closely with Neary, then a medical student (now a doctor), who joined me in the waiting areas, who chatted with patients, their family members, and hospital staff, and who accompanied me at a few of my interviews with radiologists and health officials. As a medical student and daughter of a midwife, Neary had unique expertise and insight into medical education and health care in Cambodia. She connected me to the ultrasound ward at the National Center for Maternal and Child Health and to the private clinic Sorphea VIP. Our dialogues shape this book.

My research also took me to other spaces in the city. I spent afternoons looking at Khmer and French audiovisual media at the Bophana Audiovisual Resource Center and reading medical journals at the National Archives of Cambodia. My interest in the broader visual sphere drew me to art exhibitions, film screenings, and lectures at the gallery Reyum (sadly, now closed), the Royal University of Phnom Penh, Sa Sa Gallery, Java Café, and Chinese House, among other sites. I talked to diverse people about ultrasound imaging: waitresses, tuk-tuk drivers, academic researchers, nongovernmental organization (NGO) workers, and people doing their evening exercise at the park. My visible pregnancy and occasional fieldwork with an infant son opened up space for conversation about prenatal ultrasound imaging in unanticipated ways.

Another important person to this research was Socheat, a former soldier and United Nations Transitional Authority in Cambodia (UNTAC) interpreter, with whom I studied Khmer in the late afternoons. Socheat helped me translate some documents and films, arranged meetings with monks, and helped to interpret and guide during my conversations with monks. His perspectives on recent Cambodian history, postconflict development, and vernacular health care helped me to think through many questions in this book.

Most of my research was conducted in Khmer or English. I have competency in Khmer, but I could not understand everything that was said in clinical settings. I also did not always ask for clarification if it seemed like it would interrupt an appointment. In some instances, I relied on Neary and Socheat to help me with questions after the fact, to interpret during interviews, and to puzzle through my ideas. Conversations with friends, lawyers working on the Duch trial at the Khmer Rouge Tribunal, and former colleagues of mine and my partner, Thomas, at the World Health Organization (WHO), the US Centers for Disease Control and Prevention (CDC), and the Banteay Meanchey Provincial Health Department were also important to my understanding of postcolonial and contemporary modernity in which ultrasound imaging is situated.[10] I first became interested in ultrasound in 2004, when I was living in Sisophon, a town in Banteay Meanchey Province about forty-five minutes (on the road at the time) from the Poipet border crossing to Thailand. I accompanied Rouen, a warm, practical, irreverent woman who cooked meals for us during the week, for an exam of a large abdominal lump. She had been hesitant to go to the doctor, she did not trust that she would receive good care, but as her discomfort and worry increased, she agreed to go to someone recommended by a colleague. The ultrasound exam led to a diagnosis of a uterine cyst and recommendation for surgery in Phnom Penh. Rouen had the surgery and recovered to full health. As I sat in the pink-tiled consultation room of the government doctor's private practice, on the ground floor of his *pteah lvaeng* (apartment/shophouse), translating between Rouen and the doctor, I wondered about the forms of affect and care, the hierarchies of class, race, and expertise that shaped the exam and its outcome. Across these different times and places, my methods are grounded in forms of attachment that are friendship, though they may be unequal and involve economic and gift exchange (Ramírez-i-Ollé 2019).

Ashley Thompson (2006, 200) observed that indirectness is "generally characteristic of Cambodian culture." Though I will not go so big or so far about Cambodian culture, I must acknowledge a form of indirectness in my own writing about Cambodia. Perhaps "an aesthetic practice of the oblique" (Thompson 2006, 201) is proper to writing about Cambodia, or, at least, acceptable as a refraction of a Cambodian style of expression with my own refusal of the effects of different genres of directness: exoticization, whether by abundance of ethnographic particulars or reduction of ethnological generalizations; abjection, by stubborn health and poverty indicators; and haunting, by survivor testimonies meticulously transcribed for the court.

The role of ethnography, as I see it, is description as well as imagination and theorization from description. The danger and romance of ethnographic description is that it may create a sense of otherness valid only to itself, so deeply contextualized that it becomes a separate world that precludes translation, dialogue, or "engaged contest of thought" (Klima 2002, 196). Following Alan Klima (2002, 198), ethnography takes alternative practice as "a source of theoretical insight" rather than "a source of empirical global variation." But the genre of theorizing that ethnography inspires, following Annemarie Mol (2017), does not aim to be empirically encompassing or universally valid. Klima and Mol write from different intellectual traditions and in different styles, yet they both find Walter Benjamin to be a good guide. For Klima (2002, 8), who draws on Benjamin's notion of *Geschichtsphilosophie* (philosophy *made out of* history), philosophy is made out of ethnography. This means that ethnography is the concrete, frankly visual (even if textual) material of theory. Mol (2002, 183) draws upon Benjamin's *Arcades Project* as an exemplary case for theory that is situated in time and place. *Fixing the Image* attempts to draw on specific cases of practice in contemporary Phnom Penh as telling, in ways that are suggestive.[11] The stories in this book do not necessarily proceed in a conventional form of academic argumentation and are intended to open up problems for thought about health technologies in the majority world (Alam 2008) and the force and appeal of imaging the body's interior.

TECHNOLOGICAL FIXES

One way to understand the desire for new technologies in postconflict and postsocialist Cambodia is in relation to a long history in which the invention, use, and abuse of technology is intimately tied to judgments about the capacity and potential of Cambodians and Cambodia. Cambodia has a colonial and postcolonial history in which technology figured as symbol and tool of civilization, progress, and modernity. In the colonial period, these categories were racialized such that advanced technology was associated with white colonizers. In the postcolonial period, advanced technology was associated with building a modern independent nation.[12] Both colonial and anti-colonial practices were rooted in notions of technology as somewhat independent from society and capable of producing a particular kind of social change. There is no written history of technology in Cambodia, to my knowledge, and what follows is a sketch of colonial and postcolonial history centered on the question of technological modernity.

Since the sixteenth century, North Atlantic ideals have defined civilization and progress in terms of the invention and use of technology.[13] Cambodia's encounter with Europe began in the early sixteenth century, after the Portuguese conquest of Malacca in 1511 (Groslier 2006, vii). Portuguese and Spanish merchants and missionaries went to Cambodia in the 1550s (Groslier 2006, 20), though the Spanish attack on Srei Santhor in 1596 marked the beginning of the end of Spanish influence (Boxer 1969, 130). The first French missionary, Father Georges de la Mothe, landed in the Mekong Delta in 1585 (Norindr 1996, 3). Supportive relations between Catholic missionaries and the French navy over the subsequent three hundred years were to become central to French intervention in Cambodia and mainland Southeast Asia.

French control became formal in 1863, when Cambodia signed a protectorate treaty with the French that gave mineral and timber concessions in exchange for protection against the Siamese and Vietnamese imperial courts, which had been jousting for control of Cambodia for centuries (Au 2011, 16). Two decades later, in 1884, the French colonial administration in Cochinchina forced King Norodom to sign a treaty that extended French control. Cambodia was a colony in all but name. There was a popular revolt against this treaty, and historian of medicine Sokhieng Au (2011, 16) argues that it was the threat of popular insurrection that explains the slowness of French colonial programs, such as infrastructure, public health, education, and economy; the French were wary of pushing Norodom too far, as he had the power to quell revolt. After Norodom's death in 1904, the French concentrated economic and political control of Cambodia. It was in these early decades of the twentieth century that the French developed medical infrastructures, such as hospitals, vaccine programs, and midwifery trainings (Au 2011). During the early period of French colonization, French medicine was being reconfigured by germ theory and the rise of laboratory science and by growth of population health thinking in health and medicine (Au 2011, 25). Science was produced through colonial practices and sites, notably, the Institutes Pasteur in the Union Indochinoise and in French colonies in Africa.[14]

The late nineteenth and early twentieth centuries were the high points of French, Dutch, and British colonialism in Asia and Africa and of elaboration of scientific theories of human difference and social progress. Technological transformation realized modernity on a practical level, for example, in the ways that changing modes of production, transportation, measurement, and rationalization transformed the life and labor of people

(Abraham 2006; Mrázek 2002). Science and technology reinforced colonial and neocolonial dominance, for example, as a rationale for taxation and corvée labor to build public works (Padwe 2020, 95) and facilitating mapping, mining, weapons, forestry, plantation agriculture, and tropical medicine.[15] These interventions and institutions were contested by peasants, healers, elites, and Indigenous groups and sometimes, too, by colonial doctors and administrators. It is important to emphasize that resistance to public health and infrastructure programs of colonial administrations was diverse in form—including violence, protest, refusal, silence, partial accommodation, and escape—and particular to social, material, and technoscientific context.[16] As Sokhieng Au (2011, 58) describes, in the 1920s and 1930s, Cambodians accepted the smallpox vaccine, which was introduced early in the colonial period and whose method of administration resembled local variation practices; Cambodians and Europeans resisted the cholera vaccine, which was unreliable in quality and had significant side effects.

Technological modernity was central to the "global view of things" (Anderson 2006, 7) of colonial doctors and bureaucrats and to the identities and aspirations of anti-colonial movements, which, in some cases, were led by doctors (Pols 2018).[17] Technology was part of the new "global dream space" (Tsing 2005, 84) of postcolonial heads of state as well as the "global feeling" (Tadiar 2009, 334) at the end of the Cold War about the failure of liberation movements. Colonial logics about what it is to be modern, developed, and sovereign imbue postcolonial governance in the form of public works, public health, education, communications, agriculture, conservation, and resource extraction. Sihanouk, the leader of post-Independence Cambodia, sought to appropriate technologies—to harness the powers of cinema, X-ray, modernist architecture, mass media—and make them Cambodian (Keo 2019; Ly and Muan 2001). Across newly independent nations, resistance to state development projects could be dismissed as unsupportive of the decolonial project or standing against national development and sovereignty.[18]

There can be little doubt that technology changes society structurally, biologically, and morally. But technology does not evolve on its own, leaving humans with one sole option: submit. This is what Martin Heidegger called the "inexorability of its limitless reign" ([1962] 1998, 137), the idea "that modern technology could speak forth a demand the realization of which humans would be unable to bring to a halt or even survey and control as a whole." In *The Question Concerning Technology* (1977) and, more concisely, in "Traditional Language and Technological Language," his 1962 lecture to science teachers at a vocational school, Heidegger reflects on what is "peculiar" to technology.[19] He summarizes the standard conception of technology in two "mutually dependent moments" ([1962] 1998, 133–34): technology is *anthropological* in that it is designed and used by humans and co-configured with human knowledge practices, namely, the sciences, and technology is *instrumental*, in that it is a means produced and used for a definite end. The end, for Heidegger, is calculability, a challenging forth of nature, "placing it [nature] at our disposal and securing it as natural energy" (137–38). This challenging forth takes the form of a demand, one that is not peculiar only to technology, or even to science. Rather, for Heidegger, it is the demand of our time.[20] This demand can be glossed as instrumentality, and one genealogy of science and technology studies (STS) could be framed as a critique of instrumentality.

For a technology such as ultrasound that has been so thoroughly normalized in health care and especially prenatal care around the globe, the inexorability of its reign seems like a foregone conclusion. But what does this mean? It is not everywhere the same, yet global scholarship on prenatal ultrasound documents important similarities. Ultrasound is enrolled in the commercialization, medicalization, and control of pregnancy and the making of "modern women" and modern medicine.[21] Ultrasound has been theorized as an instrument of colonial control over women's bodies (Frost and Haas 2017) and as a pedagogy for learning how to see who exists in the world (Haraway [1992] 2004). It is this question of subjectivation that animates ethnographic studies in particular; who (or what) is the fetal subject, and how does it become with imaging?[22] What are the effects of this subjectivation on pregnant women and on the determination of worthy, desirable, and unworthy lives?[23] In *Fixing the Image*, ultrasound imaging sparks questions about technological modernity after colonialism and the Cold War that diverge from a straight narrative of instrumentality or inexorability. One of the possibilities for this is the work of the ultrasound image.

IMAGES THAT STABILIZE

My concern in *Fixing the Image* is to understand the stability and instability of images and their referents and the aesthetics of the ultrasound image. By stability and instability of images, I mean both the stability of the *claim* the image makes about the present state of tissue and the material stability of the *image*, how it holds up in environmental conditions. The stability and instability of referents has to do with the bodily matter that reflects ultrasound waves, the referent of the picture. How dynamic is this matter? Can ultrasound affect it and, if so, how? Patients' and doctors' attention to aesthetics, the way an image looks, are a clue to the ontologies of images and the ontologies of referents and hint at the multiplicity of the ultrasound image. Ultrasound is a medical image with particular expectations for truth and aesthetic conventions for being a good image, and, in the case of prenatal ultrasound, it is also an image of kin, of a baby-to-be, with its own expectations for truth and aesthetic conventions for being a good image. I arrived at this point of inquiry having drawn insights from interdisciplinary scholarship on mechanical images as stabilization of knowledge with a special authority to define being—in terms of medicine, race, gender, morality, and more.

Mechanical images, such as photography and cinema, have been central to definitions of life as composed of biological and mechanical elements. Medical images help to isolate and hold steady these elements for the production of scientific and medical knowledge (Cartwright 1995). This holding together is temporary but important for the coordination of different diagnostic practices into a diagnostic category (Mol 2002). In some cases, the unreliability of images due to mechanical issues, or training, means that a medical image's contribution to diagnosis is minimal, if diagnosis is possible at all (Street 2014a).

Ethnographies in laboratory settings show how scientists produce and use images to argue for the existence of a natural fact and simultaneously describe natural facts about the ordinarily unseen, in some cases as if they already exist separately from their technological apprehension.[24] In the late nineteenth century, photographic vision became a metaphor for objective truth, not because photographs *look* true to nature—paintings often looked more real, if only because of color—but because the camera seemed to eliminate human agency (in the form of judgment, selection, imagination, theory). Lorraine Daston and Peter Galison (1992) trace this to the proliferation of machines elsewhere in Europe at the time, such as in manufacturing, where machines solve the problem of the human who tires, who performs better on some days and worse on others, who may tinker with technological practices. In short, machines standardize and replicate. It is in this moment, around the turn of the twentieth century, that *non-intervention* becomes more important than *verisimilitude* for making truthful depictions of biological bodies and processes (Daston and Galison 1992, 120). What Daston and Galison show, through historical study of different ways of depicting and debating depictions, is how a good and true image requires learning to see it as such. The seeming non-intervention of mechanical images is part of what makes them an authoritative representation of the body, what Daston and Galison call *mechanical objectivity*.

The extent to which "non-intervention" is important to objective representation has been a central conversation in feminist and postcolonial science studies and in visual studies. One strand of this conversation has to do with the way sight does not encounter the object with the intimacy of touch and taste (see Mol 2021 for an undoing of this in regard to taste). Vision permits distance, as the argument goes, and is required for differentiating a subject from an object. In colonial contexts, optical tools are technologies of watching the colony and the colonized as well as the self. Rudolf Mrázek (2002) conjoins Dutch and Indonesian interest in photography, mapping, lighting, microscopy, and display as central to the late colonial moment. Airplanes and trains, too, are optical tools, affording new visions of the landscape and its human and nonhuman inhabitants. Mrázek likens "the numbers, the maps, and all the other gadgets of the watching technology" (120, 121) to the instrumentalization of nature more broadly in the late colonial period. For Mrázek, colonial watching technologies and the perfection of optics were a making trivial, a distancing of the world so that "matter is not touched" (120). In chapter 4, I offer another model of seeing as one that is a skill of managing interference. It is not a detached gaze, whether from above or outside, and it requires other senses and reading a response. Michel Foucault ([1963] 1994), too, posited a sensorial seeing, a medical observation emerging in the nineteenth century that alternated the gaze with language, forging observation as a "fine sensibility," a seeing that is skilled but a-theoretical.[25]

Another strand of critique of mechanical objectivity emphasizes the ways in which its distance and supposed non-intervention of mechanical observation are very much interventions into the world. This is an ontological and political tactic of differentiating subjects and objects. Trinh T. Minh-ha's (1989) and Fatimah Tobing Rony's (1996) critiques of ethnographic film strike directly at visual projection of a dehumanized, othered objecthood. For poet and post-Independence leader Léopold Senghor, remaining at a distance, privileging vision above all else, subtends white supremacist subject/object dichotomies and practices of sensory engagement with the world. He proposes an alternative "African" sensibility that involves holding objects at a distance but also looking, smelling, and care, to hold an object in its vibrancy, not to fix or kill (Senghor 1964, 72, quoted in Mavhunga 2018, 8).[26] Frantz Fanon's (1967, 109) widely quoted passage about being sealed into "crushing objecthood" describes how the white colonial gaze is bound up in an essentialist definition of ontology that excludes Blackness: "The movements, the attitudes, the glances of the other fixed me there, in the sense in which a chemical solution is fixed by a dye. I was indignant; I demanded an explanation." In this book, following people's desire for particular kinds of ultrasound images leads us to the heart of tensions in medical imaging, indeed, in representationalism. Representationalism, in Karen Barad's (2007, 28) terms, is the "idea that representations and the objects (subjects, events, or states of affairs) that they purport to represent are independent of one another."

The genre of the mechanized medical image calls for fidelity to material reality, even as the image is involved in bringing reality to the senses. This puzzle of co-construction of reality between human and more-than-human others, technologies, and animate and inanimate nature is of central concern in ethnographic studies of science and medicine, particularly imaging studies and feminist new materialisms. Medical images travel outside of clinical, research, and laboratory contexts and are a part of a visual world in which they shape understandings of what it is to be human and normal. Correspondingly, medical images produced in clinical, research, and laboratory contexts are themselves shaped by this broader visual world and understandings of what it is to be human.[27] A key cultural logic that drives medical imaging is what Isabelle Dussauge (2008, 15) calls the "Western cultural utopia of the *transparent body*." Joe Dumit (2004) shows how positron emission tomography (PET) brain images become removed from their scientific or clinical context and travel beyond their intended use, in forums such as *Vogue*, courtrooms, and films, where they are taken seriously as revealing facts about the brain and about personhood. PET brain images have this mobility in the United States because of cultural logics about brains, personhood, and imaging: a brain scan can stand for a brain; the brain can stand for the person; the person is biologically determined; the medical image depicts a truth (Dumit 2004, 100; see also Joyce 2008). Studies of visual technologies in science that produce race and gender (Bailey 2016; M'charek 2013) emphasize the relational dynamics of objects under study, the political economic conditions under which images come into being, the ways images circulate, and the knowledge and care projects into which they are enlisted (Hausken, Papenburg, and Schmitz 2018, 4).

Critical studies of photography and cinema have pointed out the ways in which mechanical objectivity functions ideologically in scientific and colonial images as a means of constructing and maintaining white supremacy and heteropatriarchy. White colonizers had the tools to define others and the power to back it up as authoritative truth. However, vernacular uses of photography do not merely replicate the ideology of mechanical objectivity. Neither distance nor non-intervention is central to what makes a meaningful picture of a human (Campt 2017; Klima 2002; Pinney 2003; Strassler 2010). The truth of an image of the human depends on what it *projects*, its soundings and emanations. Photographs and photography as practice are also conduits of spiritual power. Photographs *reveal* the presence of entities that exist outside of one material form, and, in doing so, photographs become "electric" with presence (Wright 2008, 370). These insights—the portrait as projection as well as documentation, the photograph as conduit of spiritual presence—help me to understand aesthetic practices of relating to prenatal ultrasound images, but there is still the puzzle of the referent. People relate to prenatal ultrasound as a live connection to the child-to-be, in some cases, a being *that was brought out by the image.*

An image is a powerful way of making something manifest, even if showing involves hiding or bringing forward some realities and not others. The structure of the relationship between the seeable and stateable (Foucault [1963] 1994), and the presence of that which cannot be seen, has been theorized as haunting (Gordon [1997] 2008), wildness (Apichatpong 2010), and opacity (Glissant 1997). To access these presences that are not present, scholars advocate methods of listening to (Campt 2017) and touching (Marks 2000) images and more general acts of noticing (Tsing 2015), desiring, and living with/through images in desire's deferral (Fuhrmann 2016). *Fixing the Image* centers on a modest and temporary sense of making manifest. The medical image presents a reality, makes a reality, but it is never the final image. Imaging practices involve wrestling with the mutability of images and relating images to other medicine practices, such as looking at bodies, touching bodies, and listening to bodies (Harris 2016; Kazimierczak 2018) and to patient stories.

In the early days of photography, fixing the image was one of the puzzles to figure out. Henry Fox Talbot's experiments with image production were excited by the possibility of freezing an object or event in time. Historian of science Chitra Ramalingam (2008, 86) quotes Talbot's writing in 1839: "The most transitory of things, a shadow, the proverbial emblem of all that is fleeting and momentary . . . may be fixed for ever in the position which it seemed only destined for a single instant to occupy." Ramalingam notes that "fixed forever" was merely hopeful at that point. The chemical processes did not stabilize an image on its medium. But in time, these technological and material problems were solved such that the image did stabilize, at least a bit (Batchen 1997).

The ubiquity of digital images redirects concerns for stability of the image to the fleeting nature of the cascade of images in daily life, to the speed and paths of circulation, and to its openness to digital manipulation. The broader visual digital economy (cf. Poole 1997) is not the subject of this book, but it is worth mentioning that ultrasound imaging services were proliferating alongside other digital images in Phnom Penh. Internet cafés and digital photography studios were primary sites for people to produce, circulate, and consume images. The digital landscape has changed quickly; since at least 2017, mobile phones are the primary way people access the internet. Over ten million phones were connected to the internet in 2017, out of a population of around sixteen million people (Kem et al. 2019, 8).[28]

In sum, mechanical images produced by colonial science and statecraft "fix" knowledge and identity for the purpose of classification and domination. The radical task in social theory has been to unsettle this fix, to show how knowledge and beings can be fluid, mobile, changing form, refusing the categories imposed upon them. The ideology of mechanical objectivity that is important to scientific and documentary images depends on *distance* between the technology and the object, between the image and the object, and between the image and the beholder. Scientific and documentary images entail temporalities of the moment and its past. This is what your cyst looks like today. The radical task in STS has been to show intra-action (Barad 2007), enactment (Mol 2002), co-enactment (Åsberg and Lum 2010) of matter, images, and instruments, rather than distance and separation, and to do so with attention to the specificity of the matter (Abrahamsson et al. 2015) and racial and gender formation (Hinton, Mehrabi, and Barla 2015; Roy and Subramaniam 2016). In another tradition, the anthropology of photography has challenged representationalist assumptions premised on distance and separation to show how the image and object may be fused, how the image may be performatively effective (Pinney 1997, 178–79) and entail temporalities in which the image is not only a document of a past presence but also an ongoing presence and even a projection of future possibility.[29]

FIXING THE IMAGE

I use the title *Fixing the Image* to convey the instabilities of the image and the desire and practice to make better, despite the uncertainty of results or effects. The fixing of the image is compelling; it is a promise, the image an allure. Both are like a drug we cannot get enough of, whose effects are anticipated but cannot be utterly controlled.

In the chapters that follow, I describe how people's encounters with imaging technology are inflected with experience of different kinds of instability over time. This includes a history of violence and upheaval, a present of dispossession, opportunity, and dizzying change toward a future unknown. *Fixing the Image* is an ethnography of medical imaging in a moment of its proliferation, in a context of authoritarian capitalism. The chapters move between scales, from nation to the health system; to health care in the waiting area and appointment room; to the different kinds of seeing that happens between doctors, monks, machines, and patients; and, finally, to the ultrasound image and the relations of viewers and referent to the image.

Lisa Stevenson (2014, 11) argues that we think and live through images—photographs and films but also memories, phrases, dreams, and sounds. One way to think of ethnography, then, is the encounter with disparate kinds of images and the attempt to articulate their resonances, their soundings (Campt 2017), what they might have in common. Stevenson (2014, 12) credits Benjamin (2006) for a capacious understanding of image not tethered to vision and Foucault ([1963] 1993) for his understanding of the image as "a language that expresses without formulating."[30] The image of thought as ethnographic method and writing is useful for those problems and relations that resist the austerity sometimes required by statements of fact. Furthermore, an image of thought "can capture uncertainty and contradiction without having to resolve it" (Stevenson 2014, 10). With an expanded sense of image, one that is not narrowly visual, we can grasp gestalt slices of the world.

Many of the chapters in this book propose an image of thought as a visual-conceptual form of theorizing and as a loose unifying mechanism. For my purposes, Stevenson's "image of thought" permits a method of juxtaposition of sources, such as conversations, films, memories, reports, sayings, and photographs. More specifically, the image of flickering presence of technologies does two things. It counters an imaginary of Cambodia as always lacking, and it disrupts an imaginary that technological modernity follows North Atlantic tempo and form. As I explore in the following chapters, it helps us to understand the desire for a material fix that an imaging technology is potentially able to fulfill.

The first two chapters of *Fixing the Image* focus on histories and political economies of imaging technologies in relation to health care infrastructures. In chapter 1, I trace a genealogy of technology in medicine since Independence in 1953. The image of flickering presence of technology conveys not only the dichotomy of presence and absence but also a presence that is not steady, one that is susceptible to being blown out by chance or by circumstance or by intention. The image of thought conveys the spectacle of a new X-ray machine donated to a state-of-the-art hospital, a *vaste cité médicale*, in the 1960s and a new ultrasound machine donated to that same hospital in the 2010s. Between these shiny material presences are decades of material uncertainty and instability: neglect and destruction of machines, indeed the absence of the imaging ward and health clinic in the 1970s; the spectacle of need that motivates humanitarian donation of a used ultrasound machine in 1989; and the non-spectacle of an X-ray machine that silently seeps radiation in the 1990s (Grant 2018). In other words, a flickering presence and absence is an image of thought, and it is material and mechanical. When is anything going to stay put? My argument is built from analysis of speeches and conversations, medical journals and promotional films, stories of doctors, government officials, and donors trying to fix Cambodia with and through medical technologies, the imagination of Cambodia as a place in need of fixing, a place that can be fixed.

Chapter 2 explores another instability of significance to ultrasound—the relationship between public and private health care. I argue that ultrasound had a role in elaboration of private health care at a time when the relation between public and private was not an object of explicit political ideology, as it had been in previous organizations of health care. A speculative mood infused decisions about value, and ultrasound machines, images, and appointments were valuable things to be exchanged. To elaborate how ultrasound participates in what I call post-political care, I use an image of thought inspired by conversation with a health official: the relationship between the government and the private sector, he told me, was like that of mother and child, involving relations of authority and intimacy, care and value, that were continuously being worked out.

The question of care with ultrasound is at the heart of this book, the hinge that conjoins the histories and economies explored in chapters 1 and 2 with ways of seeing in medicine and practices of relating to images of body and person explored in chapters 4 and 5. Based on ethnography inside and outside of the imaging ward, chapter 3 describes practices of over-care and under-care, too much and not enough care, arguing that it is difficult to settle on what good care with ultrasound can be. Care, here, is practice with respectful attention, *yok chett tuk dak*.

In chapter 4 I use the image of thought of the echo to juxtapose ways of seeing that are tangent to ultrasound. Ultrasound exists in a rich field of visual practices and among human and non-human entities whose vision supports diagnosis and healing, sometimes causing ill health. I propose a concept of medical vision as a *skill of managing interference*. Doctors, monks, and the ultrasound machine offer a way to think about expert vision as a practice of sending something out through a medium or matter and receiving a response that must be made sense of. In this framing, vision is an unstable achievement involving a seer, a material, and an action.

This understanding of vision as a skill of managing interference reworks vision rather than jettisons it, in alignment with work in feminist science studies (Haraway 1991) and postcolonial visual studies (Rony 1996) that brings the seer, matter, and act of seeing into a situated and non-totalizing frame. Imaging technologies stabilize this skilled vision, seeing as managing interference, in a mechanized image. The stability of the image is not permanent, nor is the matter that it depicts, yet it enables intervention toward etiology and diagnosis.

Chapter 5 focuses on the ways that women relate to prenatal ultrasound images and to their aesthetics in particular. Medical images are a genre of image that carries particular expectations for how it represents, how it relates to its referent, and who can make and understand it. However, medical images are part of a broad visuality, a modernity saturated with images. A selfie on a phone, a picture of a corpse on the front page of the newspaper, an identification photograph for an official document, or the same identification photograph framed on the wall as a portrait of kin—these carry different expectations about truth, affect, audience, and expertise. In the case of prenatal ultrasound, the ultrasound is a medical image *and* it is a portrait of a child-to-be. It is a document of what is and a projection of what may be. It is an expert and a family image. It is care, in a rich and multiple sense. Medical images offer a temporary but consequential stabilization of the inside of the body. The multiplicity of genre in some medical images amplifies their portent, bringing together multiple representational and ontological commitments.

CHAPTER ONE

FLICKERING HISTORIES

2010

ON THE MORNING OF THE CEREMONY, THE PARKING LOT OF THE KHMER-Soviet Friendship Hospital, commonly called Russian Hospital, was cleared of cars, tuk-tuks, and people, creating a somewhat eerie and expectant quiet. I greeted the hospital director, deputy directors, and German medical equipment distributor with a formal *sompeah*, palms held together and head bent forward, and joined them in waiting. Two large Lexus SUVs—one black, one gold—and a long black sedan pulled up. The US ambassador and representatives from the US multinational corporation General Electric (GE) emerged with bright, serious smiles, accompanied by staff in suits.

I walked through the main courtyard of the hospital, past the open-air payment and waiting area to the meeting room, which was filled with mostly male hospital staff. I sat next to Dr. Pen and Dr. Chandy, radiologists I knew from the imaging ward, who were partly interested but mostly obligated to be there. The chitchat and dull hum of florescent lights were punctuated by the occasional blast of Khmer pop music, a phone ringtone. Some read the newspaper, others watched videos on their phones, one looked through an anatomy textbook. After ten minutes or so, the main doors opened and figures silhouetted by the fierce sunlight entered the room. GE staff, ministers of health, and hospital staff took their seats on the small stage.

The first to speak was the director of Russian Hospital. He spoke in Khmer, pausing for an English translator. The equipment was brand new and high quality, *thmey thmey kunpheap l'a*, and the hospital could not have afforded it on its own, he said. The hospital was "delighted and grateful."

"Most equipment donated to us [before] has been used," he said through the translator. "It had problems or did not work. When broken, these machines were difficult for the hospital to repair because there were so many different types. This is the first time in the history of the hospital for receiving such support. Russian Hospital is committed to maintaining the machines." In closing, the director wished "good health and success" to GE staff.

The second speaker was the vice president of GE corporate citizenship. He spoke in English and in more narrative form, telling the origin story of the Developing Health Globally program in Cambodia and how it had grown beyond expectations. "Two years ago, we began working to improve access to quality health care for the average Cambodian. We hope the additional resources and technology will help dedicated staff at such a large hospital. I know the equipment will be put to good use. Despite our original goal to work at three to four hospitals in Cambodia, by the end of the year, we will have worked at twenty-three hospitals: an X-ray for every CPA 3 hospital in Cambodia!" In closing, he wished the audience well. "Please use the equipment to care for people. I want to unofficially rename this the Khmer-GE Friendship Hospital!"

* * *

The audience laughed at the joke. But what was happening here? There was a substitution: GE replaced the former world superpower, the Soviet Union, never mind that the superpower was half the Cold War and built the hospital in which he stood.[1] Prior to the substitution, there was an erasure. The hospital director praised GE's donation as the first time the hospital had been given new equipment. What about the Soviet Union having equipped the entire hospital that it built?

In this chapter, I explore the pasts that this scene depends on. I sketch a history of medicine centered on technologies to show their promotion, their neglect, and their linkage or not to the vitality of the nation over the dizzying succession of regimes following Independence from France in 1953. X-ray was the star medical technology in the 1960s, and for thirty years, it was the only technology that could see inside the body. Ultrasound enters the story in 1989 and 1993 (there are multiple origin stories). I follow a conventional political periodization because political periods structured different arrangements of capital, infrastructure, and notions of the public good in Phnom Penh. In medicine, four imaginaries mark each successive period: development, destruction, reconstruction, and humanitarianism.

DEVELOPMENT	DESTRUCTION	RECONSTRUCTION	HUMANITARIANISM[2]
Sangkum Reastr Niyum (1955–70)			
	Khmer Republic (1970–75) Democratic Kampuchea (1975–79)		
		People's Republic of Kampuchea (1979–89) State of Cambodia (1989–91)	
			UNTAC (1991–93) Kingdom of Cambodia (1st decade, 1993–2003)
Kingdom of Cambodia (2nd decade, 2003–13)			

The danger of any chart is the erasure of differences within categories. Within periods of optimistic development are practices of improvement of health care infrastructure and education and neglect of patients and entire rural areas. Within the bleakest period of destruction of the medical system, Democratic Kampuchea, there were field schools training medical practitioners, and hospitals in towns continued to operate for high-ranking cadre. The Khmer Republic may be better characterized as a period of undoing, at least from the perspective of medicine and technology. Medicine was practiced but amid draining of human and material resources.

I propose an image of thought for this history of technology as one of flickering presence and argue that this image of thought helps us understand the tempo and form of technological modernity as well as how ultrasound machines come to be or not to be in hospitals. My argument is built from analysis of speeches and conversations; medical journals and promotional films; stories of doctors, government officials, and donors trying to fix Cambodia with and through medical technologies; and the imagination of

Cambodia as a place in need of fixing, a place that can be fixed. By *flickering presence* I mean categorical assessments of presence and absence—Does the hospital have an ultrasound machine or not?—as well as the continuum of what counts as a functioning presence—To what extent can it be used in diagnosis and care?[3] The latter question becomes more pressing after humanitarian need for technologies and infrastructure to provide basic health care after the wars transitioned into development need for a sustainable health care system. Donated used equipment fills a short-term lack but not a longer-term program of care. Just what this longer-term program of health care, the health care system, should look like was very much under debate at the time of my research. It was a high point of health-related development aid from bilateral, corporate, and NGO donors that was intended to support public health. But, occurring as it did in a postsocialist moment, the beginning of an authoritarian elite capitalism, this aid was met with continued retreat of the state and rise of a private sector not orientated to public health.

Receiving donations of X-ray and ultrasound machines is one way to fix a health care system, as we see in the 2010 celebration. But what looks like a fix is not always a fix. Remember two points in the director's speech: *thmey thmey kunpheap l'a*, the equipment was brand new and high quality, and "Russian Hospital is committed to maintaining the machines." The images in the films and texts that follow, and the interlaced statistics and stories, tell one story of machines and labor. However, when donations or purchases are secondhand and do not work, when new hospitals are emptied of their new equipment to move on to the next photo op, this creates what Tess Lea and Paul Pholeros (2010) have called visual-discursive surrealism. In their analysis of Indigenous housing in Australia, they argue that a house is a house only if it has power, water, and sewage. The picture of a house, or calling something a house in a budget or report when it does not have the necessary infrastructure to function, is not a house. Its existence as a non-house serves just about everyone but the recipient (Lea and Pholeros 2010). Similarly, a hospital's donated technologies do not function without the proper maintenance. As the director of Russian Hospital said in his speech, old, used equipment does not fix the problem as intended because it is so difficult to maintain. In the end, the hospital, lucky enough to receive the donation, is responsible for its dysfunction. Thus, not only the absence of technologies but also their presence can be trouble, a kind of trouble that is difficult to account for in donor reports, government strategic plans, and a WHO complementary package of activities. As a flame needs oxygen, technologies require not only maintenance but also infrastructure and skill to be functional. How to represent this in the press release or the ledger?

Finally, flickering as an image for thought suggests how absence and presence contain and condition each other. For GE, Cambodia is an "emerging market" that has endured both underdevelopment and acute annihilation of its health care infrastructure. This underdevelopment and destruction, this "damage," "saturate[s] . . . the fantasies of outsiders" (Tuck 2009, 412) and of insiders. Russian Hospital had X-ray and ultrasound machines and patient monitors, but it received new ones because the image of lack enables an intervention on the part of GE and the Ministry of Health and the hospital. A donation, and a welcoming of the new, as if it were the first time. The Japanese government's foreign aid program, Japan International Cooperation Agency (JICA), found many machines in public hospitals but few of them working (JICA 2010). The lack here is a lack of guidelines for accepting donations and absence of training in equipment maintenance and repair.

Thus, the image of flickering presence of technology conveys not only the dichotomy of presence and absence but also a presence that is not steady, one that is susceptible to being blown out by chance, or by circumstance, or by intention. Flickering also hints at a presence that may be toxic.[4] A low flame may leak gas, an X-ray machine might seep radiation (Grant 2018), a ward with an ultrasound machine may be considered a functioning imaging ward from the perspective of donors or administrators, but if the machine is broken, this is a false presence that exacts a toll on the labor and morale of health care workers and on the health, trust, and pocketbooks of patients.

Juxtaposing different moments in Russian Hospital's biography, we can grasp something of the organization of health care in Phnom Penh, the centrality of technologies to development projects and values, and the shifting roles of foreigners and Cambodians in public health, as well as tropes of "starting from nothing," which are used to mobilize an array of projects.[5] We can also grasp a present for ultrasound imaging that is shaped by a history of concerns about sovereignty over medicine and technology, the histories that development practices promote and the histories that they silence, and how these histories relate to the material presence, absence, and working of technologies. What were the beginnings of this medicine in Cambodia?

1907

French medicine arrived late to colonial Cambodia and Laos relative to Annam, Cochinchina, and Tonkin and remained underdeveloped during the protectorate (1863–1953).[6] The year 1907 marked the beginning of the first sustained medical system aimed at the general population in Cambodia, the

FIGURE 1.1. Medicine as spectacle at the waning of French empire. In the courtyard of a wat, stupas visible in the background, a crowd gathers around the mobile Disease Control Unit as it conducts a medical procedure. A white French man and two Cambodian men bend over a man lying shirtless on an elevated exam bed. The procedure is unclear. Behind them is a truck of sorts, trunks of supplies ajar in the back, medical crosses painted on the side and *Krom Roksa Chomngeu–Srok Khmae* (Disease control unit–Cambodia) painted on the front. The semicircle of observers includes children; some look at the camera, others at a man filming the scene with a camera mounted on a tripod, barely visible at the right. Le Service de Santé en Indochine 1945–1954, box 365, Archives de l'institut de médecine tropicale du service de santé des armées (AIMTSSA). Courtesy of AIMTSSA. Photographer and date unknown.

Assistance Médicale (Au 2011). With the exception of drugs, French health care and its technologies were not alluring to the majority of Cambodians. Historian Sokhieng Au (2011) argues that French and Cambodian fields of medical culture and practice were separate; they did not mix. French medicine circulated through contested vaccination campaigns and largely unsuccessful midwife training programs (these were more successful in rural areas). Later, in the 1940s, traveling medical clinics, such as the one depicted in figure 1.1, were something of a rural spectacle, if only for the presence of the cameras used to film the event.[7] Cambodian doctors went to Hanoi for medical education until Phnom Penh's École des officiers de santé was established in 1946.[8] Dr. My Samedy, a retired radiologist and one of the first graduates from the medical school, told me that students were Cambodian, Vietnamese, and Lao, and teachers were French, Vietnamese, and Cambodian. The course of study was the same program as in Viet Nam.[9]

Only in the waning days of empire did France beef up its medical efforts in Cambodia, perhaps, as Anne Guillou (2009) suggests, emphasizing science and technology in an attempt to regain its political footprint after World War II. The Pasteur Institute established a site in Phnom Penh in 1953, though a microbiology laboratory had been opened earlier, part of the "high-performance network" of labs supervised by Pasteur Institutes in Saigon, Nha Trang, Hanoi, and Dalat (Dedet 2008, 31). However, until Independence in 1953, medicine and biological research were still largely undeveloped, and for access to advanced technologies such as X-ray, Cambodians had to travel east to Viet Nam. Figure 1.2 depicts the armed services' X-ray ward in Saigon. The multi-racial composition of patients, technicians, and medical officers in these scenes suggests that military and medical circuits of French empire were still active. But the box at the archive of the Armed Services Institute of Tropical Medicine, dated 1945 to 1954, locates the scene at the tormented end of French Indochina.[10] Of the three main medical projects enacted during the ninety years of French colonization—the military health service, the civilian health service or Assistance Médicale, and the Pasteur Institute—only the Pasteur Institute continued operation after Independence.

1960

The grounds of the Khmer-Soviet Friendship Hospital teemed with ministers, foreign dignitaries, and hospital staff in white coats. August sun was blazing, and overlapping conversations in Khmer, French, and Russian pulsed with the electricity of anticipation. Sihanouk, the prince and elected leader of post-Independence Cambodia, was beaming with achievement: a brand-new hospital, the largest in Southeast Asia, a *vaste cité médicale* with cutting-edge equipment and training. Dancers waited to perform ballet in the opening ceremony, sweating under costumes and make-up, gold headdresses glowing, green and red silk radiating.

The USSR designed, constructed, and equipped the hospital buildings as a gift to the government and people of Cambodia.[11] Occupying a site in the southwest of the city, a former sanitarium for those with contagious diseases such as cholera,[12] the new buildings were massive, symmetric, and aspiring,

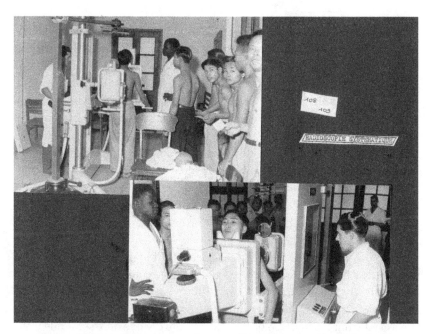

FIGURE 1.2. A front and back view of a room filled with men, the majority of whom look Vietnamese, Cambodian, or Lao, and a large X-ray machine. The caption, *Radioscopie systématique* (Routine fluoroscopy), suggests this is a scene of routine imaging. A man stands for a chest fluoroscopy between the X-ray machine and the fluoroscopic screen, with a technician on either side. One technician, who is Black, stands hands on hips, and the other, who is white, stands behind a screen and control panel. Along the wall is a line of shirtless men, waiting for their exam. Some turn their heads to look at the camera; some hold a slip of paper. White shirts and a hat are piled on chairs. In the bottom photo, the X-ray machine takes center stage; the patient, chin up, looks calmly ahead, and the technicians look at him, or at the machine, or at each other, it is hard to tell. Le Service de Santé en Indochine 1945–1954, box 365, Archives de l'institut de médecine tropicale du service de santé des armées (AIMTSSA). Courtesy of AIMTSSA. Photographer and date unknown.

"like a bird with two wings," the Russian ambassador said in his speech to the crowd assembled for the inauguration.[13] Concrete but permeable, the hospital's structural elements, such as open-air passageways, lattice walls, and louvered windows, shaded the sun and allowed air to flow. Modernist in material, tropical in form, multiple in language, the hospital was a delicate composition at a time when the Cold War had not yet crushed Cambodia's struggle to remain non-aligned.

The idea for Russian Hospital came to Sihanouk during his 1956 visit to Moscow,[14] as a part of the post-Independence government's priority to develop a modern health care system. The Sangkum Reastr Niyum (1955–70)—commonly translated as "the People's Socialist Community" but literally "community favored by the people"—was Sihanouk's political party and ideology.[15] Sihanouk and official publications referred to this ideology as "Buddhist socialism" or "Khmer socialism." This socialism was officially described as following the "middle way" of Buddhism, emphasizing social equilibrium, mutual assistance, and individual merit.[16] Practically speaking, this meant a state-controlled economy but without land collectivization and with mixed ownership in some domains to stimulate private savings and investment and protect the vulnerable from exploitation by both foreign and national capitalist elites (Slocomb 2010).

In health care, the middle way expressed itself in the growth of both the government health care system and the private sector. This entanglement of government and private health care returned in the 1990s and exists today, in a different amalgamation of capitalist free market and authoritarian state control. During the high Cold War, the Buddhist value of "the middle way" performed as the ideological foundation for both capitalist-socialist features in domestic policy and neutralism in foreign policy (Ewing 2019; Slocomb 2006, 389). Cambodia joined the United Nations, and Sihanouk was an official speaker at Bandung and a vigorous advocate for the non-aligned movement in the 1950s and 1960s.

Russian Hospital was born in a time when the Sangkum government was doing what it could to build the new nation. "Friendship" named gifts given by both sides of the Cold War.[17] Cambodia was one of sixteen new countries in Asia and Africa targeted by the USSR for "non-capitalist development," which meant development of the state not necessarily associated with a communist revolution.[18] A part of this development involved educating foreign nationals in the USSR and establishing training institutions in targeted countries (Tsvetkova 2008). Cambodian students and officials welcomed Soviet aid in fields that seemed politically neutral, such as medicine and technology, and rejected aid in fields perceived as overtly ideological, such as education (Tsvetkova n.d.). In the 1950s and early 1960s, Cambodia also received significant military and other aid from the United States.[19] In 1959, the Khmer-American Friendship Highway from Phnom Penh to Kampong Som was inaugurated, followed a year later by the Khmer-Soviet Friendship Hospital.

* * *

After introductory speeches, the inauguration ceremony moved on to a performance of Khmer dance by the Royal Ballet Corps with a song composed specially for the occasion.[20] The first two verses of the song are:

> Welcome to his Excellency, the Minister,
> Please convey our sincerest thanks
> To the people of Russia, our friends
> Who have the generosity to help the Cambodian nation.
> Friends, you have given the gift of a hospital,
> A great building of 500 beds,
> All the equipment needed for care
> And treatment of all types of diseases.

Note that "equipment" receives special mention: "all the equipment needed for care / and treatment of all types of diseases." (Recall as well the Russian Hospital director thanking GE for its 2010 donation of equipment: "the first time in the history of the hospital for receiving such support.") The lyrics are remarkable, too, in how they detail the number of beds: 500. Russian Hospital had seven units: general medicine (150 beds, 10 for radiotherapy), surgery (60 beds), maternity (40 beds), women's health (20 beds), tuberculosis (120 beds), infectious disease (60 beds), and pediatrics (50 beds).[21] Of the 500 beds, 200 were for patients able to pay a fee, and 300 were for free medical care for the poor, monks, and civil servants who earned less than 25,000 riel. The USSR pledged to donate medicine for two years, to support twenty-four Russian staff (doctors, nurses, technicians, and translators), and to fund twenty scholarships for Cambodians to study medicine in the USSR.[22] What a gift! Radiologist Rethy Chhem (2018), who completed some of his training at Russian Hospital in the early 1970s, called Russian Hospital a significant act of medical diplomacy.

X-ray and radiation therapy were star technologies at Russian Hospital. An eleven-page spread in the government magazine, *Cambodge d'Aujourd'hui*, covered the origin story of the hospital, inauguration speeches, images from the ceremony, statistics on service capacity, and special sections on surgery, radiology, and general medicine.[23] The radiology section includes two images: one of an X-ray machine in the exam room and one of a cobalt therapy machine "in use." There are no credits; this is how I read the image: A patient lying down, shirtless, is attended by four clinical staff in white coats and caps and a large white machine. A Cambodian man and a Russian woman stand on either side of the cobalt machine, stabilizing the machine over the patient's abdomen with graceful hands. A second Cambodian man leans forward, hands on the patient's right shoulder. A third man stands just behind, intently observing the machine in use. The scene is one of international cooperation and competence in technological care.

It is possible that in 2010, the director of Russian Hospital and the GE VP for corporate citizenship did not know the story of how the hospital got its name, what was involved in its construction, or that it was a pillar of the Sihanouk government's campaign of developing modern medicine and health care. "[A]mnesia is more likely to be induced by the desire for reconciliation" (Kammen 1991, 13), whereas memory is more likely to be activated by contestation. A donation ceremony is a coming together, a ritual (Grant 2017b) of friendly relations between government and corporation, Cambodia and the United States, doctors and bureaucrats and businesspeople, capitalist and formerly socialist imaginaries. Amnesia, for what it contributes to an image of thought, is also an agonist of ethnography.

1968

> It is with great pleasure that I observe how the Khmer medical profession dedicates itself to scientific research and to making its work known at the international level. This is, for me, a cause of immense satisfaction because our superior work shows that Cambodia has taken its place amongst nations that contribute to the progress of humanity. (Norodom Sihanouk, 1968)

By 1968, much had changed in Phnom Penh medicine since Independence. There were health professionals, hospitals, clinics, periodicals, medicines, and machines. These advances were intimately linked to the vitality of the new nation-state. Between 1955 and 1964, the number of doctors in the government health service, "national doctors," increased from 5 to 87, health officers from 72 to 186, and nurses from 630 to 1,432 (Crochet 2008, 371). The previously French-administered Royal School of Medicine became the Cambodian Faculty of Medicine in 1962; though the language of medical training and administration remained French, the course of study continued to be modeled after the one in Viet Nam,[24] and Cambodian physicians continued to train in France.[25] This growth in medical infrastructure and professionals would not find its return for forty years.[26]

In addition to professional training, the construction of buildings and publication of health-related periodicals were central to Sihanouk's program for improving public health and the health system. In 1955, there were 119 hospitals, district health centers, commune infirmaries, and dispensaries in

Cambodia. Fourteen years later, in 1969, there were 656 of these health facilities, including an over fourfold increase in hospitals. Between 1955 and 1967, the number of pharmacies increased from 24 to 300 and the number of rural birthing centers from 60 to 644 (Guillou 2001, 119). During the 1960s, the government published reports on "Public Health in Cambodia"[27] and periodicals for health workers,[28] and the Royal Society of Medicine published a bulletin[29] about its activities. By the end of the 1960s, medical tools and medications represented 3 percent of foreign commerce, predominantly with France (Crochet 2008, 373). Advanced technologies were one of the things that drew young people to the medical profession in the 1960s (Guillou 2009, 182). Also during this period, local companies began to manufacture medicines and some materials, such as compresses, which were advertised in the pages of the *Annals of the Khmer-Soviet Friendship Hospital.*

The spectacular increase in the number of medical professionals, institutions, and materials was documented in film and print media, educating a public on how to understand its belonging to the nation. *Actualités* (newsreels) and promotional films from the Sangkum depict medicine as part of the making of modern Cambodia and the modern Khmer woman in particular.[30] *Cambodian Women in the Time of the Sangkum* is a twenty-four-minute Khmer-language film made in 1960 by the Sangkum communications bureau. The film depicts women manufacturing pharmaceuticals in a factory, operating an X-ray machine, assisting in surgery, and performing experiments in a medical laboratory (in addition to sowing rice, dancing, teaching, playing basketball, sailing, painting, and performing military exercises).[31] An undated *actualité*, most likely from the early 1960s, devotes two of its five segments to health-related activities: women being trained in modern midwifery at a Phnom Penh medical center and "A day at the Ta Khmao health center," which tells us that the United States, WHO, and Cambodia are working together in health prevention and treatment. We are also shown that in addition to breastfeeding mothers, a maternity ward, and children receiving vaccinations, the center has a laboratory and microscopes so that "health will rise up and blossom."[32]

The objective of the government was technological modernity and the international circulation of knowledge and reputation enabled by techno-modernity. Indeed, as historians of medicine have shown, Sihanouk was not unique in promoting technological medicine, clinical research, and public health care as core to biodevelopmentalist nation-building (Lock and Nguyen 2010). Similar initiatives were undertaken by new governments in postcolonial Africa, South and Southeast Asia, and the Pacific.[33] Future histories of medicine in Southeast Asia would benefit from tracing decolonial ideals and

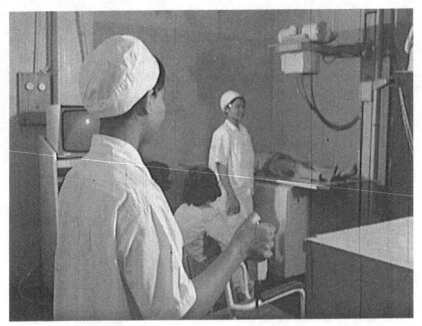

FIGURE 1.3. Woman operating X-ray machine, Democratic Kampuchea. This color image, a still from the film *Scientific System of Instruction under the Khmer Rouge*, depicts an X-ray exam room in a hospital. In the frame are an X-ray machine; two technicians in white coats and caps, both women; one patient lying on an exam table; and two women, perhaps parents or relatives, sitting facing the patient. One technician stands in the foreground, her back to the camera as she faces the X-ray machine. She holds a control in her right hand and seems about to "click" it. The other technician stands by the exam bed, turned slightly to face the camera. *Scientific System of Instruction under the Khmer Rouge*, DDC_VI_001358, Bophana Center. Courtesy of the Bophana Audiovisual Resource Center.

practices across regions; Southeast Asian and African medical histories still have much to tell each other.

At Russian Hospital, Cambodian and Soviet doctors, nurses, technicians, and translators collaborated throughout the decade on clinical care, training, research, and publication. The *Annals of the Khmer-Soviet Friendship Hospital*,[34] Cambodia's first medical journal oriented to cosmopolitan medicine, was published in French between 1961 and 1971. It contains case studies and epidemiological reports co-authored by Soviet and Cambodian clinicians, X-rays, photographs, and other forms of writing and imagery. In their 1962 case study of esophagoplasty for a twenty-three-year-old who was unable to eat, Soviet physician Mokchniouk and Cambodian physician

Thoeun offer a step-by-step description of diagnostic process, selection of surgical intervention amid a range of options, rationale for treatment choice, surgery, and follow-up. They offer three different techniques of imaging the body: drawing, photography, and X-ray. This case study is an exemplary representation of the scientific, didactic, cooperative, and pragmatic tone of many of the articles in the journal (Grant 2017a). The prefaces by ministers of health and even Prince Sihanouk (an excerpt from his 1968 preface is quoted above) attest to the prominence of scientifically and technologically advanced medicine as a national project. It is telling that Sihanouk's administration refused an offer from China to train barefoot doctors, despite close diplomatic relations (Guillou 2001, 114–15).

Toward the end of the 1960s, there was rapid depletion of public finances, increasing corruption, and persecution of those who advocated political economic alternatives to the Sangkum (Chandler 1992, 191–204). Furthermore, the health infrastructure numbers mentioned above may give a false impression. According to Au (2011, 182) and Crochet (2008, 370–71), new buildings and their technologies were hollow symbols of progress, spectacle without function. Hospitals were emptied of medicine, staff, and equipment soon after their opening in order to furnish the next inauguration. Furthermore, development was vastly uneven. While Phnom Penh received hospitals equipped with modern technologies, the "theatrical symbol par excellence of Sihanouk's modernism" (Guillou 2009, 182), facilities and care for the rural population remained underdeveloped.

Sometimes the gift, however generous, is costly. Guillou even writes of the gift of Russian Hospital as "a little poisoned" (2001, 117): despite free medicines and Soviet technical experts, the Cambodian government was responsible for operation costs, and as the decade progressed, these costs were difficult to support. Officials explicitly confronted the costs of medical equipment donations to the government health system in the 2010s. These were on a much smaller scale—ultrasound machines, patient monitors—but when used and with a limited life span, parts were hard to find and repair was expensive.

When images or words claim a particular reality—a new hospital, a new machine—that does not obtain, what to do? Some scholars respond by unmasking a façade built on false consciousness; some respond with the surreal (Lea and Pholeros 2010) or with haunting (Gordon [1997] 2008). Lea and Pholeros (2010) advocate doubling down on empirical realities or what they call "dirty materialism." The point is not new—that presence may not be what it seems, that it may be the shell of an absence, a mask of something else—certainly not in Marxist and psychoanalytic thought (see Gordon

[1997] 2008). What to *do* with the absence or false presence is the interesting question. Bringing together numbers, texts, images, jokes, memories, and mourning to understand an image of thought is my strategy, which for me complements the dirty materialism of others, the reports and testimonies that expose what was actually there and what happened.[35] The story of the Sangkum as a high point of medicine and the Russian Hospital as its shiny core is, for many health professionals, a shell around the unspeakable discouragement that followed.

1971

In this period of enormous difficulty of all kinds caused by the aggression against our country by the North Vietnamese and Vietcong, the persistence of scientific activity is a guarantee of our will to survive the annexationist appetite of the Foreigner. (So Satta, 1971)

So Satta wrote these words in the 1970/1971 preface to what would be the final issue of Russian Hospital's medical journal. Though the *Annals* ceased publication, Russian Hospital stayed open after the 1970 coup that ousted the Sihanouk government and during the Khmer Republic. Newsreels from the beginning of the Republic depict health activities but not in the idiom of "national development." Rather, we see reel after reel of blood donations, military hospitals, and physical rehabilitation for soldiers, indicating the new government's focus on the civil war.[36] If the Sangkum was oriented to building public services, the Republic was characterized by the disruption of services, including damage to infrastructure, shortage of materials, and only sporadic humanitarian support for refugees on the city outskirts.

Radiologist and historian Rethy Chhem told me about the intensities of studying medicine in the early 1970s: "It was a very particular time to train as a doctor. Training during wartime builds character! The courses were on and off. The city was shelled by rockets from the communists. We had a lot of exposure to trauma, [and] we spent a lot of time in the operating room. However, we were young and this was the only world we knew. Weekends would be one day an impromptu party—daytime only because of the curfew—and one day volunteering in the refugee camps."[37] Chhem led the youth section of the Red Cross, every weekend taking a group of students to the refugee camps on the outskirts of Phnom Penh to do sanitary and anticholera work. Humanitarian medicine for internal refugees would become an erratic but recurring mode of health care in Cambodia: different humanitarian actors did different work in the early 1970s, the early 1980s, and the 1990s. The civil war between the Republic and the Khmer Rouge, behind whom Sihanouk had thrown his support, and the devastating US bombing in the north and east of the country had propelled the first of many mass displacements of people. In the early 1970s, refugees flooded the cities, primarily Phnom Penh. In 1975, the cities would be forcibly emptied by the Khmer Rouge. After 1979, people would return to the capital, by bicycle or on foot.[38]

Dr. Chhem's father was killed in 1974 by a grenade attack at a wedding. Phuong Monich, a prominent radiologist and family friend, was the one who told Chhem the devastating news: "'Your father has been killed. Go and bring him home,' he said. I picked up my father's body on Monivong Street. Instantly I grew up. I was the oldest son."

The situation in Phnom Penh became worse and worse. The medical school was more often closed than open; there was very little teaching going on. Chhem saw a lot of corruption in the hospital. He shook his head as he described nurses and doctors selling medicine and rich patients getting a room while poor soldiers were left suffering in the courtyard. Across the city, similar forms of corruption, as well as the buying of diplomas and jobs, tarnished the public's image of doctors during the Republic (Guillou 2009, 52). There was no future for Chhem's medical training in Phnom Penh. But his mother was there. He was torn.

"I asked my mother about leaving. She said, 'I would rather have you go and study than stay with me. You cannot shield me from the rockets. Go.'" Chhem decided to join his younger brother, who was in Paris on a fellowship. Two of his sisters went to Laos, where they had a family connection. Chhem left Phnom Penh on 13 April 1975, on the last commercial flight out of the country.[39]

Many doctors responded to the hardships of the civil war by leaving the country or retreating into private practice. A few joined the revolution, the most prominent being the director of Russian Hospital, Dr. Thiounn Thioeun, whose biography would offer an alternative history of medicine in Cambodia. Thiounn was a highly regarded surgeon, scholar, teacher, and administrator. He was an advisor to the *Annals* and authored or co-authored sixty-three articles between 1961 and 1969, including the one described in the previous section (Grant 2017a). He was dean of the Faculty of Medicine at the University of Health Sciences. Thiounn joined the revolution following the coup in 1970 and established field schools for health workers. Thiounn returned to Russian Hospital as minister of health during Democratic Kampuchea (Ovesen and Trankell 2010, 127). Thiounn, however, was an exception; the majority of doctors worked in medicine as a way to earn a good living, with the security of a government position. Anne Guillou (2009) calls this formation *les médecins fonctionnaires-entrepreneur*, the doctor as civil servant–entrepreneur. If we follow her assertion that the entrepreneurial spirit was as compelling, if not more, than the spirit of public service (imperfectly realized within the state bureaucracy), we can see why doctors may not have been enamored of a leftist politics, nor leftist politicians of doctors.

1975

> Our children and youth spent all their time making war and
> gathering food. . . . Let us not forget that later we will need a more
> advanced technology. But scientific education and technology
> should obey this orientation: our technicians and scientists should
> first forge themselves in the mass movement. (Khieu Samphan,
> c. 1975; cited in Slocomb 2010, 203)

During the Khmer Rouge period, the vitality of the nation-state was not linked to health through technomedicine, and a good life was not to be found through private enterprise, including medical practice. Ownership of private property was abolished, along with money, markets, Buddhism, family relations, and schools. Instead, "the revolution itself was a public health enterprise" (Guillou 2004, 10). The nation would be independent, modern, and developed, echoing the glory of Angkor, once Cambodia was self-sufficient in rice. Khmer Rouge films focus on activities oriented toward this goal of self-sufficiency, particularly farming and dam and irrigation construction. Medicine does not feature prominently, though amid the silent black-and-white films at the Bophana Center is a short color film with voice-over, *Scientific System of Instruction under the Khmer Rouge*.[40] It depicts a laboratory of traditional medicine and orderly piles of pellets, ampoules, and glass bottles. Everyone in the lab wears a pristine white coat, as do instructors and students in a classroom and on a hospital ward. The X-ray machine makes an appearance too. It is operated by two women, who scan the legs of a child at the Revolutionary Children's Hospital. Every cooperative, district, and city has a hospital, the film claims. Another film depicts bags of serum and small glass jars of liquid, but there is no other information to confirm what the medicines are.[41]

Across the country, a two-tiered medical system was enforced: one for the people and one for high-ranking cadre (Ovesen and Trankell 2010).

Illness was defined as the inability to work and thus morally suspect. The public, if a notion of the public applies, received "traditional" medicine from minimally trained providers. As medical expertise was linked to ideological purity, the ability to practice medicine was awarded to those with favorable politics, often the young and those untainted by bourgeois or imperialist ideology (Guillou 2009).[42] However, hospital and indeed technological medicine was not absent. Elites and their families received care from trained doctors in urban hospitals (Ovesen and Trankell 2010). Russian Hospital, renamed the April 17 Hospital for the date Phnom Penh fell, was reserved for high-ranking cadre, along with two other government hospitals in the capital, Calmette and Preah Ket Mealea.

My Samedy's memoir, *Survivor for the Surviving* (2000), vividly illustrates who received care and from whom. Before Democratic Kampuchea, My was a radiologist with a private practice in Phnom Penh. After being forced to leave the city with his family, My's survival depended on his ability to diagnose and treat, and even to repair an X-ray machine, when called upon and to hide these abilities when not. He would be taken away from his village without warning or information, terrified that this meant his death, and end up in a provincial city required to treat a family member of high-ranking cadre. Unlike in the revolutionary hospitals, where treatment failure was the fault of the patient, here, if the patient was not cured, it would be My's fault, evidence of his disloyalty to the revolution. In other words, fixing an old GE X-ray machine, or treating a sister of an elite, was a question of life or death.[43] Then, back at the village, My had to labor in the fields like everyone else and take care not to arouse the suspicion of those who thought medical or scientific expertise was a sign of bourgeois betrayal of the revolution.

1980

In January 1979, the Khmer Rouge were ousted from Phnom Penh and thus political control of the country by a coalition of former Khmer Rouge and Vietnamese armies. Medicine as mode of nation-building returned, this time in the idiom of socialist reconstruction. In films from the People's Republic of Kampuchea (PRK, 1979–89), the gendered nature of how reconstruction would proceed becomes clear. In contrast to the film about women in the Sangkum, *The Role of Women in the Reconstruction of the Country*[44] emphasizes four duties for women in the PRK:

1. encourage husbands to return from the forest (i.e., defect from the Khmer Rouge and come out of hiding);

2. allow your sons to become soldiers for the government;
3. give birth; and
4. reformulate the education system for children.

The section about giving birth depicts an operation and a checkup at Russian Hospital, and the voice-over tells us that women are now able to have children again rather than suffer the threat of death to themselves or their newborns. In the film, medicine returns the ability to reproduce, which was robbed from women (and the nation) through malnourishment, overwork, and lack of medical care under the "dark regime." The PRK was a brief period of pronatalism, similar to postwar Viet Nam (Gammeltoft 2014), in which the government strongly encouraged reproduction, and medical technologies as tools for reproduction, to compensate for deaths and lack of births.

"Mother's milk will flow again." This poetic imagery, in a half-hour film from 1980, is both promise and command, hope and obligation. The film depicts the reopening of the medical school—"Thank you, revolution!"—and people being examined in a doctor's office, in addition to the reestablishment of other institutional (post office, library, school of dance) and non-institutional forms (wedding ceremonies, swimming, street performances, rice farming).[45] Another film from the PRK depicts medical exams, surgeries, and a male doctor thoughtfully studying X-rays of the chest and leg.[46] The Khmer-language narration states that since liberation, the Ministry of Health has struggled tirelessly, night and day, to fulfill its duties to the health of the people and that it will use modern technology and materials to achieve these goals.

Many doctors, nurses, dentists, and pharmacists were trained during the PRK as the government sought out those with some medical experience who were able to teach. Not only were there few teachers and materials, but there were few even qualified to be students.[47] My Samedy was asked to be dean of the reopened medical school in 1979, and he described the time as extremely challenging. Out of 3,400 medical students in the early 1970s, only seven or eight remained after Democratic Kampuchea. Only five or six in pharmacy. Only one dentist. Only fifteen doctors.[48] This was primarily due to death but also because of the large numbers who fled the country in the early 1970s, before the fall of Phnom Penh.

In *Rebirth of Kampuchea*, My leads a group down an open-air passageway of Russian Hospital, explaining that hospitals are open and providing care for the people.[49] One can see the white-and-yellow checkered tiles that still line the floor of the imaging ward waiting area. An interior scene shows a white man and a Cambodian woman in white coats, looking together at an X-ray. Later a different man holds an X-ray up to the light to examine its contents. The film cuts abruptly to a snowscape—snowball fights, laughter, Cambodian and Russian young adults in fur caps walking arm-in-arm. The life of Cambodian students in Moscow.

In the 1980s, only a select few were able to pursue higher education in the USSR and former Eastern Europe. The first generation of twenty or so students studied medicine, linguistics, economics, and civil engineering, and many of them held senior positions in hospitals, government, banks, and universities.[50] At the time of my research, the directors of the medical imaging wards at Russian Hospital and Calmette had studied medicine and radiology in Kiev and East Germany, respectively.

Dr. Chhum, the head of imaging at Russian Hospital, started working there in 1987. Things were in bad shape then, he told me.

"Doctors did not communicate well with each other," he said. "Diagnoses were vague, and scans were only ordered once a diagnosis was provided. But diagnosis is what the scans are for!"

Dr. Chhum was frustrated that X-ray interpretations were different across doctors. Problems with interpretation (*kar bakbrae*), quality (*kunpheap*) of materials, and poorly maintained machines meant that during that period, he says, "X-rays were not so useful."[51] He was unable to practice the medicine he had been trained for in Kiev.

Students are no longer sent to Kiev for medical school and specialization, and the German Democratic Republic no longer exists. If students train abroad, they go to France, Japan, sometimes Australia, Viet Nam, or the United States. In 1989, the Soviets withdrew support for reconstruction, and the Vietnamese authorities and army left Cambodia. The new State of Cambodia (1989–91) faced the problem of what to do about the ongoing war with resistance factions that were operating out of refugee camps along the Thai border, armed by China and the West. The 1991 Paris Peace Agreements formally ended the civil war and made the country a UN mandate. From January 1992 to 1993, the UN Transitional Authority for Cambodia, or UNTAC, controlled significant areas of administration, including defense, foreign affairs, information, and finance, while preparations were made for democratic elections, held over six days in May 1993 (Slocomb 2010, 231).[52] During the UNTAC mandate, NGOs came to the country to manage repatriation of over 300,000 refugees from the border camps in Thailand and to provide humanitarian, especially health-related, aid.

1989/1993

At this moment, when postsocialism and postconflict humanitarianism meet, it becomes possible to narrate a history of ultrasound in Phnom Penh. Until this point, X-ray was the only way to see inside the body. There is no singular origin story of ultrasound, though the two that I heard involve foreign humanitarian aid. Was the first machine donated to Calmette Hospital by the French toward the end of 1989 or to Russian Hospital by Japan in 1993?[53] Does it even matter which was first? The director of the imaging ward at Calmette told me that their first ultrasound machine was used in obstetrics, following training by a French gynecologist. This machine was old, and it broke within two years. Calmette Hospital then bought two ultrasound machines for itself, one "expensive, good, new" (*"thlai thlai l'a l'a thmey thmey"*) and another secondhand.

The donation story told by the imaging director is of a genre, one could call it "the genre of the humanitarian machine, 1993." A decade and a half later, another story. Around the time of GE's Developing Health Globally donation program, one of Neary's professors, the director of a large government hospital in Phnom Penh, told her he was not interested in magnetic resonance imaging (MRI) or computerized tomography (CT) machine donations. If the donor did not supply training, staff would not know how to operate and maintain the machines. If the machine broke, it would be too expensive to fix. His hospital had received a donated CT machine. It broke two weeks after it was donated, as the doctor trying to use it had not been trained. The professor told Neary that he and his staff felt embarrassed that they could not make use of such a gift. It would cost US$100,000 to fix, an impossible sum to pay. So, radiology staff pretended it was not there, and the hospital carried on its work as if it did not have a CT machine.

Compare these stories of donation, noting the suspicion, embarrassment, and pretending that they entail, to the stories of the new X-ray machine donated from the people of the USSR, told by the government in 1960, or of the new ultrasound machines and patient monitors donated by GE, told by the Russian Hospital director in 2010. Even if a machine is new, its presence is no guarantee of better health care. Are the people—technicians, doctors, nurses—trained to use the machine? Is the environment humid, or dusty, and is the electrical current protected from surges and failures? Are there resources for cleaning and maintenance, including training for mechanics and spare parts for repair? The fix for health, and health care, must be more than a machine, but this is often beyond the ambit of humanitarian aid. What, then, does development look like? After the Paris Peace Agreements, the NGO was to become a central actor in health-related development and service provision. But the NGO is rarely in it for nation-building. Which actor takes on the building and repair of water and sewage systems (see Jensen 2017), electricity grids, hospitals, or university programs?

1993

The specificity and significance of the humanitarian and development aid of the post-UNTAC period was made clear to me in Montréal, of all places, where I attended the 2011 American Anthropological Association meetings. I took a taxi from the airport to a friend's apartment and had a sociable driver, Lim. Lim was born in Cambodia and came to Canada as a refugee in the early 1980s. We spoke in Khmer about his life in Canada, his vacation house in Costa Rica, his daughter studying film and animation, and my research in Cambodia. I used the term *âphivadd*, development, and he laughed and said he hadn't heard that word before. I said it in English, and he shook his head, eyes moving between the road and me in the rearview mirror.

"Strange word! Is it Sanskrit?"

"How would you say 'development'?" I asked.

Lim shrugged. "I don't know, before you would just say *cheuan leuan*" (to be developed, advanced).[54]

At the turn of the twenty-first century, development became a Sanskrit-sounding noun, one that conferred an almost scientific legitimacy to innumerable activities of NGOs, governments, universities, multilateral agencies, and corporate foundations working in Cambodia after UNTAC.[55] Lim was amused by the jargon; his lack of familiarity with the term *âphivadd* marks how these forms of development existed in a distinct postconflict, postsocialist time-space (and one that did not include refugees).

Following the decade of socialist reconstruction and isolation from the West, the UNTAC period was experienced by many in Phnom Penh as a sudden and dramatic influx of new people, resources, objects, and activities. Old practices were allowed again, including traditional medicine and private medical practice. Buddhism was not only permitted but encouraged and declared the national religion in 1989. As someone told anthropologists Jan Ovesen and Ing-Britt Trankell (2010, 15), "UNTAC released all the spirits."

Cambodia's experience with humanitarianism co-occurred with postsocialist structural adjustment in the 1990s, a decade after many economies of Africa and Latin America were shocked into neoliberal immiseration. For Cambodia, the scope and texture of this shock is hard to comprehend. The socialist economy had started to liberalize in the late 1980s, along with Viet

Nam's market reforms, but even so, the state had been the sole provider of many public services. Structural adjustment meant reducing the public-sector workforce, lowering public salaries, cutting public-sector budgets, removing subsidies and price controls, selling state-owned services, and weakening labor and environment regulations. All this after a decade of the state trying to build itself and its public.[56] In health, adjustment took the form of user fees, private insurance schemes, outsourcing government services to NGOs and private entities, and decentralization, practices discussed in more detail in the following chapter.

2010 (MAINTENANCE AND REPAIR)

What did *âphivadd*, Cambodia's particular configuration of postconflict development, mean for medical technologies such as ultrasound? Twenty years after the first ultrasound machines came into use in Phnom Penh, tropes of absence that motivated patchwork donation of equipment in the 1990s and early 2000s were making way to tropes of breakdown. From categorical presence—"Are there machines or not?"—to continuum of presence—"Are the machines functioning?"—doctors, donors, and officials voiced concern about the quality of equipment and the capacity to manage and maintain it.

The Ministry of Health developed their medical equipment management guidelines with JICA. JICA's MEDEM2 project followed MEDEM1, which started in 2006. MEDEM1 found that "there was no clear concept of medical equipment management" (JICA 2010), according to Takeshi Matsuo, chief advisor to the project, thus MEDEM2's objective was "to train users in the maintenance and up-keep of medical equipment." The following excerpt from a JICA column describes the poor condition of equipment and relates this condition to development practices following the civil war.

> In many public Cambodian hospitals, we see unused medical equipment, much of it broken with spare parts impossible to find.
> The medical equipment in question includes varieties such as X-ray diagnostic equipment, ultrasound scanners, operating tables, and infant incubators. Not all the equipment is used every day but it is important that it is ready to be put into use at any time. But according to a survey of 22 public hospitals in this country, only 43% of all the medical equipment was in good condition. 38% were "fair" and 16% were broken. Mr. Matsuo said, "It is surprising that less than half of the equipment is in good

condition." After the civil war, a lot of medical equipment was sent to Cambodia through both governmental and nongovernmental cooperation, however there was no training in terms of maintenance. "Some of it was used equipment so its life span was limited and parts were especially hard to find," Mr. Matsuo said. JICA wants to establish a guideline for accepting such used equipment. (JICA 2010)

This brief statement makes explicit how donation became a problem: multiple actors, governmental and nongovernmental; machines, but no training in maintenance; used machines with limited life span; parts that were hard to find. The Ministry of Health's Technical Working Group on Health (TWGH) added cost to this list of problems. In the minutes of a 2011 TWGH meeting, the chairman stated, "[the MOH] does not encourage and gradually reduces the import of second hand electronic medical equipment owing to the fact that they are difficult to fix or very costly" (Ministry of Health—TWGH Secretariat 2011, 3).

Perhaps now it is easier to grasp why, in 2010, the director of Russian Hospital emphasized the newness of the equipment donated by GE. At the time, the cumulative problems of multiple donors, fragmented donation, and the costs of maintenance and repair were at the forefront of people's minds.

2010 (SUBADDITIONALITY)

From today's vantage, the time of my research was a high point of health-related development aid to Cambodia—or more accurately, to NGOs working in Cambodia. This was generally the case for low- and middle-income countries around the world at the time. Globally, "development assistance for health," or DAH as it is known in health economics, quadrupled between 1990 and 2007, with particular acceleration after 2002 (Ravishankar et al. 2009). DAH comes from public sources, such as the WHO and other UN programs, but the more striking increases in DAH came from private sources, such as the Bill and Melinda Gates Foundation, US NGOs that mobilize private philanthropy, and multinational corporations. "In particular, *corporate drug and equipment donations* have expanded substantially" (Ravishankar et al. 2009, 2121; emphasis mine).[57] Though not dealing exclusively with Cambodia, Cambodia is included in the analysis, and the time frame of the study is that of Cambodia's re-entry to the Euro-American development scene after almost twenty years of sanctions and isolation.

One outcome of increases in DAH is that Ministries of Finance tend to reduce domestic health spending, a phenomenon intriguingly called "sub-additionality" (Lu et al. 2010, 1383). If DAH continues to increase, and government health expenditure as a share of general expenditure continues to decrease, what does this mean for government health programs over the longer term? How does a Ministry of Health plan for subadditionality, when funds are controlled by the Ministry of Finance? The Cambodian Ministry of Health operates in cooperation with many "development partners" to support basic services for the poor. In the 2010s, the Ministry of Health collaborated with twenty-two bilateral donors,[58] seven "global health partners,"[59] two multilateral partners (GAVI and the Global Fund), the Association of Southeast Asian Nations (ASEAN),[60] three universities,[61] as well as dozens of local NGOs. The National Cancer Center at Calmette Hospital, opened in 2018, was funded by the governments of Cambodia and France and by the International Atomic Energy Agency (Amaro 2018). Ministers did not belabor to me the intricacies of these collaborations, but one can only imagine the challenges of integrating different policies, priorities, and standards for reporting, monitoring, evaluation, and ethics review. Government hospitals are sites where it is possible to witness the struggle of administrators and clinicians to raise money and to create transparency and accountability.[62]

At Russian Hospital, there were visible signs of transparency efforts and improvement in infrastructure after a long period of stagnancy. New signs in the lab and imaging ward listed services and their prices. New centrifuge machines took up counter space in the newly renovated laboratory. A new patient wing was under construction, and new mental health and methadone centers were completed in 2010. On my monthly visits to the lab while pregnant, I noticed small tweaks in blood draw protocol as they worked out their new systems.

These changes, which indicate an influx of funds and materials, prioritized infrastructure and machines over more mundane technologies and basic materials. Medical staff performed duties that in other contexts might be automated or performed by subordinates. I spent my first morning of fieldwork at Russian Hospital with the head surgery nurse and medical students cutting and folding gauze to make compresses for the day's surgeries. As a patient in the lab, I learned the cause of the blood splotches on the sleeves of patients in the imaging ward—the lab did not provide Band-Aids or tape after draws. I, too, stained my shirt sleeve, distracted enough not to apply a minute of pressure to the stick.

New centrifuge and ultrasound machines came before compresses, tape, or Band-Aids. Russian Hospital must prioritize what to spend money on, of course. Centrifuges are crucial to the reliability, safety, and accuracy of laboratory work, which is absolutely crucial to diagnostic and therapeutic work of the hospital and to the everyday labor of doctors, nurses, and technicians.[63] The interesting question is, How are priorities determined, and by whom? Through what negotiations between wards, hospitals, the Ministry of Health, the Ministry of Economy and Finance, bilateral donors, development partners, foreign universities, corporations, and NGOs?

One place to see the effects of increases in DAH intertwining with postsocialist transition is in the donation ceremony that opened this chapter. DAH assumes that Ministries of Health will take over the cost of and responsibility for health programs and infrastructures. Market transition from socialism presses the other direction, that the government will relinquish the cost of and responsibility for health programs and infrastructures to private entities, smaller municipalities, and perhaps back to development partners again. Subadditionality is a conundrum for donors, but is not retreat of the state the goal of structural adjustment and market transition agendas? Ultrasound machines seem to slip through without too much trouble, in this time of subadditionality.

2010 (RUSSIAN LEOPARD)

According to the *Financial Times*, in 2010, Cambodia was pro-business. Corporate tax was 9 percent, and there were no laws prohibiting 100 percent foreign ownership of companies, though only Cambodians could own 100 percent of land. Douglas Clayton, the founder of Leopard Capital, a "frontier market fund manager" that invests in "overlooked, transitional economies," placed Cambodia within a regional development trajectory: "Cambodia is where Thailand was 30 years ago, and where Vietnam was 15 years ago. There is a lot going on" (Moore 2010).[64] In Clayton's words, investors were "lured" to Cambodia because of political stability under Hun Sen and the country's "undeveloped natural resources."

Around the time of Clayton's interview in the *Financial Times*, I met Benny Widyono, a former UN diplomat who served as governor of Siem Reap province during UNTAC. It turned out he was now an advisor for Leopard Cambodia. When I told Widyono I was working at Russian Hospital, he said, "Ah, Russian Hospital! Leopard Capital tried to buy Russian Hospital a few years ago."[65] I was intrigued. What would an investment fund want with an old government hospital, one still named for its Cold War donor? Widyono did not know the details of Leopard's plans for Russian Hospital, but in any event, Prime Minister Hun Sen scuttled the deal for reasons that were unclear.

Leopard Capital's attempt to buy Russian Hospital conveys how health care relates to the "entrepreneurial turn" in which development has become explicitly centered on making money in contrast to the 1990s and 2000s mantra of building civil society or promoting democracy.[66] This case also illustrates the supreme authority of Hun Sen over seemingly decentralized entrepreneurship, entrepreneurship that includes health care. "No strings" aid was a key word in Cambodia, referring to Chinese, Korean, Vietnamese, Malaysian, and Thai modes of doing development, in which direct investment guarantees access to natural resources and cheap labor without the "democratization discourse" of Western (i.e., US, Canadian, European, Australian, IMF, World Bank, and UN) donors.[67] "No strings" means no pressure on the government for democratic reform.[68] Prime Minister Hun Sen has long been a critic of aid conditions such as protection of human rights, freedom of press, freedom of assembly, and transparency in governance. Prior to the 2009 annual meeting of the government and international donors, Hun Sen said that Western conditions on aid threatened Cambodia's sovereignty more than the Vietnamese overseeing of the country in the 1980s.[69] These concerns about sovereignty are not new to Cambodia, not to Cambodia's leaders nor their health care officials. Somehow the freedom to make and spend money is more central to post–Cold War, "post-political" configurations of society than other practices of freedom. The "Russian Leopard" story brings forward how a major government hospital nearly became privatized through a foreign fund manager. The government prevented this move, staving off what would have been yet another dramatic turn in Russian Hospital's biography. Yet the privatization of other public goods roars along, and it is not the case that privatization obviates the need to consider sovereignty. Rather, the nature of privatization of public goods resembles the subimperialism described by Kuan-Hsing Chen (2010) in his analysis of de–Cold War, decolonial, and de-imperial practices in Asia.

CONCLUSION

At the time of my research, Russian Hospital was large, imposing, and relatively bare. A place for the very sick, the poor. Where people go to die. But it was not always thus. And it was becoming something else. In this chapter, I traced a genealogy of technology in medicine and proposed flickering presence as an image of thought to understand this genealogy. The image of thought of a flickering presence conveys the spectacle of a new X-ray machine donated to a state-of-the-art hospital, a *vaste cité médicale*, in the 1960s and a new ultrasound machine donated to that same hospital in the 2010s. As the GE commissioning ceremony at Russian Hospital ended, I photographed a moment in the disassembling. A woman in a formal silk sampot and white blouse removes decorative flowers. A donated patient monitor remains at the edge of the frame. The letters on the felt banner were partially taken down.

Between the shiny material presences of technologies in 1960 and 2010 were decades of material uncertainty and instability. In some regards, this is what Noémi Tousignant (2018, 14) calls "a familiar story: that of abandonment" of public health and health infrastructures by the state. In Phnom Penh it includes neglect and destruction of machines, indeed the absence of the imaging ward and health clinic in the 1970s; the spectacle of need that motivates humanitarian donation of a used ultrasound machine in 1989; and the non-spectacle of repair of X-ray machines in the 2000s (Grant 2020). In other words, a flickering presence and absence is an image of thought and it is material and mechanical. When is anything going to stay put? If things stay put, will they work?

Grounding this genealogy in a biography of Russian Hospital, my primary fieldsite, I relied on the memories of doctors who were medical students in the 1960s and 1970s; government films from the 1960s, 1970s, and 1980s; the decade of its medical journal, the *Annals*; Ministry of Health documents; donor reports; news media; and conversations with prominent radiologists My Samedy and Rethy Chhem and with officials in the Ministry of Health. I used these materials in juxtaposition with my ethnographic work: mornings in the hospital each week over two years and attending GE commissioning ceremonies across town. I also imagined—the sound, the sparkle, the heat, the bustle, the excitement of a new hospital. In addition to a sensory portrait, I hoped to convey the centrality of technologies to development projects and values, the shifting roles of foreigners and Cambodians in public health, and tropes of "starting from nothing," which were used to mobilize an array of projects.

This chapter lays out a present for ultrasound imaging that is shaped by a history of concerns about sovereignty over medicine and technology. The post-Independence government pursued technologically advanced medicine as a means of decolonization and nation-building. One of the modes through which the government enacted its neutralism in the Cold War was through aid and trade with capitalist and communist nations, which generated islands of materials and expertise as well as nested sovereignties over health care, medical sciences, and equipment. These are the postcolonial, Cold War antecedents of what Richard Rottenburg (2009) has called "archipelagic formations"—island-like areas of medical resources and expertise, often with distinct or conflicting sovereignties. In the 1980s, the public good was expressed as socialist-inflected *samkki* or solidarity, a responsibility of the state and the people working together.[70] In the 1990s, responsibility for the "public good" remained in the government health care system, supported through humanitarian aid, NGOs, and wats. The fix for health, and health care, must be more than a machine, but this was beyond the ambit of humanitarian aid. The 2000s look different than the 1960s and the 1990s in that there are more actors involved—corporations, NGOs, universities, public-private partnerships—but they work at middle scale. No donors today are giving just one used machine to a hospital; a donor today is building a new government hospital, equipping it, and training its staff. What comes to the fore in this chapter are discontinuities in the availability and value of medical technology as well as similarities in practice—prioritizing, neglecting—across politically and temporally distinct periods and a history of equipment donations that come with strings.

CHAPTER TWO

MOTHER AND CHILD

THE NEW CLINIC

THE FIRST TIME I WENT TO SORPHEA VIP MATERNITY HOSPITAL WAS JUST after lunch on a Thursday.[1] The streets of the centrally located middle-class 7 Makara district of Phnom Penh were thinning out as people returned to work. In contrast, the lobby of the clinic was bustling with bodies, movement, and conversation. Women, from young adult to middle age, and a few men occupied rows of chairs, the aisleways, and the open space in front of the reception counter. Some women held carbon copies of ultrasound orders while others carried a single orange box of metronidazole, a flowered box containing a vaginal douche, or a sheet of red vitamins.[2] Two reporters carrying notepads, voice recorders, and a camera hovered nearby in an attempt to catch the buzz in the air if not to amplify it. I moved to the side of lobby, where a flat-screen TV glowed on the wall, like an aura for the substantial spirit house that sat below it. The spirit house was adorned with iridescent peacock feathers, a brass frog, and red and gold banners in Chinese script. I inhaled sweet and smoky fumes from the clutch of incense and bouquet of fresh flowers at its base. The room was vibrant.

It turned out that I had visited during the opening of Sorphea VIP's new building. As part of the special promotion for the event, a visiting OBGYN from Viet Nam was providing free physical exams for general disease, *chumngeu toutov*, and free medicines for mild conditions. Free ultrasound exams and blood tests were available to those with more serious conditions. Follow-up visits for test results would be scheduled at Sorphea VIP, or patients could go to Viet Nam for serious cases such as cancer. Medicines and douches were promotional giveaways, and many women had more than one item. I asked a group of women how they heard about the event. They told me that they came to the clinic at the urging of their neighborhood leader, who had been told by the district chief, who himself had been told by the clinic directors to spread the word.[3] Here, the clinic was an important site of overlapping spheres: the private clinic tapped into its relationship with public authorities in order to draw in attendees as well as its transnational connections with medical clinics in neighboring Viet Nam.

Sorphea VIP had all of the excitement that comes with what is new and modern, as well as the imprimatur of established institutions. Sorphea VIP was the literal offspring of Sorphea Maternity, a well-known but older and somewhat drabber private clinic just up the road. The director of Sorphea Maternity opened Sorphea VIP with her son, Dr. Nov Rattana.[4] Like other medical professionals in Phnom Penh, Dr. Nov was also a physician at a public hospital, Maternal Hospital. His business card, on offer at the reception counter, spelled out these connections. The Khmer side listed Dr. Nov's private affiliation, the name and address of Sorphea VIP, and a blue cross, a common symbol indicating a medical clinic. The English side displayed his government affiliations, the Ministry of Health and the Maternal Hospital, and two different symbols: a snake and staff for the medical profession and a royal crown with rays of light emanating from it denoting the Kingdom of Cambodia. Sorphea VIP had it all: family patronage, medical qualifications, government connections, international connections, and a good reputation from the start. And it now had a beautiful new building.

From the outside, the clinic looked like one of the dozens of new high-rise apartment and commercial buildings mushrooming sporadically across the city at the time. Its verticality was a material symbol of Phnom Penh's future: prosperous, modern, urban, Asian.[5] On the inside, too, it looked like these other new spaces of life and commerce with an elevator, air-conditioning, and TVs in the lobby and post-delivery rooms, which ensured that families could visit comfortably. The consultation rooms were clean, bright, and private. The heavy, lacquered wood chairs that lined the wall, symbols of wealth and good taste, were for companions of patients waiting for an exam, not strangers, as in a government hospital imaging ward. Posters on the consultation room walls conveyed prosperity through depiction of happy, healthy-looking children, and cosmopolitanism through the US flag and a Christmas message in English. Some months later, Neary, my research assistant, teasingly said that I liked working at Sorphea VIP because of the posters: a white baby in a red beret holding a US flag; an Asian girl in a pink tutu with the caption "Merry Christmas" in small silver letters. We both knew that I was not the intended audience for these images, of course. The posters and furniture, along with the Chinese zodiac calendars that sat in a neat pile on the desk, showed care for the experience of the Cambodian middle class.

The ultrasound machines at Sorphea VIP were nice too. On one of his evening shifts, I chatted with Dr. Sophal, a colleague of Dr. Nov at Maternal Hospital, about the large, cream-colored machine on wheels: "Medison, from Korea," he pointed out.[6] It had a wide keyboard panel, a reasonably sized monitor, and a second monitor on the wall at the foot of the bed so the patient lying down could watch the scan in process. The machine had three sensors: a rounded one for obstetric exams, a wide flat one for abdominal scans, and a long narrow one, still in bubble wrap, for vaginal scans. When I asked about the bubble wrap, Dr. Sophal said that women typically do not want this type of exam: "They don't like the probe."[7] On the day of the promotion an ultrasound exam was free, but on normal days one must pay US$5 for a color printout. This was roughly the same price as at other private clinics and the same price as a color printout at government hospitals.

Sorphea VIP was a clinic of new machines housed in a new building. In contrast were other private clinics with their secondhand ultrasound machines and exam areas separated from the entryway by a rattan screen rather than a thick wall and a door that closes. The owners of those clinics may not have positions at a reputable government hospital. The attending health professional may not be a doctor but most likely is a midwife or even a pharmacist. What draws a patient to these spaces of private health care? What compels a practitioner to open a clinic, when there are so many sprouting around the city?

This chapter explores the conditions under which ultrasound services become available to patients. I examine the intertwining of public and private health care in relation to a broader system that has been reshaped by transition from socialism to authoritarian elite capitalism. The image of thought that animates this chapter is the relationship of mother to child, which foregrounds relations of authority and intimacy, care and value, as well as the limits of "freedom" in defining good health care in contemporary Cambodia. The mother-child relationship is material as it is productive, as illustrated in the case of Sorphea VIP: a mother helped her son open the clinic. The relationship is metaphorical and instructive, as when a Ministry of Health official invited me to compare the relationship between the private sector and the Ministry to the relationship of mother to child. The minister's comparison is provocative in that it inverts what might be expected: the child in this relationship is not the clinic, but, in fact, it is the Ministry of Health and the government bureaucrat (Grant 2014) who emerged in the postconflict and postsocialist period of rebuilding the country. The mother figure is the private sector, which *re*-emerged in the same period but, as I argue, was prefigured in the post-Independence *fonctionnaire-entrepreneur*, the doctor who is both civil servant and entrepreneur.

In the 2010s, the relationship between private and government health care was being worked out, far from settled, and as I contend, ultrasound services played a part in shaping it. This "reciprocal adjustment" (Akrich 1992, 207) of technology, people, and economy is a premise in STS and one that often gets framed as a question of politics. I explore what ultrasound can teach us about the politics of post-political health care, in which the ideologies of the old order have been reshaped by the demands of the market. The end of the Cold War resulted in different paths in different contexts, yet in many formerly socialist countries, diagnostic imaging services were the first green shoots of private practice.[8] Ultrasound continues to be an easy entry into the health care market because it does not require much capital and infrastructure and labor costs are low. Ultrasound machines produce a tangible product for patients—something to show for your money and thus are more like a pill than words on a piece of paper. And in the case of prenatal ultrasound, the image serves interests beyond diagnosis or screening as the scan depicts kin as well as tissue.[9] It is the specificity of *both* ultrasound technology *and* the structure and imagination of political economy in health care that are the subjects of this chapter.

After revolutionary and reconstruction socialism, the private sector in Cambodia was nourished by the discourse and practice of the free market, speculation, and patron-client relations, a mixture I call authoritarian elite capitalism. In the 1990s and early 2000s, freedom, democracy, and choice translated into the freedom to open a private clinic, to buy an ultrasound machine, or to choose your health care provider. These freedoms became entangled with practices of global neoliberalism, a key feature of which is "a planetary search for new assets in which to speculate" (Hall, Massey, and Rustin 2013, 6). After revolutionary and reconstruction socialism, speculation animated markets in land and real estate. A doctor's complaint, "Anyone can sell land and buy an ultrasound machine," locates private health care within these wider logics of speculation. Financial gain comes from the exchange of an ultrasound scan for riel or dollar, and thus value accrues not in the qualities of the scan, but in the quantities of it in the fact of the exchange and the exam-for-money transaction. Whereas the doctor-as-speculator bears the financial risk of buying an ultrasound machine, the significant risk, both financial and bodily, is borne by the patient. At the end of this chapter, I propose that these practices can produce care that is extractive and untrustworthy. Following feminist technoscience scholars (Mol 2008; Puig de la

Bellacasa 2011), care is concern both for the *manner of doing* care and for the *object* of care. There is always excess to an exchange, but in the case of the scan and the riel, care should not be about excess. Care must be the point and the purpose.

I begin with an introduction to the language and symbol of the mother-child relation, to the forms of authority and dependency with which it overlaps, and to the figure of the civil servant–entrepreneur in the post-Independence period. I describe features of market transition from socialist medicine to situate the figure of the civil servant–entrepreneur in Phnom Penh's present configuration of government and private health care institutions. I then turn to material and regulatory features of government and private health care. The work of an equipment distributor who sells ultrasound machines to government institutions and to doctors in private practice and regulations of the Ministry of Health for purchasing and managing ultrasound machines reveal a normative and symbiotic intertwinement of public and private interests. Furthermore, a broader economic logic of speculation infuses the purchasing of ultrasound machines as low-risk investments for the selling of images and, perhaps, more care. Intertwinement of public and private enable practices concern some officials and health professionals, who criticize the siphoning of public resources for private gain and the difficulty of ensuring standards of care. It is hard for the child to regulate the mother; the mother is the life force and the authority, and, in relations of such intimacy, freedom is constrained. Thus, we find that freedom to choose a health care provider, or freedom to buy an ultrasound machine, is gossamer that obscures the ways that value flows to the mother.

THE MOTHER AND THE CHILD

At the end of our conversation, Dr. Sovannarith, director of hospital services, told me, "Cambodia is different from your country, because the history is complicated."[10] We were sitting at his desk in his office in a new wing of the Ministry of Health. Dr. Sovannarith located his department's struggles to regulate the private sector in a narrative of the recent past and as a past particular to Cambodia. He described hospitals, clinics, and individual private practice being closed during the Khmer Rouge period. He then described the difficulties of the 1980s socialist reconstruction period in terms of minimal human and material resources. With the formal advent of market transition following UNTAC, the 1990s presented a different challenge—a generation of health care providers had been trained in Cambodia and abroad, but "there were no policies. There were many practitioners, mostly careless. There are no standards, yet." Dr. Sovannarith was not saying there are no policies or regulations. His job, in fact, was to develop and enforce them. He was saying there are no standards of complying with regulation. He paused and then shifted from historical narrative to metaphor: "We can compare the relationship to that of mother and child. It is difficult for the child to control the mother."

I was confused. My confusion betrayed my assumption that the Ministry of Health was the "mother," in the form of the state that disciplines and cares. But no, it was quite the opposite. Just as it is difficult for the child to control the mother, it is difficult for Sovannarith's Department of Hospital Services, which has only been around since 1997, to control the more established and wealthier private sector.

In Khmer, hierarchical relations are often described in familial terms. The mother-child relation is a widely recognizable frame for the patron-client relation, and as Erik W. Davis (2008) writes, there is a specific linguistic and symbolic overlap between the mother and patron.[11] "[M]others have long been a symbol for patrons on whom one is forced to depend too much. . . . The closer and more intimate a relationship, such as that of mother and child, the more absolute the relationship of authority. . . . Like a patron, a mother can be authoritarian, unquestionable, and disobeyed only with risk" (Davis 2008, 226).

Dr. Sovannarith's use of the mother-child metaphor for a non-familial hierarchical relationship illuminates an intimate authority and dependency between government and private health care. In a straight political economic history of Cambodia, private medical practice is supposed to come later, after socialism. But there was private practice before socialism too. In the 1990s, the Ministry of Health was a postconflict creation supported by and a conduit for foreign aid. So, what then is this "mother" figure in the form of the private sector? When was she born, and how did she come to be in relations of capital and kinship?

Before Independence in 1953, there was no model of Cambodian professional medical practice (Guillou 2009, 45). During the French protectorate (1863–1953), the medical profession attracted relatively small numbers of Cambodians because it required one to study abroad for a long period of time under the control of the French (often through Vietnamese superiors who operated as intermediaries). Medical work was also associated with an unpopular civil service and low pay (Guillou 2009). After Independence, things changed. The establishment of the medical school in Phnom Penh eliminated to need to go abroad to study medicine. Instead the length of study became an investment, and one's association with the state guaranteed a form of protection from risk as did the ability to open private practice following training, which was lucrative.

Doctors developed a socio-professional role in Cambodian society, or what Guillou (2009, 48–50) calls "*les médecins fonctionnaires-entrepreneurs*," in the post-Independence period of the Sangkum Reastr Niyum (1955–70), often associated with a new Cambodia and a flourishing of modernity. This figure was composed of both civil servant (*fonctionnaire*) working in a government hospital or clinic who was also an entrepreneur in private practice. In addition to the doctor as civil servant–entrepreneur, government and business were intertwined in health care through other relations, usually through kinship. Doctors married merchants and officials, and the children of merchants and officials studied medicine (Guillou 2009). These connections of marriage and blood linked doctors to the capital and influence they needed to open a private clinic and to advance in their government positions. Guillou (2009, 50) writes that these kin networks organized hierarchies in medicine, more so than titles or professional activities.

The private sector was outlawed from 1975 to 1985 during the Khmer Rouge and the first half of the People's Republic of Kampuchea (PRK). After the ouster of the Khmer Rouge in 1979, the PRK faced the arduous task of rebuilding a devastated health system while under severe economic sanctions from most nations outside the Soviet Bloc.[12] Health system reconstruction, like other domains of economic and cultural life, was along socialist lines, particularly Vietnamese socialist ones. In 1985, the PRK formally recognized the private economy.

The socialist period was neither long nor was it totalizing. Transition in economic practices, such as decollectivization, began in the late 1980s. In contrast to this period of "silent perestroika" as one Russian diplomat put it, the changes in political, economic, and cultural structures during the two-year UNTAC period were incredibly abrupt and dramatic.[13] Soon after private medical practice was legalized in 1993 (World Bank 2011, 41), additional privatization policies began to accelerate the shape of the public health system.[14] In this context, technologies became more widely available, commercial advertisements for medical services became commonplace (see figure 2.1), and together these helped to generate greater demand. The commercialization of health care was part of an expanding consumer economy and the commercialization of other spheres of life in the 1990s.

What Dr. Sovannarith was telling me, through his historical narrative and through the metaphor of the relationship of mother and child, was that the system of government hospitals and clinics and private practices and clinics was organized through intimate relations of dependence and

FIGURE 2.1. "Free ultrasound services." At the center of this photograph of a street scene in northern Phnom Penh is an advertisement on the back of a tuk-tuk taxi. The tuk-tuk is parked at the curb of a small traffic island of manicured grass and short bushes. The advertisement is white with blue, red, and black text, and a color photograph of a mobile ultrasound machine is at the right underneath a blue cross. The text says NSC Clinic (in Khmer and English)—Free color ultrasound exam (*Pinity echo poar ât kit thlai*). It lists clinic hours—7–9 a.m., Monday–Friday—and two phone numbers. The limited service hours suggest the medical professional running the clinic has another day job. Photo by author, 2010.

authority. Control and regulation of the private sector become difficult given the Ministry's subordinate position: Ministry / private sector = child / mother. Furthermore, this arrangement yields a combination of interests. Government control of the private sector may work against the interests of other, more powerful government actors—for example, politicians in the ruling party who own or are related to owners of private enterprises among which include clinics. What we see then is that these personalized structures of authority combined with the restructuring of public health in post-conflict, postsocialist market transition co-produce an underdevelopment of state institutions that serve the public. We can further build upon Sovannarith's mother-child metaphor: private and public health care are part of the same family, sharing blood and an entwined destiny.

Since UNTAC, which oversaw the peace agreements in Cambodia in the early 1990s, public health policy in Cambodia has been closely aligned with WHO policies and articulated in the language of health economics. In the Ministry of Health's *Strategic Framework for Health Financing 2008–2015*, for instance, the overarching future goal is stated as one that can "achieve universal coverage of the population with funded pre-payment mechanisms" (Ministry of Health 2008, 2), or what has become the country's social health insurance program. The *Strategic Framework* calls for increasing the health budget, decreasing reliance on donors, harmonizing donor and Ministry of Health activities and priorities, and removing financial barriers at "point-of-care."[15]

The *Strategic Framework* was developed within a transition economy at a time when health care was "fast becoming a commodity open to market forces with a resultant cost escalation" (Hardeman et al. 2004, 279).[16] Free services for all but the very poor were phased out after the 1996 Health Financing Charter introduced scheduled user fees at public facilities (World Bank 2011, 44). By 2008, almost all government health facilities had user fees (SAC/D 2016). The government experimented with different "cost recovery mechanisms," from user fees, to Health Equity Funds (qualifying poor have their inpatient services paid for by an NGO), to community health insurance. As fees go up, insurance schemes and equity funds are supposed to cover costs for the poor, or so the logic went.[17] However, Dr. Sovannarith, the director of health services, told me that micro-insurance pilot programs have shown little success.[18]

User fees and insurance schemes are market fixes to a centralized, government-controlled public health care system that is also chronically underfunded. Compared to countries with similar levels of income per capita, the Cambodian government spent less on health infrastructure, materials, and salaries, so much so that Cambodians provide a higher proportion of health care funding than the government. In 2009, the government spent 2.5 percent of GDP on health, of which half was funded by donors. As points of contrast, donors provide 20 percent of education funding and 70 percent of funding for the transport sectors. Government funding (including donations) was only one-third of total spending on health care, and the rest was out-of-pocket (all figures from World Bank 2011, 23).[19] The level of *total* government spending in Cambodia is similar to that of countries with comparable levels of income per capita. However, when compared to countries with similar populations, the total number of doctors and teachers are low, as are their wages. This is not so much a matter of resources as it is one of allocation. Some civil servants are doing fine, including those who work in security and military after the Cambodian government "dramatically" increased their wages (World Bank 2011, 20).

At the time of my research, public health institutions (or more broadly *rot*, government) were organized into 20 municipal and 4 provincial health departments. Within these were 76 operational districts, 83 referral hospitals, 1,024 health centers, and 121 health posts.[20] In Phnom Penh, there were eight national hospitals[21] (*monteyrpety*, hospital) and two specialty hospitals, the National Center for Maternal and Child Health and the National Center for TB/Leprosy. Several of the hospitals were in the process of becoming or already were "autonomous," a special status that grants greater financial independence and responsibility than typical government hospitals. The private sector, *aekchon*, was and is much larger, made up of private practices, many of which are individually owned and referred to by the French term *cabinet*, or *pikroeah chumngeu* in Khmer. The private sector also includes private hospitals and clinics as well as drug sellers and pharmacies. In 2009, the Ministry of Health counted 169 private hospitals, clinics, and polyclinics with 758 inpatient beds. There were reportedly 2,300 *cabinets*, of which 80 percent were registered with the government.[22]

A *cabinet*'s operating hours are restricted and can only be outside of government work hours (typically 5–7 a.m. and/or 5–8 p.m.). A physician must be present during operating hours, and the owner cannot employ additional nurses or physicians as staff. *Cabinets* may provide minor treatment but not surgical, inpatient, or pharmacy services. It is less expensive and less complicated to open a *cabinet* than a clinic, in terms of bureaucratic procedures involved and taxes paid to district and ministry authorities. A clinic is a larger space and can be open even when the primary doctor is not there. It usually has a board of directors, a staff made up of nurses and other doctors, and provides a wider range of services, including surgery.

The trend is to push national referral hospitals to become semi-private or autonomous so that they can recover costs and compete with the private sector "because we have a free market," in the words of Dr. Sovannarith.[23] Calmette was the first hospital in Cambodia to become autonomous. Russian Hospital and Maternal Hospital have begun this process. Autonomy is intended to decrease government involvement and increase local responsibility and efficiency. The logic is that if hospitals cannot rely on or be held back by government (and donors), they will have to improve the quality of their services in order to attract patients. The effort is also intended to appeal to patients who would otherwise go abroad to Viet Nam, Thailand, or

Singapore for care.[24] Yet commitment to market principles and practices remains ambivalent. Although autonomy is encouraged by the Ministry of Health, hospitals must go through the process of securing final approval from the Council of Ministers as well as the prime minister (Ros 2009).

Fees for medical services at autonomous hospitals have increased over time, even though they remain lower than the fees for services at a private clinic. The government still pays monthly salaries at autonomous hospitals, but salaries can also be supplemented by the hospital, depending on the number of patients seen. The amount of the supplement is determined based on position and rank and is the same throughout the hospital; for example, all midwives get a set amount no matter the ward in which they work. A midwife at Maternal Hospital told me that all workers are happier with this aspect of a hospital's autonomy. However, there are problems. Her government salary was typically paid on time (in her case, US$80 per month as a senior midwife), but on the day of the biweekly hospital wage supplement, the person who distributed the money was often absent. The previous week, staff hadn't been paid on Thursday and had to go without pay on a three-day weekend, which required gifts of money for the autumn moon festival.[25] People were unhappy, especially as the hospital was very strict about staff clocking in with the thumbprint machine and sent monitors every few hours to determine whether staff were actually working. These practices of accounting and monitoring are directly linked to the total amounts on their paychecks.

Autonomy, along with user fees and social insurance schemes, are live experiments that involve the transfer of resources and responsibilities for health care. The Ministry of Health's *Strategic Framework*, discussed above, prioritizes deconcentration and decentralization, which, in general, provide overarching strategies in other domains for transitioning socialist economies to market economies.[26] In Cambodia, decentralization has been an explicit policy in the realm of politics (Un and Ledgerwood 2003) as well as education (Un 2012). Paradoxically, decentralization has unfolded alongside greater consolidation of state resources. Political scientists (e.g., Cock 2010; Un and So 2011) document the intertwining of public and private in politics and economy, diagnosing this relationship as neo-patrimonial capitalism. This system is organized by patron-client relations that work together with legal reforms and weak bureaucracy to abet the elite capture of public goods, such as land. In health care, these public goods include training, medicine, materials, machines, and perhaps also patients.[27]

A concern about dual practice is the most obvious when it comes to conflict of interest in patient referrals. For example, a health worker in a public hospital can refer a patient to their own private practice for further care or send the patient to a friend. This referral usually takes place in the exam room, so when it happened in the waiting area of the imaging ward in Maternal Hospital, I took notice. A young woman came out of the exam room and spoke to a nurse named Mony. She said that she had been told by the doctor that she needed to pay more if she wanted to get a color ultrasound scan. She explained to Mony that she had taken "the abortion pill" but there was still some remaining tissue leading to an infection in her uterus. Mony told the woman that if she wanted to do the removal of this tissue in the comfort of her own home, she had a friend who could provide the service.

"Why does Mony keep talking?" I whispered to Neary. "The woman is clearly not happy."

"Because if she refers to her friend, she gets a 40/60 split," Neary whispered back.

The Ministry of Health is worried about these practices, if not for the undue pressure on patients, then for the loss of revenue to its hospitals. In the *Strategic Framework* (2008, 11), one of the desired outcomes is "[s]pending from the private/informal sector redirected to the public health sector."

DYNAMIC PHARMA CO., LTD.

To better understand how ultrasound machines circulated in public and private health care, I talked to Cambodian and expatriate medical equipment distributors about their businesses. These distributors worked with imaging wards in government hospitals and with doctors in private practice. In complement to the previous chapter, which centered aid practices such as donation of ultrasound machines and development of equipment maintenance guidelines, here I foreground the private sector version of these practices. In the medical technology field, as in commercial real estate, inter-Asian currents are central. The growth of biosciences and biotechnology industries in South Korea, Singapore, India, and China means that technologies, medicines, sciences, and services, from health care to polymerase chain reaction (PCR) genotyping, are centered in Asia.[28] Asian *commerce*, rather than European, Australian, and North American aid, are the main circuits through which ultrasound machines circulated in Cambodia. Dynamic Pharma Co., Ltd. was the largest distributor in Cambodia at the time and sold Mindray and Toshiba machines designed and manufactured in China and Japan, respectively.

Mr. Long Phirum, assistant sales and service manager at Dynamic, provided insights on how machines circulate as products and investments. He cared very much for the specific qualities of his technologies and the skills needed to use them. When I went to meet Mr. Long at Dynamic's office in Phnom Penh, security was tight, conveying a sense of protection for the activities and materials inside.[29] The building would have stood out on the block of Norodom Boulevard near Mao Tse Tung Boulevard given that it is a tall peach concrete structure, shimmering with blue reflective windows. But it was set back from the street and concealed behind a substantial gate. There was no sign on its exterior with the exception on the front door of the building in small script framed by Chinese New Year decorations. A security guard in the standard dark blue uniform asked me about the purpose of my visit and escorted me across the courtyard, opening the mirrored glass door with a passkey. The secretary at the front desk was expecting me and guided me down the hall into a conference room after greeting me warmly and offering me a glass of water. I sat at the large oval table, facing a wall lined with neatly stacked boxes and few machines covered in clear plastic tarps. Mr. Long entered almost immediately. He was a tall, slender man in his early thirties with short hair gelled in a neat, classic style. He wore dark framed glasses and an ID badge on a blue ribbon around his neck, as did everyone at Dynamic. Mr. Long introduced himself, handed me a business card and a few brochures for ultrasound machines, and told me to call him Phirum.

Phirum was trained and had worked for a long time as an engineer and only recently had been promoted to working in sales. His new position entailed selling ultrasound machines and other equipment as well as providing onsite operation training to customers on how to obtain high-quality images. Dynamic sold two brands of ultrasound machines: the Toshiba Nemio XG, which was manufactured in Japan and cost US$48,000, and Mindray, which was manufactured in China and cost US$24,000. The machines had similar capabilities, though Phirum said the Nemio offered slightly better image quality. His clients generally preferred Japanese to Chinese manufacturers. For training on new models, Phirum had gone to Singapore, the Toshiba ASEAN hub, and to China, for Mindray.

For the most part, he sold the Toshiba Nemio ultrasound machine to big clinics with "famous" doctors who wanted the best image quality and the Mindray machine to smaller clinics and sites in the provinces, though a majority of Phirum's customers were from Phnom Penh. For Phirum, a famous doctor was someone known for producing good scans and reports to whom other doctors would refer patients. Provincial customers had to travel to Phnom Penh in order to buy ultrasound machines, as there were no distributors in the provinces at that time. The majority of his buyers were individual doctors, or what he called "end users," at private clinics, but Dynamic also had a team working with the Ministry of Health, JICA, and NGOs such as the Reproductive Health Association of Cambodia (RHAC), which operated reproductive health clinics throughout the city. The Ministry of Health had bought three ultrasound machines for Russian Hospital, whereas the fourth, he said, was "donated by France."

I asked Phirum to walk me through a sale. He said that he discusses the following issues with clients: For what purpose will the ultrasound be used? What kinds of probes are required? What is the budget? How many cases [patients] per day? The last question helped the doctor figure out how long it would take to get a return on their investment. Famous doctors see enough patients to cover costs, but even then, the Toshiba was prohibitively expensive for the majority of doctors, making it hard to sell. Many people instead bought secondhand machines.

One of Phirum's frustrations was that the majority of doctors buying for their private practice had minimal knowledge or experience with imaging, and they could not take advantage of the capacity of the machine. "Doctors want a machine that prints color images, they want a 'big one,'" he said. "But in actuality they should buy a simpler machine as they only use a small portion of its functions." He pointed to the Mindray catalog on the table, indicating the simpler and less expensive of the machines he sold. Then he spoke about the purpose of ultrasound: "Of the main purposes for ultrasound—screening [such as blood flow], diagnosis, and guiding surgery or biopsy—diagnosis is why ultrasound is overused. For example, someone has stomach pain. The doctor referred her to get an ultrasound exam. If she had only air in her stomach, there is no value in the ultrasound!"

In obstetrics, Phirum continued, ultrasound helps identify structural abnormalities in the fetus, such as in organs or to the nose and face. Phirum moved his hand in front of his face, spreading his thumb apart from his fingers to stretch across his nose, from cheekbone to cheekbone. He was gesturing to the face as a site of meaning for fetal anomaly. But just because ultrasound is useful in prenatal exams, it doesn't mean it is needed every month. "Three scans, one each trimester," he said, which aligns with best practices at Russian Hospital and Maternal Hospital. Echoing the words I heard from imaging ward doctors, Phirum said that because there are no sanctions against seeking or providing scans in both the public and private sectors, professionally agreed upon guidelines are often not followed.

I saw Phirum twice after our conversation, and both of these encounters illuminate the paths that machines and professionals travel between public and private sectors. A week after we spoke, I ran into Phirum at Calmette

Hospital. I was there to meet with the director of the imaging ward, and Phirum was there to sell imaging machines. More than a year later, I ran into Phirum in the parking lot of the GE Cambodia office. He was locking a large, black pickup truck and balancing a small box on one arm. I said hello and asked how he was doing. Phirum smiled, asked after my child, and told me that he had a new job with GE. He had joined the big newcomer in the medical equipment business. When, sometime later, I drove by Dynamic's office, I saw that another company had taken over the building.

ANYONE CAN SELL LAND AND BUY AN ULTRASOUND MACHINE

In the private sector, ultrasound machines were leased or bought, as Phirum described in his work for Dynamic. Government hospitals used more diverse and laborious means of obtaining ultrasound machines: they could partner with a development partner to obtain a machine, or they could buy or lease a machine directly. All paths required convincing those higher in the hierarchy—hospital directors, donors, the Ministry of Health, and the Ministry of Finance. The regulations and guidelines around purchasing, use, and training in ultrasound machines created a space of both no control and overlapping, irregular control.

Neary told me a story one afternoon after school that struck me for how it conveyed the frustration of this space and the absence of a fix. We were talking about her exams, which had been postponed due to the death of His Excellency Dr. Uon Sabo, the founder of International University. She would have more time to work with me that month than what she had earlier expected. She had mentioned to a couple of her professors and fellow students her work with me, and their conversation about exams shifted abruptly from evaluation of students to lack of it in the broader medical field. Neary said that her professors "feel angry and complain to us that anyone can sell land and buy an ultrasound machine. All you need is money." Because of the rise of land prices in Phnom Penh and across Cambodia more broadly, land provided the capital necessary to fund devices that bolster the prevalence of private clinics.

Anyone can sell land and buy an ultrasound machine. What concerns brought together real estate and medicine in so sharp and succinct a complaint? One register of the professors' complaint has to do with regulation in health care. The National Assembly passed the first law regulating private medical and paramedical services in 2000 (WHO and Ministry of Health 2012, 5), yet the enforcement of the law is uneven and unpredictable.

For some health professionals, uneven regulation in the context of post-socialist transition is evidence of state retrenchment of support and protection of their professions. That the state seems unwilling to or uninterested in regulating the circulation of ultrasound machines signals to doctors devaluation of their medical training and expertise in the provision of ultrasound services. Uneven regulation permits an array of practitioners to enter the health care field, including those who have training and those who do not. All you need is money.

Anyone can sell land and buy an ultrasound machine. Another register of this complaint has to do with broader economic logics, perhaps an economic affect. What would lead one to sell land, historically an important source of value in Cambodia, for an ultrasound machine, which is also tangible but arguably much less durable? How were real estate and medicine linked in the postsocialist market transition? Both land and ultrasound machines are objects of speculation.[30] In the mid-2000s, buying and selling land was at a fever pitch, vividly illustrated in the words of Sylvia Nam's (2017a, 650) interlocutor, an attorney: "You couldn't talk to a motodop [motorbike taxi driver] without him telling you where to buy land, and you could buy this piece of land and double your money in three months. It was all true."

One could see medicine and real estate coming together in other ways. Billboards in a high-end satellite city under construction in the north of Phnom Penh hailed, in English, the coming of "Cambodia's best medical facilities" as well as the "Manhattan Shophouse."[31] In these new developments, health care went hand in hand with shopping. Many projects featured amenities such as private medical care as an index of the good life. Over the course of my fieldwork, I could see the performing, and in it the forming, of the new middle class at Sorphea VIP. This was evident in the way staff and patients interacted with each other and how patients dressed. They arrived in cars or on expensive motos and parked in front of the floor-to-ceiling lobby windows for all to see both inside and out.

The Ministry of Health tries to regulate the private sector through law and licensing. The existence, and thriving, of private hospitals and the practice of *chor chmouh* are two examples of how law and policy do not dictate health care practice. I was surprised to learn that the law set by the National Assembly prohibited private hospitals. As Dr. Sovannarith, director of hospital services, said, it is "difficult to explain" how private hospitals have been established outside of the constitution. In order to open a private *cabinet* or clinic, you must be a physician with a diploma recognized by the Ministry of Health, and you must apply for a license from the municipal health department. In order to have a clinic with inpatient services, you must ask for leave of absence from the government. For this reason, many appoint a retired doctor as the figurehead of the clinic, who can "stand behind the name," or *chor chmouh*.

It is important to understand that the thriving private sector does not indicate the absence of law. In health care, as in real estate (Nam 2017b) and land reform (Un and So 2011), laws and policies do exist. In fact, an excess of policy and regulation may actually create the terrain of uneven enforcement of policies. The variability of cost and quality of services in the private sector is a source of worry and, sometimes, scandal. Donor reports and newspaper articles detail serious incompetence and abuse.[32] The effects of enforcement and non-enforcement practices are open empirical questions, but there is no question who remains the most vulnerable in a health care system that functions under an uneven enforcement of standards and policies: the poor. This is disturbingly illustrated in a study by Hardeman et al. (2004) of health expenditures following a dengue fever outbreak in Banteay Meanchey Province. Not only did costs of private vs. public services differ greatly—an average of US$103 vs. US$8, respectively—but there was variability in what people were charged: in the private sector, poor people were often asked to pay more than others for the same service (Hardeman et al. 2004, 273). The authors found that even modest expenditures lead to indebtedness in poor households, requiring people to use savings, sell assets such as land and animals, and borrow money at high interest, thus intensifying a cycle of poverty.[33] Though the private sector may obscure the workings of class—the wealthy, middle class, and poor all go to private clinics—the benefits and harms tend to fall along lines of class.

The Ministry of Health tries to regulate the private sector through licensing, though Dr. Sovannarith told me that his department has no control over technical aspects of services, including purchasing and maintenance of medical technologies and training on their use. It also has little control over the costs of services. Ultrasound machines and other materials are supplied to public health facilities according to their complementary package of activities (CPA) level as iterated in the *National Guidelines* (Ministry of Health 2006).[34] Dr. Sovannarith described a hypothetical case: Calmette Hospital (a CPA 3 hospital), which is among the largest in Phnom Penh, is in need of an ultrasound machine. The director is supposed to make a formal request to the Ministry of Health, which then discusses that request, along with other requests for materials and equipment, with an expert advisory committee. This includes foreign aid agencies. For instance, at the time, JICA, which has long funded Cambodian infrastructure projects, was a key player on this committee. The advisory committee will then make a recommendation to the Ministry of Health's Department of Budgeting and Finance. The Department of Budgeting and Finance puts together an annual plan and submits this to the Ministry of Economy and Finance. The Ministry of Health must negotiate its budget each year with the Ministry of Economy and Finance. Dr. Sovannarith emphasized this "bottom up" trajectory; hospital directors "do not jump up" over the heads of superiors to request money for ultrasound machines directly from the Ministry of Economy and Finance. Once the purchase of materials and equipment is agreed upon by all parties, the logistics are handled through the Central Medical Store, either the one near the Ministry of Health or the one in Chaom Chao, on the outskirts of Phnom Penh. The Central Medical Store then distributes materials to hospitals.

All CPA-level hospitals are supposed to have an ultrasound machine, but this is not possible because of shortages of money and trained staff. As Dr. Sovannarith said, "In general, the Ministry of Health has an insufficient budget to purchase enough ultrasound machines to supply those referral hospitals. In general, we have to find different development partners [aid agencies] to assist us. Each hospital [the larger referral hospital] has its own budget, and its own development partner, to assist."[35]

Obtaining ultrasound machines (and presumably, other equipment and devices) in the public sector becomes an achievement in itself. There are so many factors, so many departments, organizations, and individual personalities to manage: guidelines and budgets, Ministry of Health officials, hospital directors, and sometimes even imaging department heads, the Ministry of Economy and Finance, and international "development partners" or "funding partners." And connections, strategy, and a bit of luck never hurt. The bureaucracy works for those who are politically well connected, at a CPA 3 level hospital, or facing a generous Ministry of Finance. But guidelines can be impenetrable. Political connections are not always reliable. Furthermore, the Ministry of Finance is subject to diverse forces with shifting priorities: the ruling party, international investors, the World Bank, individual patrons and their clients. Hospital directors may establish relationships with development partners (which include private corporations, such as GE) to assist their hospital. In the end, if one is unable to assemble resources to purchase, or align allies to receive a donation, one might just go rogue. Directors of two different imaging wards told me that they purchased an ultrasound machine for their hospital out of their own pockets in order to bypass the cumbersome bureaucratic hierarchies and political hurdles.

Such dual practices—in which medical practices are a confusing mix of public and private interests and needs—are regularly the subject of critical commentary by donors, patients, officials, and even health professionals themselves. The concerns of multilateral agencies are illustrated in a 2011 World Bank report: "The Ministry [of Health] focuses on increasing the proportion of private facilities that are licensed, and is seeking to improve the reporting of health statistics by the private sector. There is still no regulation of prices or quality of private health care. *Dual practice* is tolerated but is not regulated or subject to clear codes of conduct" (2011, 41; emphasis added).

Whereas expanding public health infrastructure through the private market makes health care available to a broader swath of Cambodia, there are some real-world effects here. For one, private practices elude the accounting and audit needs of the Ministry of Health that are necessary for it to secure aid from donors. Without numbers that demonstrate outcomes, it cannot justify its own requests for assistance and materials within a context of bureaucratic demands of donors.

PRESSURE AND FREEDOM: TECHNOLOGIES AND POST-POLITICAL CARE

In 2003, the French-language paper *Cambodge Soir* published a letter to the editor written by Professor Vu, then the rector of the government medical school, the University of Health Sciences (UHS). Claiming to speak for UHS faculty, Professor Vu objected to the pro-free-market tone of a previous article in the paper that highlighted the proliferation of private universities across Phnom Penh (Kong 2003). Vu argued that choice and competition are not goods in and of themselves. Opening additional schools to train more doctors did not necessarily mean higher quality training, he argued. And many of the same professors taught at both public and private schools without improved education or public health outcomes. Rather, this privatization risked squandering resources and "sowing confusion" among students ("*ne renforce pas la qualité mais disperse les moyens et sème la confusion parmi les étudiants*"). This debate occurred around the time of the opening of the private medical school, International University.

Not all agreed that the expansion of the market into health was regressive. Indeed, free market and democracy talk were very much in the air in the 2000s in ways that held out promises that come with freedom, choice, and the quality of medical care. These promises were also framed across time periods, specifically evoking the period of scarcity during and after the civil conflict. I often heard phrases from doctors and students that explained the contemporary moment by means of a contrast with the 1980s: "Because now, we have a free market." "Because now, we can choose." "Because now, we have a democracy."

Dr. Chhoeun, a public health researcher working on rural illness and poverty, had another way of talking about freedom, choice, and the quality of medical care. I had been connected to Dr. Chhoeun by a friend who did health economics research, and he kindly agreed to meet me in his office at the National Institute of Public Health. I explained my research on ultrasound services and my interest in the relationship between government and private health care. He talked at length about the benefits and harms of the relationship. In his opinion, the positive aspect of dual practice—public and private practice—is that both doctors and patients have more "freedom." He used the term *freedom* in the market-oriented way, meaning choice in what to consume, when talking about patients. However, he used it in a different way when talking about doctors. Here, he juxtaposed "professional freedom" with "pressure." Dr. Chhoeun described three types of pressure, or constraint, under which doctors operate: "First, if a patient is too poor to pay, a doctor might not refer them for a scan, even if it is indicated. Second, patient demand. Doctors must satisfy patient demand in order to please and retain them and to maintain a good reputation. Third, there is the need, and desire, to earn more money."

I was intrigued by his articulation of freedom because it seemed to rub against the grain of public discourse about the government health care system. "What do you mean, freedom?" I asked. Dr. Chhoeun replied, "A doctor has professional freedom if he or she can treat a patient according to clinical expertise [*nav pél dael byeabal ach chroesroes tam vityea*]. In the government hospital, there is no personal incentive to send patients for an ultrasound scan if it is not indicated because the money paid for a scan is distributed to the entire hospital [rather than to the doctor]."

In contrast, at private clinics, the doctor cannot afford to lose a patient and thus may order or perform scans due to "market or peer pressure." There is more freedom to practice medicine in the public hospital because there is freedom from both patient demand and from the imperatives to earn more money.

Despite using economic language, Dr. Chhoeun stressed to me that "medicine is not commerce." Nonetheless, the presence of economic categories in the public health researcher's account is telling. Blurring needs and desires; taking "demand" to be an abstract, neutral, yet agentive force; providing ultrasound services based on ability to pay; these are practices that create a new normal, a ground from which other categories stop making sense.[36] It becomes harder to talk about free health care for all when it is opposed to freedom to choose a provider; it becomes harder to regulate private practice when it is opposed to freedom to practice medicine. It is important to think what "market," "freedom," and "choice" call for, what they symbolize and do for doctors and patients.

I came to think of the functions of these terms in Cambodian health care in relation to post-politics. Post-politics in political theory describes the global political economic condition in which there is no alternative to capitalism. Though most post-political theory concerns itself with Europe and North America at the end of the Cold War,[37] Sangeeta Kamat (2014) offers a forceful analysis of how post-politics works in the Global South through development policy and intervention. One of the features of the "new architecture of development" is that established divisions, such as between rich and poor, or urban and rural, are dissolved into seemingly inclusive categories, such as "stakeholder," "citizen," and "market." Kamat (2014, 69) argues that these categories depoliticize their contents and relations into "a post-ideological global compact on growth and democracy." Both the postcolonial state and the development subject were repositioned in 1990s development practices. "Postcolonial and post-communist countries now enthusiastically endorse neoliberalism as an economic regime in their own best interests" (Kamat 2014, 71). The citizen subject is entrepreneurial, flexible, and risk-taking rather than an abject recipient of state welfare and development aid. In the domain of technology, rather than "appropriate technology" for developing contexts, all citizens in this global market deserve "advanced technologies" (Kamat 2014, 70).

Kamat's term *post-ideological* is apt in Cambodia where the ideologies that govern the political economy are not coherent as a political platform. In Cambodia studies, the 1990s and 2000s have been termed *non-ideological* or *post-ideological* (e.g., Slocomb 2006) because Hun Sen's political economy is not legible through familiar socialist or capitalist frames. Certainly, political elites vying for power in the post-UNTAC period justified their legitimacy using the language of democracy (Norén-Nilsson 2016), which was also the language legible to donor aid agencies pumping hundreds of millions of dollars into the economy, reform, and infrastructure. Development in the 1990s and 2000s was done in terms of democratization and related principles of participation and inclusion.[38] A Euro-American origin story might term the intertwining of public and private interests after the end of the Cold War *post-political* (Swyngedouw 2009). In Cambodia, comparative political scientists use the term *neo-patrimonial* to describe the flow and mediation of power and value and the relations of accountability. Kheang Un and Sokbunthoeun So (2011, 294–95) find that accountability takes shape between individual patrons and clients, all up and down chains of authority, rather than between actors that operate between the discrete realms of state and civil society or between different government institutions. In neo-patrimonial structures, the public domain does not exist as such, as there is not a public to whom the state is responsible. These individualized networks of power and accountability are legible to doctors and patients more so because they are not specific to health care and instead crisscross all domains of life. Neo-patrimonial relations are the "capillary form" (Kamat 2014, 73) in which post-political capitalism grows.

A post-political frame is helpful because it makes visible how the seeming dissolution of political economic oppositions after the Cold War forecloses political and economic debate. In Cambodian health care, autonomy, cost recovery schemes, and public-private partnership have foreclosed the debate that is at stake, which is how to organize health care. The market is a good but also one now divorced from democracy, despite the protestations of those like Professor Vu. However, there is ambivalence about the capture of public goods for private gain. Doctors and officials criticize the diversion of public goods—machines and medicines—to private enterprise.[39] Consider the unease around the common practice of patient referral, where doctors use the public health system to acquire patients for their private practices. When nurse Mony was urging the patient to see Mony's friend for a procedure, the patient's discomfort was palpable. These cases tell us that "pressure" and "freedom" come in many different guises.

The doctor as government employee and entrepreneur, *fonctionnaire-entrepreneur*, emerged in practice and as a normative category in the post-Independence period of the Sangkum. That figure has returned in a contemporary form in a field driven by the imperatives of a political economy in which resources are unevenly distributed between public and private spheres. The period of dual practice that took place over the course of roughly twenty years was followed by its annihilation by the Khmer Rouge in a subsequent and drastic period of roughly five years. Socialist reconstruction during civil war, or roughly fifteen years, followed. By the mid-1990s, the abruptness of change in laws, processes, and actors contributed to a sense of a sudden spring, a blossoming of private practice and of traditional healing, and a flood of new images, machines, and spaces of practice. Private sector competition has become a fix to state hierarchy that cannot be questioned. Part of what makes the fix so powerful is not just the stasis of bureaucracy and mismanagement of resources but also the weakening of public institutions and foreign money that infuses health and other public goods.

The patient demand and desire of which Dr. Chhoeun spoke were created through these images and spaces of care. Experientially, private clinics may be nice—smaller and newer buildings, fewer people, people who are less sick. But private clinics do not provide the more complicated, costly, and risky health care services. How then, and where, can these services be sustained? If healthy people go to the private sector and pay for an ultrasound scan but go to public hospitals for expensive procedures that are heavily subsidized, the public system is hard to sustain. Value continues to flow toward the mother and away from the child.

My argument in this chapter is that ultrasound machines shape, and are shaped by, broader regimes of value that involve practices of freedom and speculation. Ultrasound machines, as investment objects, are one of the material forms through which the private takes shape, in turn shaping the organization and delivery of health care. When categories such as land and an ultrasound machine are interchangeable, they resemble commodities bought and sold for their value and not for their specific qualities or affordances. Speculation of this sort, in the realm of health care, becomes anticare. It reduces the multiplicity of care to a return on an investment, focused on the exchange of an ultrasound exam for riel or dollars rather than the medical needs and their techniques and the objects of evaluation along with their specificities. The machine as commodity is a condensation of exchange, an item of value because it produces value: a diagnosis, professional authority, an object/image. The consequences for health care and for the population are unknown and fade away from scrutiny even. Ultrasound forces consideration of the kinds of care, and in particular the excess of care, in conditions of transition.

Where is there better care? What ordering of money and expertise and materials permits the flourishing of good care? In Phnom Penh, user fees, autonomy, and financing schemes normalize the privatization of the public, such that other questions cannot be asked. Public and private are subject to different degrees of control and regulation, including guidelines for operating clinics, obligations for reporting, and techniques of procuring machines and other materials. Expertise, skill, and training of doctors in private and public settings are equivalent because of dual practice; the same doctors operate in both domains. However, skill and expertise are not the only factors that influence where a person might go for an ultrasound scan. There are also distinctions, recognizable to all concerned, between costs, environments, machines, and waiting times. For patients and relatives, expectations of care, such as showing respect, giving attention, and explaining results and next steps are also important. It is to this more intimate scene of care that I now turn.

CHAPTER THREE

OVER-CARE AND UNDER-CARE

WHAT CAN GOOD CARE BE, AND HOW IS ULTRASOUND A PART OF IT? Practices of freedom and speculation, the contours of post-political care, generate uncertainties about the quality of care, where to go for care, and how much to pay for it. There were questions circulating broadly in Phnom Penh about medical ethics, expertise, and technologies, what the Khmer-language newspaper *Rasmei Kampuchea* (2009a) calls "modern tools for diagnosis and treatment": "Disobeying medical ethics, lack of human resources, and shortages of modern tools for diagnosis and treatment result in a situation where many Khmer doctors are no longer considered serious providers of care for Khmer citizens."

The article focused on why people go abroad for health care. Its list of causes provides a clue as to the significance of ultrasound—a modern tool for diagnosis—to doctors and to patients. A device with broad and wondrous clinical utility, one that is relatively safe for patients and providers, that is relatively inexpensive in terms of the machine and its infrastructure (no magnets, no medical physicists),[1] and that generates a physical product (an image), the ultrasound machine has the potential to fix the problem of patient drain and the perception that doctors are not serious providers of care for citizens.[2]

Just as the contents and valence of the mother-child relation are not self-evident, neither are definitions and practices of care. In recent reviews of care in feminist science studies (Coopmans and McNamara 2020; Martin, Myers, and Viseu 2015) and critical race studies (Hobart and Kneese 2020), care is a problem for thought (Sharpe 2016, 5), an interest of the communities with which we work and think, and a question of feminist and decolonial scholarly praxis. María Puig de la Bellacasa (2017) argues that care involves three interrelated ontological dimensions: practical work, affect, and political ethics. Within these general dimensions, what care is and can be relate to its contexts, contexts that are situational—What is happening here, and who is involved?—and sociohistorical, in that they involve accretion of practice and experience and projection of expectations and refusals that are classed, raced, gendered, and abled. That is, care involves what it is to be a person in a world of others, a world of more-than-human others (Parreñas 2018). Care involves technologies and ecologies, things and beings too.

This chapter explores everyday discourse and practice of care in ultrasound exam rooms, imaging ward waiting areas, and hospitals. I argue that it is difficult to settle on what good care with ultrasound can be because ultrasound may amplify forms of care that are excessive and extractive (over-care) and neglectful (under-care). I offer a provisional definition of care as *yok chett tuk dak*, literally, "to take the heart and keep it close, safe," which denotes action done with respectful attention. Ultrasound machines and ultrasound images are a third element (Serres [1980] 2007, 53), players whose roles are patterned but unscripted in relations of care between providers and patients, patients and one another, patients and their own bodies, and hospital administrators and staff. In a broad context of distrust, so bluntly illustrated in the *Rasmei Kampuchea* article, technology is ambivalent. It automates, and it may displace the human in some diagnostic practices, such as listening, touching, and judging. The benefit is that the machine may be more accurate than a person and less able to discriminate, and this leads to better care. But the machine doesn't work without a human, and people maintain suspicion about doctors' ethics and skills.

Ultrasound images create encounters, openings for patients to discuss their health care with one another, to evaluate tissues and health trajectories. Commentary about images is a way for non-experts to engage with health care. However, ultrasound images open to lay readings are still expert images (Dumit 2004). There is a general understanding that paying experts for health care is okay and that health care and its administration need not be egalitarian. In other words, economic exchange and social hierarchy are conditions of possibility for good care. However, neither profit nor hierarchy is rationale for injustice, and patients and doctors critique the forms of injustice that come from extractive and neglectful care. I now turn to a description of exams, to provide a richer sense of what care looks like between doctors, nurses, patients, associated others, and ultrasound machines.

* * *

On a June morning, I sat in one of three blue chairs at the foot of the bed in Exam Room 1. Next to me sat a heavily pregnant woman, Srey Pouv, who was waiting for a scan, and next to her, a younger woman waiting for her grandmother's report. Two aides wheeled in a metal stretcher carrying a frail, elderly woman. The mask over her nose and mouth was tethered to a small oxygen tank, labeled "MSF," which was lying between her legs.[3] The aides, two men in their early twenties wearing khaki uniforms, instructed the woman to lie on her back instead of on her side. She complied, with difficulty, and lay open-eyed and quiet as a small group of medical students conferred with Nurse Lina about the previous patient. Nurse Lina sat in front of the computer, typing up the ultrasound exam report while teaching the students its conventions of collective authorship. Nurse Sovannary returned from getting her paycheck and washed her hands at the sink. The elderly woman, still silent, still unaddressed, turned back onto her side.

Dr. Vichet entered the exam room, put on rubber gloves, and proceeded to scan the patient's abdomen. Srey Pouv, the pregnant woman, clicked her tongue—disapproval at how the woman had been neglected? Pity for her frailty? It was unclear. Nurse Lina, Nurse Sovannary, and the students left, and the room became very quiet. Dr. Vichet did not talk to the patient nor to anyone else. The elderly woman held her eyes steady at the monitor as Dr. Vichet moved the sensor over her abdomen. Nurse Lina came back into the room as he was finishing, the open door releasing a blinding film of sunlight over us all. Dr. Vichet gave brief instructions to the aides, and they wheeled the patient away to wait for her report outside. I asked about the woman's situation. Nurse Lina said it was unclear what was going on; the woman was Vietnamese and didn't speak or understand Khmer. There was no diagnosis or condition listed on her ultrasound order, just "abdo" for the kind of scan requested.

Srey Pouv was next. She picked up the lavender scarf draped over the foot of the exam bed and asked me to help cover the lower half of her body, as she wasn't wearing leggings under her dress. Dr. Din replaced Dr. Vichet at the ultrasound machine and looked at Srey Pouv's order slip. He said aloud to Nurse Lina, now sitting behind him at the computer, "She is seven months and eight days pregnant."[4] As Nurse Lina was typing, Dr. Din asked Srey Pouv, "Is an organization helping you?" He was referring to an NGO— patients access prenatal care through multiple organizations, including local or international NGOs. Srey Pouv said no. Dr. Din squirted clear blue gel on her belly and pressed the transducer onto the site where he would begin the exam.

After a minute or so of silent work, looking at the monitor and occasionally back at the position of the transducer, Dr. Din paused and said, *"Moel kaun"* (Look at the baby). He turned the monitor toward Srey Pouv. She turned her head to the right and after a moment of looking, said, *"Ât che moel"* (I don't know how to see it, I don't understand). Dr. Din started naming body parts and pointing to black, white, and gray shadows on the monitor. "Mouth." "Nose." The young woman sitting next to me, still waiting for her grandmother's report, was getting more and more excited. She leaned forward, craning her neck to see the ultrasound monitor, a smile growing across her face. I, too, felt a pleasant anticipation. Srey Pouv looked intently at the monitor. Dr. Din switched to the Doppler, and we all could hear the heartbeat. Srey Pouv turned to me with a proud smile, and I responded, "So fast!" She was glad to hear the sound, she said, *"Sabbay"* (Happy).[5]

I chatted with Srey Pouv in the open-air waiting area after her exam. She told me it was her third ultrasound scan during the course of her pregnancy. She also said she had never been invited to look at the monitor before—she had never thought to ask. Indeed, at this hospital, where I observed hundreds of ultrasound exams over the course of two years, I rarely saw a doctor invite an obstetrical patient to *moel kaun*. Showing, narrating, and "seeing the baby" was not common at the public hospital.

At Sorphea VIP, I came to understand another component of care in which deference goes both ways. I was sitting with Dr. Sophal in his exam room for the evening.[6] Nurse Thyda brought in a patient and her friend, both women in their mid- to late twenties. The patient was slightly plump, wearing tight white jeans and a black-and-white blouse, and her companion looked fresh from work in an office, wearing a skirt and black blazer. The patient lay down on her back on the exam bed, facing the second monitor on the wall. Her friend and Nurse Thyda sat on wheeled stools at the foot of the bed. The patient looked at the monitor for the Medison ultrasound machine. She looked at her friend and at Dr. Sophal as he scanned her abdomen and her left side, where she felt slight pain. Dr. Sophal spoke softly and steadily, naming the organs that the ultrasound waves traveled through and back from. The machine provided information in English, and Dr. Sophal translated it into Khmer for the patient. He explained, *"Echo khoenh knong"* (Ultrasound can see inside the body). "It is just your kidney and spleen there, you are not pregnant. Everything is okay." The patient's period was two weeks late, and though she got a negative pregnancy test, she wanted an ultrasound exam to confirm the result.

These three cases are quite different. The sequence at Russian Hospital hints at the diversity of patients, staff, and students in the imaging ward; the diverse health conditions that present; the diverse ultrasound practices that connect health professionals to one another and to patients, patients to one another and to their own and to others' bodies. In the scene of the exam, there were patients, students, nurses, doctors, and aides, people coming and going before, during, and after exams. There was participation of unrelated others: the young woman waiting for her grandmother's results and I, the anthropologist, shared in the pleasure of seeing and hearing Srey Pouv's baby. Staff and students examined very sick people and people who were not sick at all. They worked in silence, and they talked with patients and with one another. Some patients did not speak, out of respect for status hierarchies, because they could not speak Khmer, or because they had no one to speak for them.

This sequence also depicts the varieties of attention that make up care. In one, a patient lies waiting. Were her few minutes of neglect because of language, nationality, bewildering illness, or were they because of circumstances in the ward that had nothing to do with her? Dr. Vichet had to leave the room before she was wheeled in. In his absence, Nurse Lina had to do double duty, minding the students while typing up the previous patient's report. Srey Pouv, in contrast, received the opposite of neglect. She was not sick; she was pregnant. She had been through the exam before, she knew how to handle her own needs, to cover her legs (and get someone to help her do so). Though showing and narrating the baby was atypical, doctors and healthy pregnant women held a different genre of conversation than that of doctors and the very sick. The baby is a special object to relate to, in contrast to the intestine or the thyroid or the general "abdomen." After all, Dr. Din called it *kaun*, "child," as most doctors did during prenatal exams.[7]

At the private clinic, Sorphea VIP, the patient had control over who was in the room with her—just her friend, no unrelated others, except for me. The second monitor was for her, to see the exam in real time. Dr. Sophal spoke in low and soothing tones to her, as he did to most of his patients, some who came for a prenatal exam, some, like the woman above, to confirm a negative pregnancy test. Dr. Sophal later told me that he sees people who come to him before going to their doctor. It used to be that patients would see the general doctor first, then come for the recommended diagnostic or screening tests. Now patients come first to the private clinic for an ultrasound exam and bring the ultrasound report to their doctor. Dr. Sophal felt caught between two challenges: in his public hospital work at Maternal Hospital, it is difficult to explain the exam and results to patients on account of their low education or understanding. At Sorphea VIP, clients *mean*

FIGURE 3.1. Sreylin with her child. Sreylin, a woman in her late twenties, sits on a red bench waiting for the results of her ultrasound exam area at Russian Hospital. Her child is on her lap, squirming and chewing on a plastic straw. It was the day after the tragedy of the 2010 Water Festival. Hundreds of young people returning from a concert were caught in a stampede on the bridge linking Koh Pich (Diamond Island) to Phnom Penh. Hospital staff were redirected in their duties to deal with the injured and dead. Some did not come in to work. Even though Sreylin and her husband and child were the only people in the waiting area, they had to wait awhile. We had a chance to talk about the kinds of health care she and her husband hoped for and take pictures of her child walking up and down the empty passageway. Photo by author, 2010.

omnach, they have influence, and social power, and Dr. Sophal has to take care not to offend them.

Ultrasound amplifies forms of care that are respectful and neglectful, in ways that are patterned along social hierarchies but also unscripted. What are the qualities of this care, *yok chett tuk dak*? What kind of care is Sreylin, the woman in figure 3.1, asking for? She waited patiently, her daughter wriggling on her lap, the delicate bend in her wrist a clue that the stillness in the photograph was momentary. Her look reaches out to me. Do with respect.

The different topics and concerns folded into the English term *care* are not fused into a single word in Khmer but rather spread across different words and phrases. *Pyeabal* is treatment and cure, related to health. *Âphibal* conveys a notion of care as management and administration, the responsibility of leaders. There are words for taking care of: *chenhchoem*, or raising, nourishing; *thae, thae toam, thae roksa*, or to look after, take care of. These terms have to do with practice, emphasizing the doing rather than concern (caring for) or internal stance. The Khmer phrase *yok chett tuk dak*, used by patients in the imaging ward, places emphasis on care as a style of doing as much as on a particular outcome. *Yok chett tuk dak*, literally, "to take the heart and keep it close, safe," means doing with respect. This is a style of encounter that is important in health care but not specific to it; *yok chett tuk dak* is widely recognizable in other domains of life.

It is not the work of this book to articulate a normative Cambodian form of care; however, there are qualities of *yok chett tuk dak* that may run counter to ideas of care as theorized in North Atlantic anthropology and feminist science studies and thus are important to mention, even if provisionally. Of the dimensions of care proposed by Puig de la Bellacasa (2017)—practical work, affect, and political ethics—*yok chett tuk dak* entails practical work and sociopolitical ethics. Affect is not central to *yok chett tuk dak*; that is, patients' and providers' articulations of good or bad care did not center on sincerity, authentic desire, intentions, or good feelings. This distinguishes *yok chett tuk dak* from conceptions of care implicitly associated with good feelings, a problem that Michelle Murphy (2015) identifies in feminist self-help movements of North America and in neocolonial development programs that justify their work in the name of caring about women and girls.

There is resonance, thus, between *yok chett tuk dak* and formulations of care that center practice. Annemarie Mol's (2008) theorization, based on diabetes care in the Netherlands, of persistent tinkering, doing the best one can under changing circumstances, explicitly includes technologies in care. Felicity Aulino's (2016, 2019) theorization, based on end-of-life care in Thailand, places care as embodied ritual action for others. Aulino characterizes caregivers as "simply and literally technicians of the sacred . . . attending to the gears so that the wheel of karma can freely spin" (Aulino 2016, 98). Caregivers perform their work as a ritual, that is, repetitive embodied acts in which performance matters more than internal orientation toward the performance or the object of care (Aulino 2019, 13).[8] My approach is neither praxiography nor phenomenology, yet I understand *yok chett tuk dak* to be adjacent to Mol's and Aulino's work on technical practice rather than mental states or feelings.

The quality of respectful doing *yok chett tuk dak* does not require equality or empowerment. Hierarchy is not in itself a problem for care, though patients and doctors are vocal about the ways that injustice is related to hierarchy. Nor does *yok chett tuk dak* imply recognition of lay expertise. As I show below, ultrasound images bring people into their care in new ways—relating to their own bodies, relating to the bodies of others—yet this involvement does not displace the doctor and their expertise.

Care may be small acts. Giving advice, such as Dr. Pisey telling a middle-aged man with hepatitis to drink less, because alcohol, *sra*, challenges the liver, and his liver is struggling. It may be offering reassurance, such as when Dr. Rith spent a few more minutes than usual with a young woman who was very anxious about her pain. He listened patiently while she explained her symptoms and a related dream, and he gently said, "No, there is nothing." Then he distracted her and her friend with some good-natured teasing, causing them to giggle and smile. Relief.

Outside the exam room, *yok chett tuk dak* is Dr. Chhum observing an elderly woman, silent, vacant-eyed, writhing in pain on her stretcher, and calling her in ahead of the others who had been waiting. Unfair, perhaps, but care. *Yok chett tuk dak* is also, for some patients, being strict. After Dr. Chhum barked a few sharp words of criticism to staff about slow and incomplete report writing, a man sitting next to me nodded, "*Kach* [Strict]. That is good. I like a strict doctor. It shows he is smart and focused on his work rather than on trying to please people." For some patients, quality work and moving people through the ward are more important than kind words.

Two of the elements in *yok chett tuk dak*, *tuk chett*, yield the Khmer term for "trust," and a few words must be said about trust here. Trust between health care providers and patients is not given, not in Cambodia, not in the United States, not in encounters framed by histories of discrimination, disregard, and outright harm. Eve Zucker (2013, 48) writes about *ât tuk chett* as distrust of social and moral order, of particular situations, and of both strangers and neighbors. She explains distrust as a response to years of civil war and instability, to the terror, surveillance, and even extreme violence at the hands of neighbors that one must continue to live among as well as to rapid socioeconomic change of postconflict modernity (Zucker 2013). Alice Beban (2021) argues that distrust is grounded in uncertainty about power and is actively manipulated by political elites.

The Khmer Rouge controlled language and transvalued terms to do with health, medicine, and machines, which may leave traces in how "care" happens in imaging services. Sickness was defined as being unable to labor. As such, sickness was an affront to Angkar (Guillou 2009). The enemy was not the illness within the individual body; rather, illness was the sick individual who poisoned the social whole. Pol Pot equated "treacherous elements" with "ugly microbes" that are buried, secret, and multiplying (Hinton 2004, 124). Slogans like "Angkar takes care of you all, comrades!" (Panh and Bataille 2013, 89), chanted in the face of mass starvation and terrorizing violence, produced an unreal reality of care. Disregard for the humanity of others was central to Khmer Rouge ideology and practice.

I clearly remember hearing "*Ât yok chett tuk dak!*" (This is not taking care!) articulated with force in the waiting area of the Russian Hospital imaging ward. A woman cried out, hot, wounded, and fed up after being skipped over in line while waiting for her ultrasound exam. It was not common to see anger expressed in this way. Dr. Chhum took her into an appointment room, perhaps to calm her down, perhaps to get her away from the crowd (who agreed with her even if they disapproved of her mode of expression—a display is embarrassing to all involved, even to those who merely witness it). When a despairing or offended patient cries "*Ât yok chett tuk dak!*" to call out bad care, it may be understood also as a call not for warmth or kindness but for attention to and respect for the dignity and humanity of one waiting to be seen at the hospital.

Ultrasound is not quite independent and not just an extension of the doctor. However, just its presence may engender trust. Regarding private practice, Dr. Chhum told me, "Even if it is not used, just having an ultrasound machine means people will have more confidence in you, trust you more than a doctor who doesn't have a machine." Trust lies in the ability to use a machine, produce an image, and read the image but also, importantly, how one uses the technology and the information it produces, to what ends. People trust a machine for familiar reasons, including a sense that it may reduce human error and bias in health care. Ultrasound machines see into poor bodies and rich bodies alike. "If knowledge is low," Dr. Phalla said, "if patients are uneducated, they trust the machine. If they have higher education, they trust the doctor because they understand *I* make the report, *I* see," he said, emphasizing "I" by tapping his chest.[9] Dr. Phalla believed that people understand that the ultrasound machine automates many things, but it does not work on its own; it does not do away with the need for a skilled human operator.

For Long Phirum, the engineer/sales rep at the Dynamic medical equipment company (later at GE), distrust is common among doctors as well as between patients and doctors, and ultrasound complicates this feeling.

Phirum emphasized the report; if a doctor writes a clear and accurate ultrasound report and the image quality is good, he will receive referrals from other doctors. If the report is not good, patients have to get a second opinion, which costs them money and opens the referring doctor to critique. Doctors who spent time, effort, and money to go abroad for training stressed to me that patients should trust only those with training. Untrained providers make money off ultrasound scans but cannot produce the same quality image and report, and patients may not know the difference. Dr. Phalla said that trust is spoiled when a patient meets a bad doctor for diagnosis and subsequently thinks that all doctors are bad.

OVER-CARE, UNDER-CARE

Echo pouah haoey, ah pi mun. That kbal, free.

Scan the abdomen, 20,000 riel, Take a(nother) picture of your head, free.[10]

This saying, relayed to me by Dr. Chhoeun, the public health researcher working on rural health and poverty, satirizes commercial ultrasound practices. With cynical humor characteristic of Cambodian sayings about extractive social relations, it is an iteration of the seemingly universal sales technique: "Buy one, get one free!" Pay for an abdominal scan, and the doctor will throw in a free (unusual, useless?) picture of your head! Critique of "ultrasound as commodity" is not unique to Cambodia. In late capitalist United States, in market socialist Viet Nam, in pre-war Syria, overuse of ultrasound, particularly prenatal ultrasound, has been driven by commercial interests of physicians and hospitals as well as manufacturers, distributors, and marketers.[11] This satire conveys ultrasound's role in what I term *over-care*.

Over-care is when health professionals recommend, urge, or perform care when it is not indicated. This is usually an issue of money, though economic exchange itself does not taint care. Official fees-for-service, user fees, and under-the-table payments are part of the process of negotiating health care (and other bureaucracies) in Phnom Penh. People know about these different kinds of payments and participate. The amount of an under-the-table payment depends on the service and a patient's ability or inclination to pay: usually around 2,000 or 3,000 riel (US$0.50 to US$0.75), but some patients may pay 5,000 (US$1.25) or 10,000 (US$2.50) to ensure that staff pay attention to them. Some patients justified these unofficial payments in terms of doctors' abysmal salaries. As one middle-aged teacher put it, payments to health care providers smooth movement through the system and show "kindness," *nih chea santanchett knhum*, and are needed supplements to unlivable government wages.[12]

During political economic transition, under-the-table payments become points of friction. Signs in the general waiting area of Maternal Hospital depicted in text and image that under-the-table payments are not allowed. Development reports from the 1990s and 2000s regularly focused on the ubiquity and harm of this practice. Medical anthropologists of former Soviet countries that transitioned from state socialism to market capitalism trace similar struggles over payments. Rima Praspaliauskiene observes that during socialist times in Lithuania, under-the-table payments were derided as bourgeois; during market reform and integration into the European Union, they were criticized as corrupt, or socialist even.[13] While stressfully unpredictable, under-the-table payments were a means for patients to assert a personal relationship with their provider in an otherwise impersonal, bureaucratic medical system (Praspaliauskiene 2016). Michele Rivkin-Fish (2005, 179–81) found that in post-Soviet Russia, payments and gifts to providers establish mutual obligation, giving patients a sense of influence over their therapeutic destiny and an opportunity to establish something for the future.

However, it is important to note the limits on a patient's ability to influence their therapeutic destiny. In Cambodia, patients enter a system that compels some kind of payment for adequate service, yet adequate service is not guaranteed. Is this money then a gift or a payment or a bribe? Is it obligatory or a sign of appreciation? Does it happen before or after services are provided? People talked about payments in these multiple senses: payments are exploitative and burdensome as well as a means to show appreciation and create good feeling, which can engender good care.

As specialties rely more and more on ultrasound imaging for diagnostics, patients in Phnom Penh must increasingly navigate between imaging and other wards. Stuart Blume (1992) shows how the concentration of imaging in dedicated wards reorganizes hospitals flows—of authority, of bodies, of money. In contrast, given an equal reliance on ultrasound for diagnosis in the private sector, there, at least, patients know that all services will be in one place. For patients needing more than just a scan, imaging is another node in the unpredictable journey through the hospital. Where to go? How to carry oneself? How much to pay the cashier, and how much "kindness" to pay the nurse and doctor? A person entering a hospital will usually face degrees of uncertainty and alienation. Perhaps greatest of all is the unknown of one's own body, a body that may be confounding in its alterations, or its pain. The order of things bureaucratic and biological, so to speak, is daunting in its opacity. Ultrasound is another node in a patient's trajectory in the hospital, another encounter in which *yok chett tuk dak* and possibly payment for it is at stake.

Under-care is care that is withheld, and this is also often to do with money. In the imaging ward, under-care was skipping over people who are waiting and obstacles in the system, intentional or not, with the result that people were stuck without care, having paid for services, transport, and taken time off of work. The death of Vorn Yoeub and her unborn child at Pailin Referral Hospital showed the extreme consequences of violating expectations for under-the-table payments. The story circulated widely by word of mouth and in Khmer- and English-language media (see Radosevitch and Chan Thul 2009). Vorn's husband, Mith Ran, said when she went to a referral hospital in a health emergency, midwives would not care for her unless they received 100,000 riel, about US$25, a sum the family did not have. When Mith told the deputy director of the hospital about this extreme negligence, the director replied, "Medical personnel are like soldiers. Some of them are hardworking, some are lazy." Mith told reporters, "I had no words to respond to him." The terrible injury, the unspeakable irony, is that the director paid Vorn's cremation fee, which was US$25.

In Phnom Penh, stories of money and withholding care circulate. While getting my hair cut near Olympic Stadium, hairdressers shook their heads and sucked their teeth in scorn over the story of Vorn Yoeub, "It is so bad!" Medical staff also talked about it, outside of work hours, albeit as a misdeed of others. The cases of under-care in the imaging ward were less grave than those that circulated in public discourse, yet they were linked in a public imaginary of injustice in health care.

Under-care is dealt unevenly to poor, minoritized, and colonized groups, and this is more visible in the public hospital. Neglect, as Mol (2008) writes, is bad care, so perhaps not proper care at all. However, scholars have argued that it is important to consider the negative effects of care, in terms of health and politics, rather than restricting care to the good only. Lisa Stevenson (2014) brings neglect into care through the concept of "anonymous care." For Stevenson, public health workers who focused on tuberculosis and suicide rates among Indigenous people in the Canadian Arctic treated the individual as a unit of population rather than a person with a social identity, living in relations and constraints. In doing so, they enacted harmful normativities, if not outright physical and psychic harm, on people in the name of health care.

Perhaps the most common response to neglect in the imaging ward was to swallow it like bitter medicine, to sweat it out in silence. Squinting from the glare in the waiting area, Socheata, a woman from Battambang who came for a mammogram, was moved to comment on people being seen ahead of her.[14] Socheata had first gone to a private clinic closer to home but was referred to the public hospital in the capital because of its reputation as a center of expertise. As she noticed that "better-dressed" people who arrived after her were called ahead of her, she gradually stopped talking. She called it injustice, *âyuttethoa*. "That's enough for now, child," she said as her anger sapped her interest in talking, and she became quiet.

Perhaps it is better to manage the frustration and anger by intervening respectfully. "How long?" a polite husband may enquire with the nurse. "Did you call my wife's name yet and perhaps we missed it?" "No, just wait. Soon." Or by quietly trading barbs with one another, or joking out loud, like the woman who said that she should "cheat" by pretending to faint so she would be seen faster. This was a morning when there was only one fully functioning ultrasound set up—the printer was down in Exam 1; the ultrasound machine was down in Exam 3. Exam 2 was the only room that had people moving in and out of it. The woman had made her joke as Nurse Sovannary, looking stressed, hurried down the hallway with a manual for LOGIQ, the model of the ultrasound machine that was broken.

On this morning at Russian Hospital, patients wondered aloud whether they would be able to get their ultrasound results today, given that they had not even had the exam yet. Would the results make it back to the referring doctor who sent them to the imaging ward in the first place? If patients at the public imaging wards were not seen in the morning, they would have to go home and either return after 2 p.m., when there were fewer doctors and they might still have to wait, or come back the next morning, when they might still have to wait. Whereas being skipped over in line is not particular to imaging wards, ultrasound has become an obligatory passage point for diagnosis of many conditions, particularly in gynecology and obstetrics. Another wait.

How did patients talk about under-care? Mostly in terms of discrimination against the poor. Sokuntheavy and Rouen, sisters from Kandal, came to Russian Hospital two days in a row and had yet to be seen for an ultrasound exam. Sokuntheavy was pregnant and had been bleeding for two days. She first went to a doctor closer to home, in the northern suburbs of Phnom Penh, near where she worked at a garment factory. The doctor told her to go to any big hospital in the city. Sokuntheavy's neighbor told her that Russian Hospital was a good hospital, so they came here. But on the second day here,

Sokuntheavy had not yet seen a doctor, and she was suffering. Small drop-lets of sweat pooled on her temples. I told Ming, the receptionist, that Sokuntheavy was ill. I bought her a juice from the janitor. Sokuntheavy mumbled weakly that she felt dizzy and wanted to go home. Her sister Rouen said no, they should stay.

"It costs a lot for the moto and we have already taken off work. We should stay."

Rouen looked down at her dusty pink sandal. We were silent for a moment, and then Rouen raised her head. "It is so bad!" she said. "The government complains about doctors and nurses referring patients to their private prac-tices, but the government does not complain about bad care. If I see some-one who arrives after us getting called in before us, I will complain."

Was Sokuntheavy not seen because she did not have personal connec-tions to staff, because she did not offer money up front, because she looked poor? Was it an administrative error, or was it just extremely busy? Asking my questions led nowhere. Any one of these, any combination of these, could be in play. It could also be an instance of the widespread disregard for young laborers in the city, despite garment workers being the engine of the export economy.[15] But it is important that Sokuntheavy and her sister talked about money and connections as the reasons for their exclusions, the under-care they received in this public hospital.[16]

For hospital staff, the line of patients is sometimes never ending. A col-league may not be pulling his weight, so the others must pick up the slack, doing scan after scan after scan. Dr. Sophal complained of pain from his right hand up his arm to his neck due to repetitive scanning. Nurses were bur-dened by work with minimal infrastructure and materials. Their workspace was a table, their records were a log book written in by hand (see figure 3.2). Nurses, the receptionist, and the janitor must manage the backlog of bod-ies, the fraying of patience, the accretion of suffering, the questioning looks.

In other words, it is not only patients who experience and criticize neglect in the imaging ward. At Maternal Hospital, for example, doctors were dis-cussing a problem at the hospital and the unlikeliness that it would be addressed, at least anytime soon, by those in charge. "The higher-ups go to their base, *choh mouldthan*, to the provinces, to curry favor for influence or for votes. That is where they spend their time and energy, rather than on their jobs here in Phnom Penh," said Dr. Phalla. The problem was not particular to this hospital; Dr. Phalla and colleagues were critiquing how politics are done. Most people in senior government posts, including in health care, have to be a member of the CPP, the ruling party, and have to deliver votes from particular areas of the country to keep their jobs. Cambodians working in

FIGURE 3.2. Nurses' station. The nurses' station in the ultrasound ward at the National Center for Maternal and Child Health is a simple table with a logbook, appointment book, stapler, pen, and envelopes. The table sits outside the doorway to the ultrasound room and faces a row of chairs and benches and a bright window. The nurses have to manage a lot of tasks with minimal infrastructure for record keeping and no separation from the patients. From here, the nurse answers questions, directs patients into the exam area, and advises patients where to go next. Sometimes a nurse goes over the main points of the report from the ultrasound exam with the patient here. Photo by author, 2010.

ministries, libraries, archives, hospitals, and schools are used to the erratic presence and frazzled exhaustion of their high-level administrators. That said, Maternal Hospital was not without its problems. In August 2011, a letter of complaint signed by ninety staff was published in the paper. It detailed mistreatment by the director and misconduct, including embezzlement of client fees, by two senior accountants (Khoun 2011).

Later that morning, Makara, the young technical assistant, continued where the doctors had left off. He was taking dictation from a doctor speaking from the curtained-off exam room at his left. As the doctor spelled out "légère, l-é-g-è-r-e," Makara typed and said to me, "Doctors informed higher-ups at the hospital of problems, but the director did not fix them." For Makara, neglect of administrative and managerial duties was the cause of the low quality of service in the government health system. "You can see that," he said, switching from English, which he liked to practice with me, to Khmer. "You can look from the outside (*moel pi krov*) at the problems and see them clearly (*chbas*)."

When patients at Russian Hospital experienced, and criticized, long waits in the public imaging ward as a form of status-based injustice, they narrate a violation of proper comportment within hierarchy. As Penny Edwards (2008) observes, moral understandings of social hierarchy entail the expectation that respect given to people of higher status—bodily comportment such as no eye contact, chin down, *sompeah* (bowed head and palms held together at the chest), or quiet speech—comes with the expectation of reciprocity. For the respect and money they give to doctors and nurses in a clinical encounter, patients should receive competent care. For their labor and diligence in reporting problems, doctors should have administrators who work to improve the running of the hospital. When Dr. Phalla and Makara experienced lack of change in their institution as status-based injustice (and political rot), they narrate a violation of the responsibility of leaders to their people. (Their critiques also illuminate one of the reasons health professionals embrace private practice.)

In other words, hierarchies create expectations of roles, relations, and experiences that are unequal, but hierarchies do not naturalize abuse or injustice (Beban 2021, 16). Hierarchies do not do away with the need for *yok chett tuk dak*. People are acutely aware of problems with hierarchy, but "they do not normally frame its opposite in the nationalist vision of some supposed and generalized bourgeois equality" (Davis 2008, 225). In most cases, an "asymmetric relationship between doctor and patient is natural and called for" (Sachs 1989, 336), which might chafe against egalitarian principles of scholars and health activists. Physician Baijayanta Mukhopadhyay (2016) acknowledges the challenge for social justice work in health care: people want to delegate "dealing with the decrepit, decaying body" to someone else, he writes, ideally someone who is an expert. Health care workers ought to accept this delegation, and, I would add, to do so in the manner of *yok chett tuk dak*.

CARE WITH MACHINES

One of the vigorous debates about technologies in medicine (and technologies outside of medicine) has to do with what is being automated. Which human judgments, biases, skills, and knowledges are entrusted to a machine? How will this entrustment change care? For whom? And what new medical, ethical, or economic dilemmas will the machine open up? My interest in these questions was piqued through two encounters: a training at Russian Hospital in which race correction came up (briefly, without issue) and a conversation with a senior radiologist about deskilling.

In a 2010 obstetrical ultrasound training at Russian Hospital, put on by GE Healthcare and led by an OBGYN from Paris, doctors learned that ultrasound is advantageous for use in the first trimester to determine the location of gestational sac formation, viability of the fetus, and accurate estimated due date. They learned other indications for using ultrasound during pregnancy, for example, in cases of maternal bleeding or pain, unknown due date, or if the uterine size is smaller or larger than one would expect for the due date. The training also covered the development of the embryo and its migration, implantation, and normal physiological development of the fetus. According to the trainer, ultrasound imaging is most important for determining the estimated due date, the size and development of the fetus, and "abnormal cases." "Here we have to differentiate what race is the patient, for example, America, Europe, or Asia. These have a different table of measurements. For Asia, we generally use the Japanese table: Osaka." The trainer emphasized that with new ultrasound machines, it is very important to program the correct fetal size measurement table because it can only be programmed once.

This statement brought forward what is often in the background in prenatal ultrasound imaging: the information from an ultrasound exam is not just to do with the fetus and uterine environment being scanned; it is also information about a relation to a norm. The accuracy of the measurements is subject to particular norms in the measurement scale. The norms are managed partially through race correction: program "Osaka" so that the fetus's development is measured in reference to a growth curve developed at Osaka University. There are US and European formulas in the LOGIQ model too (see figure 3.3; GE Medical Systems 2000). This programming is troubled by the diversity of what "Asian" or "European" are and how this diversity has been accounted for in the study population upon which the measurement tables were developed. This is an example of how norms are built into the machine and how it matters where, by whom, and for whom a machine is designed.

Critical theorists of technology have shown how raced and gendered privilege and bias are built into technologies, sometimes with, often without, explicit intent, such that whiteness is a norm, and non-whiteness is deviation from a norm. For example, Michael Dyer's (1997) *White* traces how photographic and film technologies were developed to depict white skin,

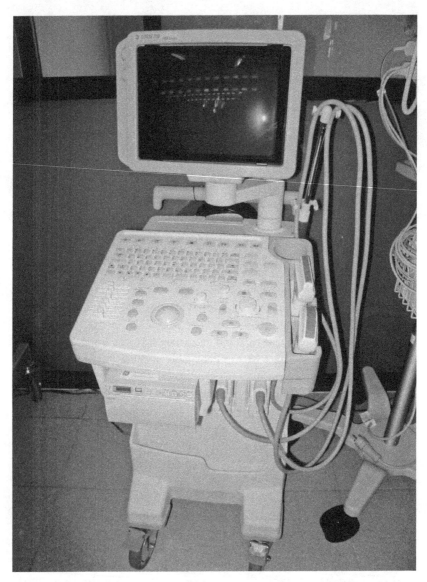

FIGURE 3.3. LOGIQ 200. This mobile ultrasound machine is one of the models that General Electric (GE) donated to public hospitals in Phnom Penh in 2009 and 2010 as part of its Developing Health Globally program. The LOGIQ 200 has an adjustable monitor, a keyboard with a trackball and controls for measurement and image capture, two kinds of sensors, and a storage drive. Photo by author, 2009.

with the result that non-white skin tones become a problem for the technician to overcome. Moya Bailey (2016) shows how medical textbooks depict almost exclusively white bodies, thus inculcating a sense of the non-white body as a particular case, not normal, for generations of medical students. Lundy Braun's (2014) history of the spirometer documents how race, class, and gender bias informed the development of the spirometer in different ways, both white supremacist science bent on biological quantification of racial and gender inferiority and business interests pursuing standards that exclude workers from illness compensation.

When racial comparison is not the explicit project, as is the case in ultrasound, race gets into the machine through the production of norms, thresholds, scales, and other practices of managing variability across and within groups. In the above story, "Asian" is a capacious and confounding category, entailing geographical location at national and continental scales, which can structure judgments about whether a fetus is developing normally or not. Race correction happens when selecting a measurement table that provides norms and standard deviations of fetal measurements—crown-rump length, biparietal diameter, femur length—as a means to apprehend whether fetal development is normal. Even when bracketing the problems with using ultrasound to measure fetal size and establish due date and pregnancy risk (see Erikson 2012 on these problems), there are so many questions. How does the machine, or the clinician, manage inter-Asian difference? And the fact that compared to other countries in Asia, babies and children in Cambodia are small?

The doctors in the training did not react visibly or verbally to the instructions to program the Osaka table. The trainer from Paris was probably not thinking about values attached to fetal size—big or small, "European" or "Asian"—her point was that accurate clinical judgments require accurate technical measurements interpreted in reference to appropriate norms. But in Cambodia the issue of small fetuses and small babies is inflected by the stigma of poverty, association of large bodies with wealth, and recent histories of serious and widespread hunger.[17] Cambodians are well aware that their babies are often smaller than Euro-American babies, and for many, this is not a positive comparison. Big babies are viewed as vital and healthy and small ones as somewhat disappointing or weak. Cambodian woman having babies with Euro-American men explained to me the need for delivery by cesarean section: "because the father is a foreigner, *barang*," the baby will be big. Which table of size measurements would this fetus require?

Ultrasound images bring patients into new care relations with their providers, with their own bodies, and with other patients. The encounter with the doctor and the ultrasound machine asks for certain kinds of awareness and knowledge from patients. If patients wanted to learn more detail about their results, they needed to know how to read and, in many cases, how to read French, which was still the professional language of medicine. At Russian Hospital, prenatal ultrasound reports were printed in Khmer as well as French, suggesting that patients would have more interest and ability to read prenatal ultrasound reports than reports for other exams. Patients were asked to articulate the sensations of the body, including reporting of general symptoms, such as where does it hurt, and how long has it hurt? The patient needed to reflect on food and drink, for example, to reply to a doctor taking an abdominal scan who asked, "Do you eat a lot of salt or drink a lot of alcohol?" They needed to keep track of menstruation to answer the question, "How long have you been pregnant?" or "When was your last period?" Most patients could answer the few questions that doctors asked them. In general, there was minimal discussion between doctors and patients, though, as mentioned earlier, pregnant patients conversed more than others. In most cases, they were not sick or in pain.

Patients also needed to know how to ask questions. Many wanted more explanation of the ultrasound exam process and what it means. They did not want to be hustled out or talked down to. They wanted the doctor to talk to them a bit more. In general, across fieldsites, I heard few questions from patients about ultrasound, what it was, what it could or could not do. Sometimes there was confusion about whom to ask: the doctor or the nurse or the technician or the woman at the front desk. I rarely saw a prenatal exam during which fetal anomaly was discovered and disclosed to the pregnant woman, a circumstance that might prompt more questions from patients and more than a brief explanation from doctors and nurses. Doctors answered patients' questions, but their questions were few. This may change as ultrasound imaging continues to proliferate.

Patients shape imaging in ways that are not easily recognized if focusing only on the content of speech. Aug Nishizaka (2011, 316) argues that doctor-sonographers provide instructions to their pregnant patients for "how to see the image" through what he calls "differentiation sequences." In these sequences, imagers juxtapose talk, gesture, and image, such as naming a fetal part with a familiar descriptor and highlighting the location of the body part with a pointing gesture. If this seems quite didactic, Nishizaka insists that women play a key role in these sequences; even silence can be generative in that it may compel the doctor to continue, to pursue a response.

However, patients did not usually look at the image on the monitor; often the monitor was not visible to the patient at all due to the orientation of the bed (in ultrasound literature this is called "low feedback"), unless the doctor turned it toward them as Dr. Din did for Srey Pouv. Some private maternity clinics had a second monitor that the patient could watch while lying down. Some patients told me they wanted to "look inside" their bodies, and others said they did not. Some expressed a shyness or fear for what they might see. Others said they didn't know how to see, *ât che moel*, and that this was the job of the *kroupet* (doctor) because he or she had the expertise.

What, then, is *yok chett tuk dak* in imaging practices? At both public imaging wards and private clinics, verbal interactions during the exam were brief, sometimes followed by a short monologue by the doctor or nurse, covering the main conclusions from the report. At Maternal Hospital, the examining doctor or Makara, the technician, gave the patient a printout of the report. Mony, the nurse at the reception desk, summarized verbally to the patient what the report said—such as whether the fetus was healthy or not, the estimated due date, information about the placenta and sex—and directed the patient where in the hospital to go next. Patients who self-referred usually got a more detailed explanation of the report than patients who were on their way back to the referring doctor. At Russian Hospital, where ultrasound was part of a general imaging ward that included mammography and X-ray, the doctors performing the scan gave only "brief diagnoses," in the words of Dr. Chhum, along with the report. Dr. Chhum explained his and his colleagues' brevity thusly: "I am a radiologist, not an internal medicine specialist. I am not qualified to talk about medications, for example. Some people may become angry upon hearing their diagnosis. My ward is not qualified to manage this response."[18]

Given that patients rely on the doctor as the expert and authority, what does the image shift? Is there some democratization of knowledge of the body or disease in which patients can participate in ways not possible before? Or is there a giving up of even minimal body knowledge, and some of the sovereignty that comes with that knowledge, if technological images are left to experts?[19] In what follows, I explore a case in which mammograms were objects for patients relating, comparing, and orienting toward the future. Patients who did not know one another compared their medical histories, estimated medical futures, detailed financial difficulties, mapped their present health problems, and dissected medical images. On this morning, the conversation involved two women who had come to have lumps in their breasts examined.

On a dry March day, Charya, Kanitha, and Samnang were standing opposite the mammography rooms at the far end of the open-air waiting area of the imaging ward.[20] Kanitha had traveled from Kampong Cham province with her sister, Charya, who needed a breast exam. Kanitha was a forty-five-year-old rice farmer with two children, a daughter in her late teens and a son in his early twenties. Kanitha was concerned about their education; her son had stopped studying, and her daughter wanted to continue with schooling in Phnom Penh, but the family did not have the resources to support her. We talked about work and leisure. Kanitha rolled up her sleeve, a peach-colored fabric decorated with brown felt and rhinestones, to show the dark skin on her forearm, *khmov*, she murmured, evidence of her work under the sun. I admired her nails, which were painted sparkly dark purple.

"My daughter did it, in her free time." She smiled at her child's skill and style.

I asked Kanitha if she and her family usually came to Phnom Penh for medical care, and she said no.

"Sometimes we go to the *krou*, because he is cheaper. But the hospital in the capital has ultrasound, so if we need an *echo*, we come to Phnom Penh."

Charya, Kanitha's sister, emerged from the mammography room and started talking to Samnang, who was sitting near us, waiting for her results. Samnang, a fiery woman from Takeo province, had also come to have a breast scan. Charya and Samnang talked about the lumps in their breasts, the size and feel of them, and the procedures they had endured to diagnose what to do about the lumps. To tell her story, Samnang lifted up the front of her black blouse and showed us her breast. She squeezed it while talking, "This hard area, it's a cyst," she instructed us. The sisters from Kampong Cham took turns squeezing Samnang's breast, commenting on the texture in comparison to that of their own breasts. They then looked at each other's mammograms. Charya said that she had had more than one scan, each picture different from the other, *rouppheap phseng phseng knea*. What to do with that? Charya and Samnang spoke in alternating loud and soft tones, shifting between excitement and reflection and back again as they puzzled together through whether they would be treated with medicine or surgery, *thnam ru veah kat*. Samnang said that she would have surgery and seemed relieved.

Consider the rich variety of practices of relating to a medical image here! The three women *compared* mammograms—Samnang's with Charya's as well as Charya's mammograms over time, which had differed from one another. They *juxtaposed* mammograms with the body parts imaged—breasts. They *felt* each other's breasts. And they *talked* to one another. They considered the authority of mammograms for apprehending lumps alongside its uncertainties: past images were different, future trajectories were unknown, how do the images relate to the feel of the lumps?

This encounter illuminates how medical images figure within practices of caring for one's health. The mammograms were available for comment by rice farmers. Patients did not wave lab results or prescriptions or products of non-image diagnostic technologies as they compared, juxtaposed, and discussed care. Yes, a prescription, too, is a visual and tangible object: a small piece of paper, signed in blue, stamped in red, ripped from an official notepad. So, too, is a lab report: A4 paper with numbers, perhaps in columns or perhaps just a list, maybe a graph. But medical images are objects of a particular kind. Ultrasound images generate relations between patients, not just between doctors and patients or between patients and their own bodies.

In describing this encounter in the mammography waiting area, I am not suggesting that Samnang, Charya, nor Kanitha could read the images as well or in the same way as Dr. Vandy or Dr. Chhum could. My interest here is in practices of relating to medical images and practices of relating to bodies, one's own body and the body of another. This is an opening for lay participation in health care. People are generally in possession of their medical documents—images, lab results, prescriptions, diagnostic reports. It is normal for patients or their family members to carry a plastic bag filled with documents or a large envelope carrying an X-ray film (see figure 3.4). This is a burden on patients, to be their own record-keeper, but it also brings medical images into people's hands. When Emily Martin (1995) asked non-experts in the urban United States what they make of micrographs of immune cells, she found that the images were points of opening to varied interpretations and even emotions of awe. In other words, the micrograph was not a reduction of complex data, or taming of a messy natural object, or a determination of one expert way of seeing. Similarly here, the mammogram is not only a pushing aside of other ways of knowing. It is calibrated alongside touch, story, hope, and uncertainty. The mammograms the women compared were not closed, nor were their implications certain.

Doing with respect. I return to Sreylin, the woman in figure 3.1. I took this photograph, one of many during the two-plus years of fieldwork at Russian Hospital. This picture stays with me. "What was I being called to by and with her look at me and mine at her?" (Sharpe 2016, 118). Her straight-ahead gaze and calm expression belie the heat of the morning, the long time spent waiting on that red bench, the fussing of her child. In returning to

FIGURE 3.4. Husband holding bag with medical records. The husband of Sreylin, pictured at the beginning of the chapter, is a soft-spoken man with a calm demeanor. He sits on the bench in the Russian Hospital imaging ward waiting area. The pink plastic bag that he is holding contains Sreylin's medical records, including prior imaging reports. At the time, patients kept track of their own records as there was no central electronic medical record system in use at the hospital, and they may see providers at different hospitals and clinics. Photo by author, 2010.

Sreylin's picture I am not pressing for your concern. That would run counter to what she would call care. I am trying to convey *yok chett tuk dak.* It is difficult to settle on what good care in the case of ultrasound could be, and this means that people are trying to pin it down, to fix care in multiple senses: to temper uncertainty about illness and income, about where to go for care, about how to move through a hospital or clinic, and about how much to pay at different sites of encounter.

Neglect is everywhere. We cannot expect a hospital to be an exceptional place. Public hospitals are the front lines of illness and suffering that are both unpredictable and inevitable. They are the front lines of illness and indebtedness, of gendered sacrifice and disregard, of hunger and exhaustion, of unequal vulnerability to accident. Public hospitals are the front lines of suffering that is uncontrollable as well as suffering that is planned, dealt by the social and economic policies of authoritarian capitalism. These policies gobble the bodies of the young in garment factories, construction, soldiering, and sex work and spit out the bodies of the old with little chance of succor beyond the wat.

Part of the question of how technologies shape care involves the issue of how technologies shape care *as an as extractive practice* of over-care and as a *neglectful practice* of under-care. Health care is already a significant source of debt for poor and middle-class families. The cost of imaging services amplifies this, raising important political questions of resource distribution, regulation of costs, and standards of care. This only presses more urgently for doing with respect.

CHAPTER FOUR

ULTRASOUND IS AN EYE FOR SEEING

Sickness is a parasitic noise. And the doctor eats by translating this noise.

—MICHEL SERRES, *THE PARASITE*

"ULTRASOUND IS AN EYE FOR SEEING, PEOPLE BELIEVE, *CHEA phnaek moel khoenh ke cheua*," Dr. Chhum said to me one morning in the imaging ward.[1] We were standing side by side at the railing of the waiting area, looking out at the dark clouds expanding like lungs from the south. He liked to photograph the sky, he told me. He liked waiting and being at the ready, the dynamic calibration of aperture and exposure time. It got us talking about other mechanical eyes, about ultrasound.

"If a doctor has the same eye as the patient, how can the doctor see inside? The doctor is also a human being; only with *echo* is he able to see inside," he continued. The riddle he was unraveling for me has to do with this technology, ultrasound, that makes images from sound, its powerful synesthesia. Seeing inside is a sounding inside. Might this way of doing also pose a challenge to ways of understanding expertise? What if Dr. Chhum was hinting at expertise itself as an echo, a way of doing that depends on an emission, its reception, and maneuvering interference?

Dr. Chhum's comments about seeing with sound underscore the elements that make ultrasound a *machine-eye*: the human, the eye, the machine, the inside matter of a body. For patients, a doctor's skill is ever more intertwined with technology. All in one breath, for some: "*Ke chumneanh, mean obakar krup kroan*" (People [at the hospital] are skilled, and they have the necessary devices), said a woman, explaining why her family—five people in

104

total—had made the long journey to Russian Hospital from Prey Veng to seek care for her father's kidney problem. *Chumneanh* means skill, ability, or expertise; *obakar* refers to devices, instruments, and materials. Indexed here is expertise as having the skills and tools to diagnose and intervene.

This chapter is about seeing with ultrasound. It situates ultrasound imaging in a dense cultural field in which seeing is a skill and in which different agents (human, machine, non-human) can be both agents of vision and available to be seen. There are long genealogies of vision and skilled diagnosis grounded in Buddhist practice and in French colonial medicine. I argue, first, that these other agents and their ways of seeing interfere with the medical gaze scripted into the machine and, second, that interference *is fundamental to seeing*. Something interesting and potentially important comes to the fore when interference is taken for granted. Skilled vision becomes maneuvering, accounting for phenomena given that there will be interference. This may provide a path around debates in visual anthropology and visual studies in STS regarding the primacy and tyranny of vision among the senses. I hope to shift the object of study in visual studies of technoscience away from critique of the ideal of a transparent body and toward the kinds of interference that looking into the body requires managing.

This proposal may be easier to imagine if we use an image of thought from a different sense—sound, specifically, the echo. Echo: a sound or series of sounds caused by the reflection of sound waves from a surface back to the listener; the deliberate introduction of reverberation into a sound recording. *Echo* is the term for ultrasound in Khmer and French; it is also an image for what mediated vision, skilled vision can be. Here I am interested in articulating an interface between two traditions of visual analysis, cultural anthropology and feminist technoscience, centering on the issues of visualist bias, of relations of seeing to authoritative knowledge, and of vision at the top of a hierarchy of senses.

Foucault's *The Birth of the Clinic* is the lodestar for analyses of visuality, knowledge, and power in medicine. His concept of the medical gaze involves a way of seeing the body that is intimately dependent upon language and sutures seeing, knowledge, expertise, and power in the institution of the teaching hospital as it emerged after the French Revolution: "The gaze implies an open field, and its essential activity is of the successive order of reading; it records and totalizes; it gradually reconstitutes immanent organizations; it spreads out over a world that is already the world of language, and that is why it is spontaneously related to hearing and speech; it forms, as it were, the privileged articulation of two fundamental aspects of *saying* (what is said and what one says)" ([1963] 1994, 121). Foucault contrasts the gaze with the glance. The medical glance "does not scan a field: it strikes at one point, which is central or decisive" (121). The action of the glance is penetrative. "The glance chooses a line that instantly distinguishes the essential; it therefore goes beyond what it sees. . . . If it strikes in its violent rectitude, it is in order to shatter, to lift, to release appearance. It is not burdened with the abuses of language. The glance is silent, like a finger pointing, denouncing" (121).

The qualities of the glance shift the "kinship" of the clinical eye from the "ear straining to catch a language" to "the index finger palpating the depths" (Foucault [1963] 1994, 122). This is the rise of pathological anatomy as the gold standard of knowledge in early nineteenth-century European medicine and the value of death to inform understandings of life (170–72). The force in Foucault's language suggests that touch is not the way out of controlling vision. Puig de la Bellacasa (2017, 20) notes that her effort to reclaim touch, or "proximal intimate knowing," as a neglected way of knowing is not an idealization of touch. For Puig de la Bellacasa, the haptic disrupts dominant epistemologies of knowledge that rely on vision as metaphor for distant knowing, distant critique.[2] It is important to remember that the medical seeing that pursues mysteries in the depth of the body (Foucault [1963] 1994) is a gaze that touches. Medical imaging displaces the authority of touch and the corpse in diagnostic labor, though as Barry Saunders (2008) notes, intrigue and the pursuit of mysteries of the body are still very much with us.

Skilled seeing of the inside of the body and of a medical image is not exclusive to medicine, not to its humans or its machines. In Phnom Penh, the authority of seeing inside the body is shared, and doctors see alongside monks, charms, and ancestors who have their own authority to see and to block seeing. The seeing and sounding of dreaming also interfere as ways of grasping what is going on inside the body, revealing the ways in which the body is in relation to other entities, such as children-to-be, or spirits. Imaging works in a realm in which seeing is powerful, authoritative, not only with the eyes, and not solely as the provenance of medicine. "Empty the visual from eyes of flesh," artist Phaptawan Suwannakudt wrote, her father's instructions to learn to see beyond sight, with imagination and with the eyes closed (cited in Datuin 2012, 211).

MOEL CHBAS, SEEING CLEARLY

Dr. Chhum used two back-to-back words for seeing, *moel khoenh*, placing emphasis on the visual: to look at and to see, to distinguish. The slippage and blending in different Khmer terms for seeing, caring, and authority structure how people understand the skill of medical and spiritual seeing.

Moel is the common verb used with ultrasound, among health professionals and everyday people outside the hospital. *Moel* folds together many topics and concerns: to look (at), watch, observe; to examine; to read; to care for or take care of (SEAlang).[3] *Moel* in the sense of "to care for" is used for looking after children—*moel kaun*. Thus, depending on context, *moel kaun* can also mean to look at the fetus through ultrasound, akin to "seeing the baby," or the everyday activity of looking after a child, what a parent, sibling, relative, or neighbor might do. *Moel* is also like the English "examine, check"; for example, *moel chheam* is a common way to talk about getting a blood test.

    Moel chbas is the phrase that people use to talk about good medical care. *Moel chbas* can be translated many ways; its multiplicity makes it generative. In the context of health, it means "see clearly or accurately." Khmer distinguishes between caring for and about, as discussed in the previous chapter with the phrase *yok chett tuk dak*, and care as an authoritative skill. *Moel chbas* is a valuation both of a doctor's ability to read ultrasound images and of a doctor's capacity to practice medicine, to do an accurate examination. Doctors can *moel chbas*, and ultrasound is a tool for *moel chbas*. Puzzling through multiple senses of *moel* with me, historian Siti Keo recalled a conversation with her aunt. They were talking about going to the doctor for consultation, and her aunt said, *"tov moel moel,"* or going to see what (the doctor) will see, or see what they find. Keo pointed out that *moel* can convey a sense of "interpretation."[4] *Moel* is also a term for the healer. Anthropologist Emiko Stock reminded me that a common saying for a *krou*, or good traditional healer, is *koat poukae moel*,[5] or he or she is skilled at looking (at a malady)/seeing (a malady). Buddhist studies scholar Trent Walker offers that "*moel* seems connected to the ontology of Khmer traditional medicine, where skilled healers are able to 'see' into the character of people, their karmic knots, and the path of unbinding them."[6] As in Buddhist visualization, the "seeing" in traditional medicine is not limited to the perceptual apparatus of the eyes. This more-than-visual seeing comes through in patients' evaluations of doctors' abilities.

    Patients used *chbas* to qualify the sort of knowing or understanding that an image may provide. *Chbas* conveys values that are separated in English— clear, accurate—and used to qualify a variety of actions and practices: speaking or hearing; seeing (*moel* or *khoenh chbas*); reading/interpreting; understanding (*yual chbas*) and knowing (*doeng chbas*). The phrase also has a lineage to the Khmer Rouge, to describe "right thinking."[7] Srey Pich, a nanny from Battambang, used *chbas* to qualify medical seeing and knowing. Neary and I talked to her in the mammography waiting area at Russian

Hospital, during what she hoped to be the final stop in her journey to diagnosis and treatment of a lump in her breast (she used the common word *dom*).[8] Srey Pich first went to a *krou khmae* in Battambang because she thought he could help and because he charged less than a medical doctor. After a half year of treatment and no improvement, her neighbor told her that ultrasound would give a clear image; it would enable her to know if the tumor was malignant or benign. She went to a medical doctor in Battambang. The doctor did a scan of her breast but was unable to tell what was wrong. He advised her to go to Phnom Penh (about 340 kilometers away, around five or six hours by taxi) for an exam at Russian Hospital. So she did, in part because of his advice and in part because, despite the journey, Russian Hospital would be less expensive than a private clinic closer to home. Srey Pich used *chbas* in two senses: she wanted to see clearly, *moel chbas*, inside her breast, and she wanted to know for sure, *aoey doeng chbas*, what was going on. Ultrasound was *the* reason she went to a medical doctor instead of a *krou khmae*, or traditional healer. Though she was angered by the long wait in the imaging ward, during which she felt she was skipped over, she was more focused on results; she wanted the clear diagnosis that she expected ultrasound and a trained doctor to provide. The doctor and the ultrasound machine together possessed the expertise that she desired.

Moel as skill and *chbas* as a quality of images are terms used outside of medicine. I regularly attended art, film, and performance events around Phnom Penh and had conversations with people in these contexts about images and the practice of looking at images. Sambath, a tall, soft-spoken man his early twenties, used *moel* and *chbas* to describe photographs at an exhibit at the Royal University of Phnom Penh. Sambath grew up in Svay Rieng and came to Phnom Penh with his brother to work as a tuk-tuk driver. Sometimes he would join me and my son, Boris, at exhibits, and one of these times was at *Photo Phnom Penh*. When we turned off Russian Federation Boulevard onto the university grounds, finally escaping the worst of roaring evening traffic, we came upon a somewhat surreal and magical scene. Tall paper cones, glowing with red light, marked a path past Vann Molyvann's iconic circular library to a courtyard. Sambath and I followed the lights toward a magnificent banyan tree, dripping a multitude of tendrils. We stopped near the tree and looked in silence at gigantic black-and-white photos hung on the outside wall of one of the buildings. After a bit, I asked Sambath what he thought of the photos.

"*Ât cheh moel*," he said, literally, "I don't know how to look at them." "*Ât chbas*," meaning they are out of focus, unclear. He could tell that the photos were taken at the university because he recognized the buildings, pointing

FIGURE 4.1. Portraits. Sambath found these color portraits, by Chhin Taingchhea, more compelling than blurry black-and-white photographs of buildings. Both were part of *Photo Phnom Penh*, an annual exhibition organized by the French Cultural Institute that features work by contemporary Cambodian and international photographers, shown in galleries, schools, and public spaces across the city. Chhin's color portraits are mounted on black metal stands, and the subjects are roughly eye level with the viewer. Most of the subjects look straight at the camera and have calm or serious expressions. The portraits flow up a wide staircase, giving the impression of an audience standing, or a crowd assembled. Photo by author, 2010.

them out around us, but he wasn't sure what to make of the images, or of what the artist wanted the images to do.

Sambath preferred the second exhibition we saw, this one inside the university auditorium (see figure 4.1). Walking in, we were faced with several dozen large color portraits mounted on thin poles, standing like a loosely ordered crowd. We walked among the figures of men and women, Sambath stopping in front of a few figures, regarding them directly. As we returned to his tuk-tuk, he told me that he didn't have a camera, but he would like one to take pictures of his friends and people he sees in his daily life, similar to the color portraits.[9]

Within both medical imaging and art photography there are images that are more or less open to reading by non-experts, as Sambath indicated when he talked more confidently and enthusiastically about the second set of pictures: clear, color portraits of people around his age. Sambath's statement that he didn't know how to see the first collection of photographs—unclear, black-and-white pictures of buildings—conveyed an aesthetic value of clarity as well as how art, like medicine, is a domain of skilled seeing, of learning to see.

RIEN MOEL, LEARNING TO SEE

There is learning to see art photographs, especially if they are semi-abstract, unclear, black-and-white. And there is learning to see the body. Traditional healers acquire their skills in *moel* through gift (Guillou 2009 uses the French term *don*) or through a combination of gift and apprenticeship. Doctors learn on the job, through lectures at medical school, brief training programs, and short internships or *stages* at a hospital. The doctor-student must also learn pathology and how to see anatomy and bodily processes in terms of categories and prompts of the ultrasound report.

The Ultrasound Diagnostic Center (UDC) was an intriguing example of an NGO that combined charity with business to teach doctors how to see with ultrasound machines. I first met radiologist Dr. Uch Soley at the Ministry of Health, when he was finishing up a meeting as I was about to begin one. He invited me to visit him at UDC, and I went with Neary the following week. UDC was located on the ground and first floors of a Chinese shophouse-style building on a busy street near the intersection of Monivong and Mao Tse Tung Boulevards. There were a few men and women waiting in the lobby, and a horror movie was playing on the TV. A younger man with a soft manner talked to us politely; he was one of two engineers at UDC. I commented on the six or so ultrasound machines covered in plastic sheaths lining the wall behind me, and he said that they were secondhand, from Japan, and available for sale. Two doctors arrived for afternoon training.

When Dr. Uch arrived, he briefly showed us two of the ultrasound exam rooms, in which training courses were underway, and then led us upstairs to his office on the mezzanine level. I asked him to tell me the story of UDC. What he told me points to the challenges for teachers and students in, as Dr. Uch put it, "learning how to see" with ultrasound, *rien moel*.

In 2002, Dr. Uch had a fellowship to study imaging in Osaka, Japan, for six months. When he returned to Cambodia, he worked at Hope Hospital as an ultrasound specialist. He noticed that doctors in Phnom Penh would not make correct (*aoey trauv*) interpretations of ultrasound, and, as a result, they would make incorrect diagnoses. For Dr. Uch, if there was an illness there, a trained eye could see it. Like Dr. Chhum, about whom I opened the chapter, the human operator matters; the machine does not perform the diagnosis—the doctor does.

Dr. Uch thought to offer training on pathology, how to write a report, and how to diagnose. He received permission from the Ministry of Health to open UDC as a *cabinet*, or individual private practice, in 2002. Conducting the training program and selling machines were not included in this license, so technically what UDC was doing was against the law, he mentioned. He ordered three types of machines from Japan, and his first class had five students and two teachers. Realizing that he needed bodies for practice, he offered free scans to bring people in. The second cohort had six people, some or all from the provinces. As people started to learn about UDC, they asked about buying machines, so Dr. Uch got the idea to sell ultrasound machines as well. UDC ran approximately four three-month training courses per year, with eight to ten people per course, paying about US$700 per person. The clinic saw between 1,000 and 1,200 patients per year.[10]

UDC had an established network of referring organizations and returning patients. Dr. Uch told me that ten different international and local NGOs referred patients to UDC, including Family Health International (FHI), Australian Agency for International Development (AusAID), Population Services International (PSI), Mith Samlanh (Friends), Khana, and Nyemo.[11] Sixty percent of his patients were pregnant women and the rest men and women who came for scans of the thyroid, abdomen, breast, leg, prostate, and uterus. Patients came from the provinces and Phnom Penh, poor and wealthy, because they knew that services at UDC were a good value (*vay thomlae trauv*) and they would receive accurate (*pit brakad*) diagnoses. To emphasize his point about UDC's reputation for accurate diagnoses, Dr. Uch used a question-answer format: Why do women come back for scans of their second and third babies? Why do wealthy people come here? Why do people come from all twenty-four provinces, when they have to pay for transport?[12] Do you know, or not? (*Doeng ât?*) Why? (*Het avey?*) He looked at me expectantly and waited after each question for me to answer. He then supplied the answer: "Correct (*troem trauv*) diagnosis."

Dr. Uch was aware of the anxiety and uncertainty patients face in finding a skilled ultrasound practitioner. He himself managed his own difficulties in his role as a teacher. His students ranged from twenty-five-year-old medical students to fifty-five-year-old provincial doctors. Dr. Uch explained that people have been trained in different countries and in different languages: Khmer, French, Vietnamese, Russian, and English. They have different levels and types of knowledge that make training, and especially report writing, very challenging. For example, young students were able to see well but had little clinical experience, whereas older doctors had difficulty seeing small things on the ultrasound monitor but had a lot of clinical experience.

Patients, too, go through a kind of training in how to be an ultrasound patient, how to be seen. Before, Dr. Uch said, his patients were afraid because they thought ultrasound worked like X-ray, that its radiation was dangerous, so one should not get many scans. Now patients understood that the radiation from ultrasound is not harmful. Dr. Uch mentioned many times that patients are scared of surgery. They want to know, "Will I need surgery or not?" The question was similar to a conversation I had with public health researcher Dr. Chhoeun, who studied ultrasound services in the provinces.[13] He said that in the future, patients will have more information about ultrasound. "People in the city will start to question the doctor," he said, "and start to realize they have something to say. And they [will] ask, why?"

Doctors are trained in imaging as a distributed seeing. They adjust to people coming directly to them for ultrasound, whether or not they were referred by a doctor. Sometimes people bring an image with them, an image made by another doctor. This is a different skill than seeing on the monitor while moving the transducer over a body, perhaps talking with and touching the patient, observing a gestalt of well-being or its absence. In short, it is different to produce an image and write a report based on an embodied interactional occasion than it is to read an image not produced through that experience. These are distinct skills that doctors are aware of and know they must learn.[14]

BECAUSE ONLY SEEING IS BELIEVING

Marketing brochures for popular ultrasound machine models in Phnom Penh emphasize the process of imaging as an embodied interaction between human, machine, transducer, and patient body. These brochures also emphasize that seeing is an authoritative mode of knowledge production. They promote a machine that can do it all; the particular human operator is less relevant, as anyone can see and then "decide with confidence." This contrasts with Dr. Chhum's and Dr. Uch's emphasis on the centrality of the human and their expertise. The Nemio XG appears like an actor ready for its starring role, solitary and spotlighted from behind, casting a long shadow across the opposite page. The promise: "At the moment of truth you can decide with confidence." On a subsequent page of sample scans, the justification: "BECAUSE ONLY SEEING IS BELIEVING."

Long Phirum, the engineer who worked in sales at Dynamic Pharma, gave me brochures for the three models that he sold: the Nemio XG Premium Compact Ultrasound by Toshiba and the DC-3 and DC-6 Expert Diagnostic Ultrasound Systems by Mindray.[15] All the machines had trademarked features for image enhancement, but those of the Mindray DC-3 and DC-6 Expert suggest a family resemblance to entertainment media technologies: iTouch provides "automatic intelligent image optimization," iBeam is "spatial compounding imaging technology," and iScape View affords "panoramic imaging." An opening quote in the DC-6 Expert brochure conveys imaging as a holistic encounter between multiple agents: "The DC-6 Expert enhances the imaging experience, seamlessly and efficiently connecting the sonographer, patient, transducers and the ultrasound system."[16]

Brochures are a means to grasp the script of the technology (Akrich 1992), that is, the imagined purposes and users built into the technology by designers. "Decide with confidence" in particular is interesting because it acknowledges that insecurity and uncertainty are part and parcel of diagnostic practice and that the Nemio XG can manage them. They simplify and optimize. They are compact, mobile, and their design reduces repetition and stress. Their "resolution" and "penetration" enable visualizations of flow, regions, and relationships. The machines are flexible and fully programmable.

Feminist STS scholars have analyzed how biotech advertising conveys understandings of life and biotechnology even if they are contradictory, for example, depicting nature as something given, passive, and fabricated (Haraway [1992] 2004) or the brain as an interior landscape to be reclaimed like a geographical terrain (Åsberg and Lum 2009). Marketing discourse about ultrasound machines also tells us something about seeing. Technologically mediated seeing enfolds technological enhancement with anatomy and bodily processes. Computer-generated (and trademarked) enhancements, such as Nemio XG's "ApliPure," become the very ground for apprehending body structures and flows, what Sarah Franklin (1995, 333) has called "slippage": "This slippage creates a complex visual-media surface composed of substantially different orders of facts, information, and imagery. . . . Computer-generated simulacra assist medical imaging technology in a manner that underscores the technologically dependent character of the entire process."

Franklin is discussing a BBC video of assisted reproduction, but "computer-generated simulacra" is also precisely what a 3D image of the fetal face is, a surface image created from composite volume measurements.[17] Amit Prasad (2005, 310) notes a similar visual regime for MRI, in which computer-generated and partial images, which he describes as "bits of data in cyberspace that can be, and are, manipulated by human beings," still make a claim toward realism. Franklin's point is not that imaging technologies falsely represent "the real body" but that their seeing increasingly defines the real body, what the body is and does.

These brochures are a foil for discussing contrasting ways of seeing with ultrasound. They do, as critical visual studies in STS note (Dussauge 2008; Joyce 2008; van Dijck 2005), present an ideal of a transparent body, knowable with confidence and the right tools. A few cautions. The brochures do not stand for an undifferentiated, monolithic "Western" or "medical" way of seeing. These brochures, given to me in Phnom Penh, are for machines designed and manufactured by Chinese and Japanese firms. So much for mapping technology's values in any comfortable imaginative geography (Said [1978] 2003) of West and Rest. Yet the Nemio and Mindray brochures do put forward a matrix of seeing, knowledge, body, and machine that prevails in medical texts, as well as social scientific critiques of medical texts, and can be glossed as *the transparent body*. Isabelle Dussauge (2008, 15) writes, "The extensive practice of medical imaging is a sign and a part of the Western cultural utopia of *the transparent body* . . . the utopia that technology enables medicine and culture to pierce, and eventually to modify, the secrets of 'nature.'" The paradoxical realism that is an object of critique in STS could be summarized thus: medical imaging, for practitioners and for brochures, produces authoritative knowledge independent of the particular seer and matter seen, yet seeing with the machine produces the matter we can see. Interventions in STS (Burri and Dumit 2008) and feminist new materialism (Hausken, Papenburg, and Schmitz 2018; Myers 2015) emphasize the importance of the *process* of producing medical and scientific images, including the embodied labor and cultural and political contexts of that labor, for scientists themselves and for scholars. (In the following chapter, I take up another concern in this scholarship, that of *matter as process* in which imaging participates.) It is easy to mess with a marketing brochure, of course. In no world is the machine alone a bringer of confidence and truth. What about interference?

SPIRITUAL INTERFERENCE

We encounter medical imaging technologies in the hospital and clinic, in machine brochures and ads on the back of tuk-tuks. They can be found elsewhere, too, and these locations and purposes can help us to understand which spiritual or protective entities are also seeing, perhaps interfering with ultrasound's sounded seeing, or perhaps co-habiting the visual sphere, see-ing in their own modes. The point is not so much that ultrasound imaging crosses between overtly medical and non-medical contexts, but that we can ask how it does so, who is drawn in, what problems are foregrounded, and who is authorized to solve them.

In conversation with patients, friends, and monks, I learned that monks, *daun chi* (female ascetics), and *krou* refer people to hospitals to get ultra-sound imaging. These healers may also be called upon to talk about ultra-sound images. Attending to how monks and laypeople talk about ultrasound images, their capacities and their incapacities, points to a richer under-standing of how this technology is taking hold, and being taken hold of, in Phnom Penh. It also tells us about the landscape of seeing and visuality in which ultrasound participates. The seeing of monks is not only with the eyes.[18] Ancestors and *khsae keatha*, the chain of amulets inscribed with Buddhist verse, see without a body even. Some of these actors, the ancestors and *khsae keatha*, can interfere with the seeing of the doctor and the ultrasound machine. All of these actors, monks, ancestors, and *khsae keatha* co-exist in a field of sensuous and capacious visual practice that involves non-expert seers, too, those who consult them.

In order to understand better how ultrasound circulates in visual heal-ing practices outside the hospital, I consulted monks who were well regarded for their healing practices. In these conversations, I learned about ultrasound and about diagnostic visual practice that ultrasound could be thought of as mimicking: the sending out of a signal and reading the response. Socheat arranged for me to meet Loak Suon, a former monk who lived at Wat Langka, where he had been a monk for fifteen years and still saw people for consul-tation. When Boris and I entered the compound, we found Loak Suon and Socheat waiting for us in the courtyard. Loak Suon was in his forties and wore layperson's clothes, a shirt and pants as opposed to a saffron robe. He led us upstairs to the first floor of the dormitory. We left our shoes in the stairwell and walked down a wide hallway, makeshift walls marking off liv-ing quarters on each side. Loak Suon's room was halfway down the hall, with a cot, neat and austere, at the right corner by the window and a cooking pot and small burner at the foot of the cot. We all sat on a mat on the floor, tak-ing up most of the space. Socheat grabbed Boris and gestured for me to start. I told Loak Suon about myself and my work and that I wanted to learn about his healing practices.

Loak Suon said he consults with four types of people: sick people, people under a love spell, people under a curse or spell to do with hatred or black magic, and people seeking to have their fortune told and to ask for good luck and success. His specialty was chanting, *sauth Pali*, to drive away poisons of various kinds, including love spells and curses. Loak Suon described a typical trajectory. It begins with pain: "First a person has stomach pain. He is unable to sleep because of the dreams he has at night. He goes to the doctor and the doctor doesn't see any problem, and says that he is not sick. But the patient believes he is sick. He is in pain. So, he goes to the monk to see if the monk can help."[19]

If Loak Suon is not sure if the person is ill or not, he may do some diagnostics, including having the patient drink coconut juice and eat betel nut. If the person vomits, it may be possible to tell what is wrong. The person may buy a *kranat*, a square, dark red piece of cloth, upon which the monk draws a yantra for the person to take with them for protection.[20] Loak Suon will chant in Pali magical verses from the Buddhist sutras, protective verses called *paritta*, or prayers from the *Kalyanamitta-sutta* (Bertrand 2004, 161).[21] The monk then sprinkles the client with holy water, dipping a clutch of small sticks into an urn of water undulating with jasmine flowers and shaking the sticks to sprinkle over the patient. These acts chase away the poison.[22]

I was originally interested in talking to monks because I was exploring the possibility of placing yantra, a drawing on cloth, with ultrasound on a continuum of visual representations of illness. I wondered if the act of creating the yantra and the patient encounter with the monk had therapeutic significance. I wondered about possible parallels between abilities to see, to produce images, and to read images. For the most part, yantra are for protection. They are about the future, but they are not diagnostic. They do not concern the present in the way that an ultrasound image pertains to what *is*, currently. A yantra could be therapeutic, in the sense that by offering protection from malevolent spirits or events, it ensures well-being. But it does not chase away poison, as does a mantra or chanting in Pali.

I asked Loak Suon if people ever talked to him about *echo*, and he said yes, people do. People come to monks when an *echo* has failed or not yielded the desired result, he said. He gave the following example: if a love spell were causing the stomach pain, then ultrasound wouldn't show any problem. In this case, the monk will chant, and the patient may buy a yantra. If the patient is happy, he or she may return with a present for the monk. The gift depends on the person's means—a few thousand riel or a few dollars, a small care package purchased in front of the wat or at a nearby market.[23]

According to Loak Suon, there are two ways that ultrasound and the doctor may fail. One is when a sick person goes to a doctor to look inside and the ultrasound does not show a problem, or *chloh at khoenh*. Loak Suon used two visual terms here: *chloh*, a rarified term, used by doctors primarily for the imaging of X-ray and other devices (in lay speech, it also refers to the shining of light or reflecting of a mirror), and *khoenh*, which we encountered at the beginning of the chapter, a common term for seeing. The doctor plus machine *chloh* but are unable to *khoenh*, so the doctor says that the person is not, in fact, sick, *at mean chumngeua ey*. Another type of failure is when a scan was not possible, or *chloh at ban*, when there was no ability or capacity to produce a scan. In this case, the machine could be materially blocked from working, such as by *khsae keatha* or by something less material and harder to manage, such as wronged ancestors.

Ancestors are beings that can see the world; their seeing is their mode of being in it, but they are not properly of the world. How does this disembodied seeing interfere with ultrasound? Venerable Hor Kemhan, a monk known for his healing, had an explanation. According to Ven. Kemhan, the spirits, *proleung*, of ancestors are related to healing, and thus permission must be sought from them. Ven. Kemhan, like Loak Suon, consulted with people who believed themselves to be sick, visited a doctor, got an ultrasound exam, but were told by the doctor that nothing could be seen in the scan. He hinted that ancestors can interfere with the machine's capacity to generate an image (whether through the sounding or the visualizing, it is not clear). In these situations, Ven. Kemhan advised, people need to make right with their ancestors by making an offering of fruit at the altar to the ancestors in one's home.

Ven. Kemhan was an exemplar of the monk who is *poukae kasang*, strong or clever at building. He lived and practiced at Wat Saravantejo in the center of Phnom Penh, which seemed like it was constantly under construction. A friend who used to live across the street told me that Wat Saravantejo used to be a kind of rough place, known for juvenile delinquents, or *kmeng steav*, dealing drugs from its grounds. Socheat, however, said that this unending construction was not a sign of things neglected or unfinished; rather, it was a sign the monks were doing well. The wat was part of the boom in religious building projects since UNTAC, which anthropologist John Marston (2008) situates within Buddhist notions of merit accrued through construction as well as nationalist visions of social reconstruction.[24] Wat Saravantejo had foreign connections too; it was the distribution point for the book *The Buddhist Way*, one in a series of Khmer translations of Buddhist texts by the Ven. K. Sri Dhammananda, supported by a Malaysian Buddhist aid organization.[25]

On the Saturday morning when Socheat and I paid our first visit, there were no *kmeng steav*. A woman sold gift packets for visitors to buy and offer to the monks; a few others swept leaves, dust, and trash from the concrete grounds; kids played games. Ven. Kemhan received us in a spacious and immaculate ground-floor room in a new, freestanding building. A small plaque next to the door indicated this was his own residence, evidence of his success in consultations and healings and his high status at the wat. His business card, which he handed to me after our conversation, contained Khmer and English text, further suggesting he was a man of resources and networks.[26] The card had rich national and religious symbolism: a photograph of Angkor Wat glowing in sunlight; the striped, multicolored Buddhist flag; and a background image of the dharmachakra, the Wheel of Law, which represents the dharma, the teachings of Buddha (McArthur 2002, 118–19). Socheat thought that Ven. Kemhan was from Kampuchea Krom, judging by his name and his accent. "People tend to think monks from Kampuchea Krom are very clever," he added.[27]

Ven. Kemhan firmly articulated healing as a Buddhist domain, with its own history and traditions. "Since the time of the Buddha until today, you cannot separate healing from Buddhism," he said. "Some sick people go to a hospital first, some to the wat. If people look very ill, I tell them to go to the hospital." He also elaborated a Buddhist seeing that is not limited to the eyes. Ven. Kemhan's specialty was giving blessings, and his primary knowledge (*vityea*) involved *sauth*, chanting Pali, and *sraoch teuk*, sprinkling holy water over the person and important objects of the person, such as a phone or moto keys. Ven. Kemhan also engaged in a bit of diagnostics through treatment: he would sprinkle water and light incense and look for a reaction. By observing a person's gestures, he could discern whether they were under a spell. In this way, he was able to see into people's hearts, *moel chett manuss*, he said.

What sort of seeing is this? Could we think of it in kinship with *echo*? It is partial. It relies on interference as an element of seeing. It involves sending something out to learn from what returns. Ven. Kemhan introduces potent material—water—and sound—chanting—to the scene of the patient and the monk. These elements have diagnostic import; they help to bring out etiology that otherwise could not be seen. The labor of coaxing, patterned yet still involving chance and uncertainty or unpredictability, nuances seeing. This is a way to think of seeing as an echo. The ultrasound machine uses sound, emitted from the sensor, passing through tissues, radiating back to the sensor. Its seeing is based on noise. Only certain materials—soft tissue, fluid flows—are passable. This seeing bounces off or passes through materials with different tendencies. Buddhist seeing involves interference; expertise is being able to see and understand the echo back, the reverberation. Here I put forward a way of thinking about skilled seeing that is informed by the mode of seeing in ultrasound and in Buddhist healing, in which translation of interference is the crux of the practice. When a metaphysics of seeing includes interference, it is also partial, as Donna Haraway ([1992] 2004) insists. Partiality admits other ways of doing, not in romantic equality, but pragmatic understandings of the multiplicity of visual practices in medicine.

MATERIAL INTERFERENCE

Loak Suon's mention of *khsae keatha* signals another kind of interference. I had seen *khsae keatha* in the ward. There was even a sign at Maternal Hospital that instructed patients to remove *khsae keatha* before scanning. *Keatha* are small, thin metal plaques inscribed with holy text (Bertrand 2004, 161) or protective formulae (Pou and Ang 1987–90, 99), rolled into cylinders, and threaded onto string. The string, called *khsae*, is worn around the waist. As Didier Bertrand (2004, 161) explains, *keatha*, like yantra and Pali chants, derive their protective power from their words, which are attributed to the Buddha.[28] During abdominal ultrasound scans, people hastily rolled the thin string down around their hips or up around the bottom ribs so the *keatha* would not interfere with the ultrasound transducer.

One morning, after watching me watch a patient push her *khsae keatha* out of the way, Dr. Vandy took it upon himself to explain: "Rural people wear them because they believe it protects them from bad spirits or ghosts, *khmaoch*. It is for psychological reassurance, *thnam phlauv chett*." Not only rural people! When I would go to visit my Cham friends in the countryside, doubting Khmer urbanites told me to wear a *khsae keatha* to protect from a curse of black magic.[29] In other words, amulets carry some stigma in urban settings as manifestations of superstition, yet city Khmers may summon their protective powers for encounters with "others," such as the Cham, who are racialized as having spiritual powers that are potentially threatening.

Patients were aware that hospital staff were dismissive of their amulets, that these stubbornly enduring materials chafe against the modernity of the hospital. Pisey, a rice farmer in his early thirties, read over my shoulder as I took notes one morning, interested that I could write in Khmer. He puzzled through my messy script and corrected my spelling as he waited for his wife, three months pregnant with their fifth child.[30] When he came to the words *khsae keatha* in my notebook, he laughed, lifting up his shirt to show me one hanging low around his waist. He got his from a monk at a wat, but you could also get one from a *krou boran*, a traditional healer, he told me. "Doctors don't believe in these," he said, lowering his voice.

Khsae keatha may be a bit embarrassing in some contexts, but they are powerful. The fact that Loak Suon, the former monk, brought up *khsae keatha* as interference suggests that ultrasound's seeing is vulnerable to them. Ultrasound's technological seeing, its strength and source of appeal, so to speak, is also its vulnerability. Seeing is a sense and a skill, one that is performed by doctors, machines, monks, and even by ancestors, these formerly human but now other-than-human entities. In all of these modes, seeing is an active, embodied, unpredictable process. It is also situated and worldly (Haraway [1992] 2004; Law and Hetherington 2003). It is an intervention.

The echo as an image of thought offers a rich and novel understanding of seeing as a skill of emitting and receiving, with attendant vulnerability to material and spiritual interference. The capacities of ultrasound machines, ancestors, doctors, and monks are different and differentiating, yet they can interfere with one another. For Michel Serres ([1980] 2007), interference, noise, which is one of three meanings (in French) of *parasite*, is always part of the signal. In his analysis of French and Greek fables, material sciences, and Christian story, interference is productive and creative in that it changes relations. Interference is not inherently good or bad. In a way, Serres articulates for North Atlantic philosophy an inherent instability of relations that resembles a given in Theravada Buddhist philosophy: the impermanence of existence.[31] Serres ([1980] 2007, 197) offers a general definition of illness that, though overly framed in terms of communications, is useful to mention here: illness is "a noise that mixes up messages in the circuits of the organism, parasiting their ordinary circulation." Translating the mix-up in messages is the job of the doctor. And, I add, the Buddhist healer. Expertise is to see with and around the interference, to sense when the interference is too much, when the problem is out of your league, as when Ven. Kemhan refers people to the hospital.

The *khsae keatha* are a material and straightforward kind of interference with ultrasound imaging. Ancestors interfere in a different mode. The skill here, the expertise, is to radiate out and see what comes back: see an image on a monitor, see the gesture of an afflicted person. These ways of seeing have ontological and epistemological entailments, to be sure, and juxtaposing them here is not to say they are the same or reducible to one another. They may be "differentiating instruments" (Bonelli 2015, 873) that make different realities; versions of seeing that participate in the "doing" of the real. Furthermore, these are practices of experts, those whose skills come from training or as a special gift. Yet ordinary people also bring ways of seeing their bodies, not only with the eyes, into relation with ultrasound and Buddhist seeing.

DREAMING

The final mode of seeing the unseen in bodies is a mode that is accessible to all: dreaming. Dreaming is powerful in that it brings forward questions and actions, understandings and suspicions about the world. Medical imaging and the seeing of monks are authoritative, carrying the status and aura and armamentaria of experts, but dreaming can interfere, inform, and communicate. It can cause a little noise, changing the course of things, bring someone to imaging even.

Saroun came for a prenatal ultrasound scan because of blood and a dream. She was forty-one years old and pregnant with her fifth child.[32] The morning I met her, she was alarmed; *thleak chheam*, she had bleeding, and her doctor had sent her to Maternal Hospital to check the pregnancy with ultrasound.

Saroun lived with three daughters in the far northern suburbs of Phnom Penh. Her fourth child, a son, had died in a road accident when he was nineteen years old. She believed this new being, this life growing in her, was her son who had died, returning. In a dream, her son had told her that he wanted her to be his mother again: *"Vea neung haoey! Vea som mok nov vinh!"* (It is him again! He asked to come back!). She went for her first ever prenatal ultrasound scan because she wanted to confirm her dream. Now, she was here for her second exam on account of the bleeding. Saroun was worried; she could not bear to lose her son again. He died one year ago exactly.

Sauron had never considered getting an ultrasound exam before, not for her previous pregnancies. It was not necessary, she said; her four children were born healthy. In fact, she did not want more than four children, and she did not care about the gender of this next child. She did care about whether ultrasound would see, in its own way, what she saw, in hers. She dreamed a beloved son's request to be reborn—Is she indeed pregnant? She saw blood—Is the pregnancy viable? Saroun's story follows popular Buddhist notions of rebirth, even if her maternal relation to the spirit that asks to be reborn is uncommon.[33] A spirit of a previously existing life chose her womb to grow into its next life. Ultrasound can see, not the dead son or his form, but a *being*. Past, present, and future family are at stake.

Dreams are not only for children, or children-to-be. Patients who were not pregnant were also compelled to seek out ultrasound imaging on account of dreaming. Bon Um Tuk, the water festival, was coming, and the imaging ward at Russian Hospital was quieter than usual. Nurse Lina led a young woman into the exam room, her order slip stating "abdo," for an abdominal scan. Lina told her to lie down on the bed and lift up her shirt. The woman pulled up her orange Izod, and the metal of her *khsae keatha* glinted in the dull florescent light. She pushed it down low around her hips. Dr. Vandy chatted amiably with her. Where did she come from? Why did she come? She said, "I have been dreaming (*yual sap*), I dream a lot. Why?" She got a scan in Kampong Cham, where she lives, and the doctor told her, *at khoenh*, he couldn't see anything wrong. But she was not convinced. "*At brakad, anhchoeng that moel.*" She is not sure, she wants to get another scan to see.

She called the doctor *loak krou*, and they talked a lot together. Vandy said there was nothing wrong; her scan was normal. He was familiar with dreams. Patients talk about them, sometimes, the sign that pushed them to come to the hospital. These stories of dreams compelling women to come for an ultrasound exam show how different orders and kinds of seeing interrelate. The seeing knits together different understandings of life as not singular and of death as not final. It suggests that information about pregnancy and illness may be conveyed through the unconscious. Clémence Schantz (2015) describes how pregnant women and men awaiting a child dream of the fetus. Dreams announce the pregnancy; they tell the sex of the baby to come and suggest the being who is reincarnated in the new body. Saroun's story knits together dream worlds and waking worlds. The machine-eye seeing with the dream eye.

WAYS OF SEEING

John Berger's 1972 BBC series and book *Ways of Seeing* explored ways of seeing determined by subject position, particularly gender and class. His materials were contemporary British advertisements and Dutch Golden Age paintings. He asked us to think about how an image is possible and what it teaches about the world, about people and objects in the world, and most importantly about social relations. I use his oft-repeated title here in an adjacent mode, a mode interested in the who but also in the what and where of seeing.

The multiple paths to diagnosis and intervention pass through the home of a traditional healer or *krou*, a one-room doctor's *cabinet*, a sprawling public hospital, an incense-clouded wat, and the common area of a village where a possession ritual extends into the night. Seeing is the path to move the afflicted out of their present state. Following discourse about ultrasound imaging into wats reveals how monks and their patients place ultrasound within other hierarchies of harmful or therapeutic agents rather than in opposition to these agents. When ultrasound and the doctor cannot produce a productive image, that is, when they are unable to see with and through

FIGURE 4.2. Looking at results. A young woman looks at her ultrasound exam results in the waiting area of Russian Hospital. The light captures the glitter on her T-shirt and gold of her thin necklace. Her ultrasound report is printed on A4 paper, with demographic and appointment details, a small black-and-white still image, and the doctor's impression, all in French. Photo by author, 2010.

the interference, monks may themselves take on the task of seeing and interfering, through blessings or chanting Pali or guiding the patient toward effecting their own intervention with ancestors. The authority of seeing maladies and their potential causes is shared; the machines and the doctors who use them operate alongside monks, charms, and ancestors who have their own authority to see, or to block seeing.

When Dr. Chhum told me, "It is only with *echo* that a doctor can see," it provoked me. A seemingly simple, literal statement: only with imaging technologies can the doctor see inside the body. Sound waves sent out and received. The image of thought of the *echo* foregrounds sound as the mode of this technology and allows us to consider a different way of thinking about seeing and what skilled seeing involves. I juxtaposed different ways of seeing: the machine-eye, the expert diagnostic system of the brochure, the skilled seeing of the doctor-student, based on knowledge of pathology, and seeing anatomy in the categories and prompts of the report. I considered the seeing of a monk, seeing the heart through gesture, for example, an indirect seeing drawn out by chanting and sprinkling with water. Seeing without the eyes, of karmic knots. Seeing and hearing in a dream. The stress on visuality is widely apparent, and when it comes to the body, its transformations, potential pregnancies and maladies, vision as a privileged sense is not just a white colonial imposition. In other words, locating the privileging of vision as a bias peculiar to the North Atlantic is at once too broad and too narrow. We miss diversity of visual practice within the North Atlantic (see Campt 2012) and the privileging of vision and visibility for personhood and healing in many parts of the world—India (Pinney 1997), Indonesia (Strassler 2010), Papua New Guinea (Street 2014a), Peru (Bonelli 2015), to name only a few. This chapter situated ultrasound seeing within other modes of seeing in diagnosis and protection. Do these diverse ways of seeing have correlates in diverse practices of relating medical images? In the next chapter, I explore ultrasound images in relation to genre, specifically, the genre of the photographic portrait.

CHAPTER FIVE

PORTRAIT AND SCAN

FADING AND ANGER

OVER THE COURSE OF THE TWO-PLUS YEARS I LIVED IN PHNOM PENH, I became acquainted with Srey Neang and Srey Noun, sisters who had a highly visible yet precarious existence in the city. They lived together with their mother and siblings on the northwest outskirts of Phnom Penh and sold newspapers in front of the Lucky Supermarket. I often chatted with them when I bought groceries, and one evening, Srey Neang asked me what I did.

I told her I was doing research on how people use ultrasound. Srey Neang lifted her chin, almost defiantly, "I had an *echo* taken." The word for taking pictures and getting an ultrasound or X-ray is the same in Khmer, *thât*. We made a date to talk when she could take a break from selling papers.

Neary and I sat with the sisters at a roadside table, sipping coconut juice from hot pink straws, and Srey Neang told us the story of her scan. When she found out she was pregnant, she went to a widow's NGO for a checkup. (She was not a widow, but organizations like this blossomed during the 1990s, after the end of the civil war, and continued, if sporadically, to provide services decades later.) The NGO referred her to the Red Cross and paid for her checkup there, which included an ultrasound scan. This was around four or five months' gestation. Srey Neang learned the baby was a boy (she was not so happy about that) and that it had no major anomaly (she was relieved). At a different health center, she was tested for diabetes and high blood pressure and given a vaccination.

I asked what she did with the picture.

Srey Neang showed the picture to her mother and family, as they wanted to see the image. She kept (*tok*) the picture to give to her son when he got older. She wanted him to have it. Srey Neang's voice hardened, her

125

few and carefully chosen words coming quickly, vibrating with condensed affect.

"The picture has faded so much. There is nothing to show him."

Srey Neang's health had not been good during her pregnancy. She described how she had to walk a lot and be on her feet all day because of her job selling newspapers. Her mother had been worried about problems with the placenta and wanted her to check again by *echo* to make sure everything was okay.

"I wanted another *echo*," Srey Neang said, "but I didn't have enough money. The widow's NGO closed, so I couldn't get free scans from the Red Cross. And I was busy working all day."

In the rare moments when she had enough money and time, "the doctor was not around." Public services were not available outside of her work hours.[1]

When Srey Neang's tone sharpened to anger at the fading image, it struck me how rarely I had sensed this. Had I ever heard it before, either from people in Phnom Penh or in the imaging literature? Not in the literature. Imaging scholarship documents the *proliferation* of ultrasound images. Analyses track images beyond the printout, the DVD, the advertisement, or the US political poster to include "keepsakes" and memorials, Facebook posts, key chains, mugs, and T-shirts. Sonographers and anthropologists are concerned about *who* is qualified to conduct ultrasound exams and *how often* exams should be done. Globally, ultrasound is relatively unregulated, and untrained providers abound. Women get many, too many, scans.[2] Images circulate and seemingly endure. There is pleasure, anxiety, desire, sorrow, confusion. But anger?

The anger tells us much. It beckons us to pay attention to how people relate to images, at times with fulsome affect, at times with unreadable silence, beyond the *content* of speech, refusing the need "to language" images (After Globalism Writing Group 2018, 35). The anger also tells us about the image and hints at its instability and its multiplicity. Srey Neang wanted to know about the placenta, the sex, the amniotic fluid. She also wanted a picture to save for her son.

How does one respond to the anger of Srey Neang, whose prenatal ultrasound image deteriorated such that it was not worth saving in an album for her son? Her frustration with the fading color—Was it from the heat, the moisture, the ink, the paper?—would perhaps be shared by anyone, but for Srey Neang its intensity was heightened by the fact that it was the only image she had. She was unable to afford another. Srey Neang's affect around the fading picture allows one to see "quotidian claims to survival, resilience, and possibility" (Campt 2017, 45). She wanted a picture for her son, a picture that looked pretty, that lasted. Listening to her anger helps us to understand how people relate to the elemental instability of images and of the beings to which images refer.

In this chapter, I explore affective and aesthetic practices of relating to prenatal ultrasound images. I found that people are concerned with the instabilities of images—Srey Neang's fading picture—and instabilities of the referent—the fetus constantly changing and vulnerable. At issue for pregnant women is how to fix, to stabilize these instabilities, even temporarily. This requires a slight shift in approach to medical imaging, a de-emphasis on fact production and "objective self-fashioning" (Dumit 2004), or the question of the reality or unreality of the fetus (Michaels 1999), and a sharpened attention to imaging as a consequential *process of intervening* into *beings that are in process* (Hausken, Papenburg, and Schmitz 2018). At base this is a fairly conventional claim: the ultrasound image is an intervention. What I hope to contribute is a method of attending to how people relate to the image's aesthetics in practice, in talk, and in affect. This method of care for what an image looks like, its material features in the printout and on the monitor, helps us to understand what is at stake for people. And indeed, stakes are different for pregnant women, their families, and their health care providers.

I advance my claim that an image is a technique of affecting the referent in four interrelated threads. The first thread is that aesthetic qualities of prenatal ultrasound that are desirable to pregnant women, their families, and doctors—color, prettiness, and clarity—relate to aesthetic histories of ordering social subjectivity. The second thread is that medical images relate to other image genres. In the case of prenatal ultrasound, this genre is portraiture. The third thread is that ontologies of *beings* guide how viewers relate to images and how images relate to referents. Even within a Buddhist ontology of the impermanence of being, a pregnant woman and a fetus are in markedly unstable states of becoming, the fetus a malleable biological and spiritual entity. Finally, the ontology of *images* guides how viewers relate to images and how images relate to referents. Material qualities of images can affect their unstable referents, possibly improving or harming them, fixing them in kinship relations. The notion of the *image-affect* conveys how images stimulate affective responses in viewers and how images affect their referents. I explore how doctors, nurses, pregnant women, and their family members want overlapping but also different things from images, and this is indicated by discourse and practice of fading, clarity, prettiness, color, and black-and-white.

When I chatted with Chenda, five months pregnant and serene, waiting to get her first ultrasound exam at the Maternal Hospital, she told me she wanted to learn whether she was having a boy or a girl and "if it had legs or not," shorthand for any physical anomaly. "What kind of scan do you want?" I asked. "Color," she replied, and when I asked why, she laughed shyly. I asked again, and she said, "*Chbas haoey s'at cheang*" (It's clearer and prettier).

For Bora, clarity was important, as it was for Chenda. Bora was a man in his mid-forties with neatly combed hair. He had come to the Maternal Hospital with his wife who was nine months pregnant.[3] This was his wife's fifth scan, and they had gone to several different places and seen different doctors. Each time they were told a different due date, even though they did see the same doctor twice, and Bora was miffed. However, despite the discrepancies in due date, he thought that ultrasound was useful for telling the approximate due date (his main reason!), the sex of the baby, position of the head, and completeness, *teang âs*, of the body. And, like so many others, Bora preferred color scans because you can see clearly, *moel chbas*.[4]

Bora and Chenda did not expect to *see* specific details on their own. They did expect the doctor to tell them certain information obtained from the ultrasound image about the fetus and the pregnancy. By far the most common expectations for fetal ultrasound were that it would tell the sex of the fetus, the due date, its health (*sokhpheap*), and its physical integrity. Less commonly, women told me they wanted to hear the heartbeat, to check the placenta, or determine if there was enough amniotic fluid. Srey Pouv, whom I introduced in chapter 3, did not expect to see the fetus, and said she didn't understand the image on the monitor, yet she was pleased when Dr. Din turned the monitor toward her and talked her through the lines and shadows of the ultrasonic nose and mouth. In the appointments I sat through at the public hospitals, this was a rare occurrence. Many private clinics, however, had a second screen monitor on the wall that the woman could look at.

Clear and pretty are aesthetic terms. *Chbas* also carries an authority, the certainty of the clinician, the guarantee of the technology, modes of seeing with able eyes. Patients used the word *s'at*, which means pretty or, in some contexts, nice or clean, to explain a valued quality of color images.

Dr. Chhum insisted that there is confusion, often strategic, about three types of color in ultrasound imaging. To radiologists and obstetricians, "color ultrasound" is a high-frequency Doppler scan, which conveys information about blood flow in blue, red, yellow, or brown. A second color is the 3D/4D volumetric images in which "surface" information, such as the fetal face and body, can be printed in "skin color" or "natural color."

A third type of color, Dr. Chhum explained, is the "platform," or background tint, a digital effect available in most 2D ultrasound machines. For a majority of patients and health professionals, this is "color ultrasound." Dr. Chhum called it "cheating": patients should not pay more for color tint on a cross-sectional 2D image because it is not an advanced clinical capability (though color ink certainly costs more than only black ink).

Ultrasound is a sonic technology, and in the digitization of sound pulses, there are gaps where color is filled in by the machine. Color is a pull-down menu. Color is a field in need of standardization to enable accurate diagnostics. A consensus report from the 2013 Summit on Color in Medical Imaging, sponsored by the US Food and Drug Administration and the International Color Consortium, begins thusly: "Today, color in medical imaging specialties is handled, with few exceptions, in an ad hoc manner with little standardization. In some areas, this presents a number of challenges to medical professionals who wish to use color images for diagnostic purposes" (Badano, Review, and Casertano 2015, 42).

For the doing of diagnosis, color challenges exist all down the imaging chain: the source of radiation, the object to be imaged, the image capture device, processing stage, image storage, interpretation, display. Color is made in all of these processes, and it must be calibrated.

Mr. Long Phirum, the engineer and sales rep who gave me the Nemio brochure, said that color scans mistakenly connote higher capability machines to patients and to doctors. Phirum predicted that demand for black-and-white images would decline to about 20 percent of the ultrasound machine market in Cambodia, with sales only to the government and NGOs. Indeed, color scanning is one reason people go to a private clinic over a government or NGO clinic, especially in the case of pregnancy, when one is not sick at all.

MÉDECIN, MACHINE, MALADE

Late one morning at the Maternal Hospital, Dr. Sophal threaded his way toward me through the standard choreography of doctors, technicians, and patients, holding out an ultrasound report printed on A4 paper. "Why do I make this in color?" He paused. The question is a genre of teaching and telling, one that does not necessarily expect an answer but rather a pause to wait for the answer from the teacher. Here, I am the student, interested in the aesthetics of ultrasound. "For the patient," he said. At the bottom of the ultrasound report was an image of a uterus in a yellowish sepia tint. There was also a little bit of blue—it was a Doppler image. Dr. Sophal smiled; the printout was an example of how his daily labor entails clinical work and work to please the patient. Color for the patient to take home, black-and-white for the patient file. Doctors are aware of different stakes. Are patients?

Dr. Sophal looked past me to examine the wall calendar, confirming whether he was working on Friday, which was a holiday, Coronation Day. Sunday was former king Sihanouk's birthday, and thus Monday was a holiday too.

"Grayscale is the *original* form of the scan, not color," said his colleague, Dr. Phalla. Dr. Phalla preferred to give his patients grayscale images, which were cheaper anyway. At public hospitals, patients pay for services in advance, choosing either color or black-and-white. They receive a copy of the ultrasound report with a color scan, but a black-and-white copy is put in the chart. Dr. Phalla explains to his patients through analogy that, in most cases, color adds no clinical information.

"An ultrasound is made from sound waves," he said. "It is like someone is talking, but in a different room." He gestured to the curtained-off exam spaces. "You can hear them talking, and you may be able to learn certain things, like their age or their sex, but you don't know what color they are because you can only hear, not see.[5] People understand this." Almost as if to illustrate his point, the Doppler-mediated sound of a fetal heartbeat throbbed from behind the curtain of one of the exam rooms. Dr. Phalla's is a remarkable strategy, for its eloquence in explaining how ultrasound works and for its troubling of the easy analogy of ultrasound's visualization to that of photography.

Dr. Phalla continued: "Color can actually *obscure* information. It makes it difficult to see some details. For example, on a grayscale monitor a cancerous tumor is black. Using a red or yellow platform on the monitor, how can you *see*?" He reminded me of the three Ms of a medical problem (in French): *médecin, machine, malade* (the doctor, the machine, and the patient). Here Dr. Phalla articulates a theory of medical diagnosis as a practice involving doctors, machines, and patient bodies. Color is important for depicting fluid flow, but when purely ornamental, such as when it is used as a background tint, color can obscure clinical information, disrupting the delicate alignment of the three Ms required to practice good medicine.

Dr. Phalla asked me about practices in the United States. I said that I thought people typically received black-and-white film images for 2D scans. He snorted, "All countries! All countries but Cambodia." In France, where

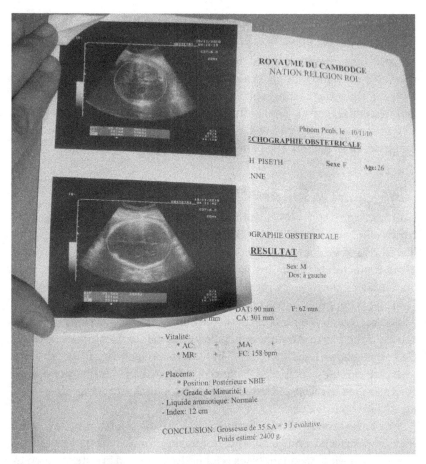

FIGURE 5.1. Report from a prenatal ultrasound exam done at a government hospital. The results are in French on A4 paper and include sex, position of the fetus and the placenta, different length measurements, assessment of amniotic fluid level, and estimated weight, among other data. Two black-and-white images of the fetus, printed on film paper, are attached. Photo by author, 2010.

he and Dr. Sophal both did their specialty training in radiology, patients received black-and-white 2D images on photo paper.

"Cambodia, Kingdom of Wonder!" he said in English, quoting the tourism advertising campaign on TV and billboards throughout the capital at the time.

"Kingdom of Color!" said Makara, the technician, smiling.

"We integrate all kinds [of practices]," said Dr. Sophal. And, referring to his earlier concern with his schedule, "We celebrate all holidays!"

Aside from the jokes about holidays, this conversation illuminates how Dr. Sophal, Dr. Phalla, and Makara work under constant awareness of their own practices in comparison to those in other countries.[6] These evaluations, and these jokes, are sensible in a system in which hospitals are co-managed by foreign development organizations, specialty training happens abroad, and "technical experts" (and anthropologists) are almost always foreigners. Color becomes another thing to explain, another thing to fix, another aberrant practice of doctors and patients.

COLOR AND SOCIAL SUBJECTIVITY

Norindr Panivong (1996) calls Indochina "phantasmatic" because of how tropes of sensory—particularly visual—excess thread through French film, literature, and exhibitions about their colonial jewel. George Groslier's vision of pre-protectorate Cambodia, as "a religious people with a passion for celebrations, for color, jewelry, music, theater, and also vanities" (cited in Muan 2001, 43), is not mine. A long tradition of critical visual studies describes the ways that color in diverse domains of film, architecture, and clothing is perceived in the North Atlantic as popular, Oriental, and feminine. Rosalind Galt (2011) shows how "the pretty" in film, which includes images that are "colorful, carefully composed, balanced, richly textured, ornamental," has been attached to raced and sexed bodies and, in film theory, to colonial-era ideas of aesthetic value.

Color also orders. White is for mourning. Saffron is for monks. Navy blue skirts or pants with white blouses are for public school students. Olive green or camouflage is for soldiers; black is for bodyguards and private security. In Cambodia, there is a history of planning your day by the color you wear. The following poem, shared with me by the poet Luoth Yin and his wife, Chanthan, prescribes the proper color for each day of the week. (Today, these colors are primarily used in royal ceremonies.) Following the ancestors' color rules, what others have deemed fitting—yellow for Monday, purple for Tuesday—will bring health, happiness, and prosperity (សុខសួស្តីដល់ប្រាណ). This is a way that color can help things come out for better or for worse.

> Sunday, dark or light red
> Monday, change to yellow, Tuesday, purple
> Wednesday, chartreuse is beautifully fitting
> Thursday, change to light green
> Blue silk, use for Friday
> Dark blue/black, or any color [ទុកសារៃសរី] for Saturday

Dress according to our ancestors' rules,
And you will have health, prosperity, and happiness in your life
[សុកស្សួស្តីដល់ប្រាណ].

This poem conveys the categories of colors, and the logics of color differentiation, that are significant in Khmer. For example, Khmer makes distinctions in succulence: Sunday, wear old or young, fresh red.

Words are just one way to understand the experience and semiotics of color, albeit a dominant way in anthropological linguistics and cognitive science. Working in Berlin and Kay (1969) tradition, yet sympathetic to structuralism, Népote and Khing (1978) gave Letracolor charts to elicit color terms from ten Cambodians living in France.[7] Based on that research, analysis of Khmer and Thai dictionaries, and cultural and linguistic studies by Saveros Lewitz (Pou) (1974), they conclude that there is enough ambiguity and disagreement around several terms—purple, gray—that Khmer does not seem to conform to Berlin and Kay's ordering of color terms. Yet there is a profound order; color terms refer to basic metaphors structured in opposition: "Cambodian culture has a very rich and significant color vision. It is a means of advancing time, of manifesting the complementarities of the components of social life, and of ordering everything in cosmic symbolism in the manner of the great societies of the Far East" (Népote and Khing 1978).[8]

In fact, the ordering of color, as a means of "advancing time" and "manifesting . . . components of social life" took an extreme turn in the 1970s and, to a lesser extent, in the 1980s. The Khmer Rouge notoriously re-engineered ownership, eating, naming, education, medicine, housing, religion, and labor. They also engineered color. When Loung Ung ([2000] 2006) and her family were relocated to Ro Leap in November 1975, they were made to gather with others in the village center to hear the rules of the new world order: "One of our rules applies to how we dress. As you see, we wear the same clothes. Everyone wears his or her hair in the same style. By wearing the same thing, we rid ourselves of the corrupt Western creation of vanity."[9]

Soldiers took the bags of belongings from the new people, those forcibly marched out of Phnom Penh and other cities. They pulled out blue jeans, pink silk blouses, yellow dresses, Ung's beloved first red dress, made by her mother for Khmer New Year. They threw all the clothes into a pile. "Wearing colorful clothes is forbidden. You will take off the clothes you have on and burn those as well. Bright colors only serve to corrupt your mind. You are no different from anyone else here and from now on will dress in black pants and shirts" (Ung [2000] 2006, 58–59).

Ordering color orders the world.

During the socialist 1980s, color was identified with advertising. To rein in its capitalist tendencies, it had to be regulated. When art historian Ingrid Muan interviewed sign painter Tim Thorn, he told her that in the 1980s, "signage and advertising were strictly controlled and shops seem to have had simply lettered signs of various colors depending on the services of goods offered by them. It was only in the 1990s that signage was deregulated and that the free-for-all array of signs which today coat public surfaces in Phnom Penh, began to develop" (Muan 2001, 464).

Ordering color orders the world.

This brief detour in color gives a sense of the complex cultural and political histories of color, which I suggest may influence the way that people relate to color and black-and-white medical images. The othering of color in colonial discourse, the Khmer Rouge obliteration of color, the People's Republic of Kampuchea restrictions on color, and cultural traditions of color order social life. Color is vanity, corruption, capitalist commerce. Color is political subjectivity and political economy. As Krisztina Fehérváry (2013) writes, color attraction and repulsion link political affects to subjectivity and to material objects and environments. Postsocialist Cambodia experienced a flood of new practices and things. And colors.

PORTRAIT AND SCAN

Prenatal images are a peculiar kind of medical image because the "objects" imaged—the fetus and uterine environment—are both interiors and exteriors. Prenatal ultrasound shows the inside of a woman's body and a fetus's body; it also shows the exterior of the fetal body. We can see the human form, recognize it in some cases, unlike we can a uterine cyst. As Joe Dumit (2004) has shown, images that are recognizable and, more to the point, recognizable as something intimate and essential to the human—PET images of brains, in his case—are more open to lay readings, circulating outside the clinic or lab. Because of this exteriority within interiority, prenatal ultrasound is also of that most popular genre of human images: the photographic portrait.

The question "What makes a good image?" is answered on different terms for the portrait than for the medical image. As anthropology of photography tells us (Klima 2002; Pinney 2003; Strassler 2010), the truth of an image of the human depends on what it *projects*. Photographs and photographic practice are also conduits of spiritual power. Photographs *reveal* the presence of entities that exist outside of one material form and, in doing so, become "electric" with presence (Wright 2008, 370). These insights—the portrait as projection as well as documentation, the photograph as conduit of spiritual presence—help me to understand aesthetic practices of relating to prenatal ultrasound images. But there is still the puzzle of the referent.

If we are open to the prenatal ultrasound as a depiction of kin, social histories of photographic portraits may help us understand how people relate with and to black-and-white and color images. So many photographs were lost during evacuations and multiple relocations of the Khmer Rouge period and the turmoil that preceded and followed that period. Forcibly lost. Portrait and family photographs depict "threads of kin and affection" (Stock 2019, 537–38), sometimes bourgeois lives, and these were counter to the revolutionary project. Thus, photographs of people from 1970 to 1990, and especially from 1975 to 1979, are rare, precious, and treasured. Perhaps there is something about a black-and-white image that is tied to that period of time, or to death and loss? Perhaps we do not need to go where so many go when Cambodia is an object of concern: to the Khmer Rouge. Black-and-white pictures from the 1970s are not static objects, not only of the past, nor purely without color. In the 1970s, they may have been colored by hand, and now they are made present through color retouching. But as I have wondered, "Why color?" some have pushed me to also think, "Why not black-and-white?" What is it about black-and-white pictures that people do not like? Perhaps it is enough to say black-and-white is gone. Color brings back?

A semiotic analysis of black-and-white takes us to more of an intermediary, liminal position. Népote and Khing (1978, 54–57) made sense of Khmer color terms with Letracolor chips in the Berlin and Kay tradition, but they could not resist semiotic analysis, even if relegated to footnotes: "Above all, several relations are expressed by their opposition or their complementarity: the opposition between black (or dark) and white (or clear) is that of the everyday and the not every day; their coming together indicates, on the contrary, essential complementarities; their combination (stripes, etc.) marks the actors/individuals ritually placed in intermediary positions; their mixture at the end: 'gray' is like a taboo."

Achar, lay officiants, wear black pants and white shirts because they are intermediaries between the mundane world and the spiritual; the elderly wear black pants and white shirts because they are in the world of the living but close to death. Might black-and-white images traffic across this intermediary position too? How does this relate to the intermediary state of pregnancy and the being-in-transformation that is the fetus?

Prenatal ultrasound tells about life in process. As studies in the anthropology of reproduction have shown, the temporality of ultrasound has to do with futurity and potential—the mixture of anxiety, curiosity, desire, and fear about what this new life might be and how it will participate in the world (see, e.g., Gammeltoft 2014). This brings us to questions of ontology—what the being is and how it becomes.

Buddhist embryology distinguishes the biological form, which develops over time, from the consciousness or spirit of a previous life. According to ethicist Damien Keown (2001, 65), conception is "the *rebirth* of a previously existing individual" but in a new physical form or, in less humanist terms, when a pre-existing life force, *vinna-na*, finds a new container. Based on work in Theravada Buddhist Sri Lanka, Bob Simpson (2010, 31) writes, "consciousness does not develop over the course of gestation, but arrives fully formed at the point of conception when a force of energy (*vinna-na*) from a previous incarnation arrives in the newly formed embryo." This is properly rebirth, not reincarnation, as one monk put it, "when there is a will to live, to still exist, life continues, even after the death of the body. . . . And it is the karmic energy that determines rebirth, in human or animal body" (cited in Schantz 2015, 48). Once the spirit has settled, the mother becomes responsible for the new life. Even after birth, rituals emphasize binding of the newborn to its family and this world. Its status is unstable.

In Cambodia, pregnancy and the fetus are not defined only by Buddhism. Other beliefs, most prominently animism but also Islam and biology, also configure understandings of fetality. Animacy exists in spirits and consciousness, beyond the human and animal. Rebirth can cross species and forms. Life is both cyclical and serial. In Ang Chouléan's (1982) terms, pregnancy is an intermediary state when a woman is more than a woman, but not yet fully a mother.[10] During pregnancy, the health of both the pregnant woman and the fetus can be affected by disease, spirits, or not following proscriptions to ensure balance. For example, pregnancy is "hot" and thus certain foods should be avoided. During pregnancy, the woman must take care concerning what she repeatedly does and what she repeatedly sees. These habits shape the fetus—shape its looks, its nature even. In the postpartum period, practices ensure that balance is restored to the woman.

Birth, like death, is termed "crossing the river," *chlong tonlé*, a hazardous and spiritually charged passage. The body is cold (Schantz 2016). The potency of this instability and transformation is evident in the circulation of stories about attempts to harness the power of pregnant women's bodies. Ghosts

FIGURE 5.2. Pregnancy's multiplicities. A woman and girl look at the paintings *A Woman Is Birth Giver*, by Kong Sovicha, part of the 2010 group show *Hey! Sister, Where Are You Going?* at Sovanna Mall. *A Woman Is Birth Giver* is two paintings, the same size, next to each other, depicting a naked, pregnant woman. One painting is black-and-white and one is color. In both, the woman's black hair is voluptuous, voluminous, flowing around both sides of her body as both comfort and adornment. She places one hand at the top of her belly and one at the bottom. Her belly is a baby, head down. The baby's belly is another baby, head up. Its belly is another baby, head down. The nested bodies convey the sense that pregnancy involves multiple beings, generates ongoing life, and draws upon power and care that extend inward, infinitely. Photo by author, 2010.

released by death of a pregnant woman or unborn fetus are particularly fearsome (Zucker 2013, 44). Stories of pregnant women killed and buried under new dams being built in the Khmer Rouge period, or under a central stupa in Bangkok (Klima 2002), show that the corpses and ghosts of pregnant women are powerful. Harnessing their power is harnessing some of the unknowable, hybrid force that reproduces life. In sum, "life" is not equivalent to singular or exclusively human personhood. More importantly for the case of imaging, fetal life involves a bio-spiritual entity that is partly stable, in terms of the previously existing consciousness, and partly malleable and in transformation.

Prenatal ultrasound mimics pregnancy's potency. One does not have to be committed to Buddhist notions of rebirth and impermanence or to new materialist ontologies to accept that fetal matter is indeterminate. Understandings of the body as plastic and malleable inform a host of biomedical interventions, from taking medicines (Dumit 2012) to hormonal intervention for menstrual suppression (Sanabria 2016). But, if we accept this indeterminacy, what then is imaging doing? For Barad (2007, 175), imaging resolves indeterminacy: "The apparatus enacts an agential cut—a resolution of the ontological indeterminacy—within the phenomenon." But is this cut fixed? Stable? Enduring?

I dwell on these convergences between process orientations in Buddhist and Euro-American theory because they can sensitize us to something interesting about relations between images and referents. If objects are made in practice (M'charek 2013) and color and non-color are different representational practices, different objects may be made by these different images. The black-and-white image is an image for health, health of the fetus and the pregnancy. The color image is for kin. Both color and non-color interfere with the indeterminacy of the future child.

The rich body of work on prenatal ultrasound shows how the fetus is constructed as a subject during ultrasound exams through signifying practices, such as excited tone of voice, smiling, silence, or positioning the body in particular ways.[11] However, the relatively minimal attention to aesthetic practices of making and relating to images suggests a certain iconophobia.[12] "The category of 'fetal bodies' is problematic in part because the collective capacity to see them critically is being worn down under pressure from an onslaught of (often) gorgeous and glamorized imagery . . . the production of computer-generated imagery overwhelms other ways of imagining and knowing fetal bodies, including those produced by embryological anatomy and the phenomenology of pregnancy" (Morgan 2011, 333). Gorgeous imagery is more dangerous than fuzzy black-and-white imagery because it displaces scientific and experiential imaginings. But does it?

In feminist critique of ultrasound as a mode of subject-production, with all the diversity of what the subject may be, there is slippage from denigration of the image as a *technique* to denigration of a *kind* of image. From critique of prenatal ultrasound as technique in prenatal care to critique of color, 3D, or 4D images. Certainly, some of the critique has to do with the question of increased radiation exposure in color and 3D/4D ultrasound and bioeffects on the fetus.[13] Most people I talked to in the imaging and maternity wards did not have concerns about risk to the fetus, though one young woman worried that repeated scans would make the fetus weak, *khsaoy*, and her doctor told her not to get too many.[14] But more generally these are anxieties about the seduction of pretty images and the numbing of political critique of the medicalization of pregnancy.[15]

If imaging is a surfacing of interiors (Taylor 2005), prenatal ultrasound is a special case because the "objects" imaged—the fetus and uterine environment—are both interiors and exteriors. I want to take Lisa Mitchell's (2001) phrase "baby's first picture" seriously, in order to think the ontology of the prenatal—of the baby, the mother, the pregnancy—with the aesthetics of the picture. This requires a theory of images, of imaging, in which images are a connection to and possible influence over the referent. This is a path between images and referents, fixity and plasticity. How clarity, color, and black-and-white animate the image and the referent differently.

THE CAT

Puthea came to my house for dinner. We sat just the two of us, eating garlicky eggplant and rice, talking pregnant life. She was almost nine months along, an enormous belly, ankles swollen, face beaming with happiness. Puthea had a decent job managing the front office of a luxury hotel on the Tonlé Sap River, and she was good at it. But work was starting to feel like a chore. Her boss was an asshole and coworkers' jokes about her size were getting on her nerves. Fatness is good, fatness is bounty.[16] But women still get teased about it, in part from envy of the bounty.

She asked me about my pregnancy, what delivery was like—*thommota ru veah kat?* (normal or C-section?). "Normal, if any delivery can be normal." I asked her about her ultrasound exams. She knew this was the subject of my research and laughed.

"Ooh, Jenna, working at dinner time!" She pursed her lips, shaking her head, pretending to scold me. Nonetheless, she told me she had gotten most of her scans at a private maternity clinic, one of the more famous in Phnom Penh. It was known for its 3D and 4D machines and obstetricians who had done their residencies in France. All of the *echo* were good; they looked clear, pretty; the baby looked fine. Then she paused.

"It's kind of silly."

"What?"

"I don't know."

"What? Tell me!"

"A couple of days ago I went to Calmette. I want to deliver there, so I went for a prenatal exam, so I would be in the system," she said. "I brought the report home to show my husband and Ming. Ming didn't like it. She thought the fetus looked strange. She said, 'It looks like a cat!'" Puthea mimicked her auntie's disgust at the abject image—mouth turned down, head tilted to the side as if avoiding an offensive smell.

I laughed, and Puthea laughed. Ming is a force of nature, the matriarch of the family. She raised Puthea and her brother after their father died in the civil war and their mother fell into gambling. Ming ran a successful guesthouse near the riverfront. She was a warm but sharp auntie to wayward souls who craved a reliable place to sleep in Phnom Penh. Puthea continued: "Ming said, 'That's what you get for always having that cat on your lap, coddling it, petting it, loving it so!'" "*Does* it look like a cat?" I asked. "No! Maybe a little bit. I don't know. It *is* a little strange. The baby doesn't look like that in the other scans."

Puthea mused on possible explanations for this image-form. Perhaps the machine at Calmette, the large, well-regarded, autonomous public hospital, was old. Perhaps the doctor wasn't good at *moel echo*, looking with ultrasound. Perhaps black-and-white machines show different things than color machines do. Perhaps they actually bring out different qualities of the child-to-be.

Puthea's strategies for scanning and delivery were typical—taking into account cost, medical expertise, facility, stage of pregnancy, kind of ultrasound image, among other things.[17] She wanted information that others also wanted from ultrasound exams: information about the sex of the child and when it is due, whether "it has its arms and legs," whether its head is up or down, the location of the placenta. However, her story of the catlike appearance in the image was unusual, and it beckoned. Khmer has a good expression for stories like these: *kuor aoy chngual*, a story one should wonder about, a story that is surprising, curious, hinting at a different reality than one is used to. I spooned more slices of red chili onto my eggplant.

"So," Puthea said, "what do you think? I can see you thinking about it. Do you think it's funny?"

"I don't know," I replied. Puthea raised her eyebrows. I added, "I don't know! Can I visit Ming? Can I see the picture and talk to her about it?"

Puthea laughed. "Why not? You know what she's like . . . she's kind of superstitious. She'll talk to you, though, I'm sure she would."

When we met in the open lobby of Ming's guesthouse, calm and quiet in the afternoon heat, Ming stood by her original assessment: "*Moel tov?*" (See?), she asked me. She showed the picture to me and then to a relative who was visiting from Canada. Puthea rolled her eyes impatiently. Ming had ideas: perhaps it was because Puthea loved her small black cat too much; she always had it on her lap, petting it, talking to it. And maybe, too, it was because

Puthea did not put up enough pretty pictures on the wall to influence the qualities of the fetus in a different direction. Surrounding oneself with nice images could help bring out vitality, health, and beauty of the child-to-be.

Puthea was caught between irritation with her auntie's "superstitious" line of thinking and intimacy with theories about practices of pregnant women influencing the physicality of the fetus. Visual and affective practices—petting the cat and perhaps loving it too much, not looking at pretty pictures—have material consequences. The idea of maternal habits affecting the physiognomy of the fetus is found in different times and places.[18]

Of course, this story is not only about the fetus. It is also about the ultrasound image. Ming suggested that Puthea's actions and affect caused the fetus to look like a cat *in the black-and-white image.* Previous *color* images had not brought out these qualities. Ming's reading made me wonder: How can an image intervene in the object, making it come out better or worse? People look to ultrasound imaging for clues about how the fetus is developing and what its nature might be. Perhaps they also hope that imaging can shift the process of fetal development, just a little, nudging, rather than resolving, ontological indeterminacy. Are women then being responsible by getting multiple scans? Is this care, good mothering? Perhaps this work on the image, from getting the image made to viewing it with others, sends something back?

Puthea's story presses me to think representation is technique for *fixing* things, in multiple senses of the term, in that it gives ontological stability to objects in process—not because there is but one singular, predetermined, or essential truth to ontology, but because this can sometimes help to improve (fix) the matters of concern.

WORKING ON THE SURFACE OF THE IMAGE

"Where do we stop, and representations begin?" (Klima 2002, 197)

Anthropological studies of photography have explored how in portrait photography, the objective is to make the photograph bring out the best qualities of the person, to call forward a potential reality. Popular practices of retouching, coloring, superimposition in portraiture are techniques of calling attention to the surface of the image. Christopher Pinney (2003, 208) argues that work on the surface of the image constructs a zone of tactility for building presences and enabling connection between the image surface and its referents and its beholders. This is quite different from the idea of the surface as an invisible window onto a body. Neither does it entail a detached viewpoint, so important to the objectivity of medical images. In Karen Strassler's (2010, 279) conception of revelatory history, the surface of the image is charged and "reveals a truth beyond our ordinary powers of perception."

The attraction of digital aestheticization of portraits for photo studios and their clients relates to the idea that the subject is contained in the photograph. Nina Hien (2014, 68), writing about a photo retoucher in Ho Chi Minh City, notes that "many people considered the photograph as not only as an index of the subject, but also as *a live connection to it*." The photo retoucher's practice brings "long standing notions about the providential qualities" (Hien 2014, 68) of photographs and an understanding of aesthetics to the use of new technologies.[19] Portraits that are beautiful, harmonious, with blemishes removed project posterity, materially and spiritually. Following a popular Vietnamese saying, "Fixing the image [could] fix the fate" (Hien 2014, 68). The image is an intervention, a projection. In the words of artist and critic Olu Oguibe (1996), a portrait may be an invocation.

Prenatal ultrasound involves multiple representational logics and different possibilities for representing well. It is for health, for the pregnancy. Doctors and patients and family members want an image of a material that is there, a document of the present. Prenatal ultrasound is also for kin. It is a document of a being that is here and a being that is in the process of becoming. How does it do the latter, how does it participate in the becoming? Writing about *ako*, a funeral effigy of the Owo of western Nigeria, Oguibe (1996, 240) articulates these tensions of "reflection" and "projection" with eloquence:

> The verisimilitude we are introduced to is a mediated gesture
> between faithfulness and faith, between reflection and projec-
> tion; it is a configuration of representation as both reflection and
> invocation beyond the limitations of transparency. For that
> which projects, that which anticipates and conjures, though
> faithful it may yet be to appearance, cannot be transparent since
> to be transparent is to convey that which already exists, that
> which precedes rather than supersedes the agency of its repre-
> sentation: to remain, as it were, within the reaches of death. The
> essence of verisimilitude here is not transparency but efficacy,
> the fulfilment of an intent beyond the materiality of the image.

Scholars of photography in the majority world describe how enhancing a portrait, coloring it, making it pretty, is about transformative possibilities, not messing up reality.

Prenatal ultrasound images operate at the seam of these multiple orders of the real. The portrait is for kin, and in being a portrait, it travels in a realm of images that have a particular relation to reality, best thought of as projection. A clear and pretty image projects goodness to the future child. This is clear and pretty and human. A black-and-white image projects a strange and surprising familiarity—resemblance to the beloved cat!—which hints at indeterminacy of the being before birth.

Puthea's story tells us how the qualities of fetuses are important to pregnant women and their families, that these qualities are not necessarily fixed, and that the image and machine may be involved in drawing them out. Imaging is a way to understand, through representing, how the fetus is developing and transforming. Representing is also, sometimes, intervening. The image-affect involves viewers and referents. Widespread belief in karma, its unknowable and unpredictable unfolding, is a backdrop of uncertainty, an uncertainty about the future that ultrasound may ameliorate, if temporarily. "Fixing the image could fix the fate," where fixing has the same meaning in the beginning and the end: improvement or repair. This is not a return to or achievement of a predetermined fate. The color and non-color images participate in a human (animal, spirit) becoming that is plastic and malleable, transforming without predetermination but not without limit.

AFFECTIVE CO-ENACTMENTS

In Srey Neang's anger about her faded scan, and Bora and his wife's seeking out of multiple color scans, I sense a struggle and a roll of the dice. Trying to know, to hold, to shift the fortune of unstable and dynamic phenomena— this is an image practice of pregnant women and their families, as it is of portrait sitters and their photo retouchers. In my terms, imaging is a stabilization but one that is temporary and incomplete. Following Stéphane Mallarmé ([1897] 2015), a roll of the dice does not abolish chance. One continues to try to put things in place, to stabilize them, again and again, even if, as good Buddhists live it, all in life is impermanent and much is uncontrollable.

Prenatal imaging can be understood within a broader range of practices aimed to find clues to fate and to fix it. For example, it was common for pregnant women to consider the Chinese astrological year of birth, and some private clinics had astrological calendars on hand for consultation. One of the years of my research was the year of the tiger, and people did not want to have children that year because of the concern that they would be difficult to marry. (Puthea later told me that her son drank milk, so he was clearly gentle, *slout*. Not all year of the tiger babies are fierce.) There are a variety of "systems and signs that people use to read present and future states of health and well-being" (Simpson 2010, 29), and prenatal ultrasound imaging is one of them.

I wonder if we have space to think of "fixing" in this context as a practice that freezes, but only momentarily. Not forever. *Co-enactment* is a term Cecilia Åsberg and Jennifer Lum (2010, 330) use to convey the work of commercial medical images and cultural understandings of disease. What my interlocutors are suggesting is something more material, of the body, of tissue.

In early photography, making the image stay was one of the central problems to solve. Stability and replicability were the struggles (Batchen 1997).[20] As these problems were solved, photography transformed into a technology for holding something still so that it can be grasped, known, a way of freezing someone or something in time. This logic of stabilizing and preserving in images and words, and its correlate that knowledge practices involve representations that are independent from reality, informs diverse fields of practice in the nineteenth and twentieth centuries, from colonial and settler ethnography, to medicine and demography, to policing, to art (e.g., Edwards 1992; Rony 1996).[21] As Tina Campt (2017, 94–96) writes, even the *desire* for photographic capture in the context of colonialism may be considered "a pernicious instrument of knowledge production," given its role in disappearance, separation, or violent "protection" of peoples and worlds. Feminist studies of medical imaging, and prenatal ultrasound in particular, have located perniciousness in what some call a masculinist colonial desire (Frost and Haas 2017) to see inside bodies. Critical studies of photography hold out the multiplicity of the image, even those compelled by power. Identification photos vibrate between the demands of state capture and the honorific, bourgeois, affective, and mobile. Even this most fixative genre of image, the identification photograph, may be seen, or listened to, at affective registers beyond the instrumental function for which they were created (Campt 2017; Strassler 2010). Vernacular uses—being sent to loved ones, memorializing the dead—and affective responses co-exist with other ways of relating to images. Prenatal ultrasound images, peculiar images made from sound, are also of different functions, different efficacies. They are for medical diagnosis, and they are for kin.

Writing "the prenatal ultrasound makes kin" is hazardous because of how it seems to settle the life politics of fetal personhood. But I have come to the conviction that the statement "a prenatal ultrasound is an image of kin" is important to continuously take on in feminist studies. I understand that the statement does not determine a particular stance on personhood, let alone subjectivity or images. To recognize Srey Neang's anger about a fading image and Ming's distaste of the catlike image is to understand prenatal images as images of interiors and exteriors, a medical image and a portrait: color for the home and perhaps a photo book, black-and-white for the clinic and the file. However, I do not want to push a dichotomy too strongly. Health comes in color, and kin come in black-and-white.

EPILOGUE

ON A NARROW, BUSY STREET BEHIND O'RUSSEI MARKET IN CENTRAL Phnom Penh was a cluster of private clinics. Their signs craned out from thickets of electrical wires, competing for attention. Banteay Srey Maternity Clinic listed its services on offer (see figure E.1). One of the services, "Color ultrasound imaging—see the face of the infant inside the belly," was illustrated by a picture of an ultrasound monitor showing the face and arms of an infant. In the south of town, a private clinic with a large canvas advertisement on its façade featured the same image. In both, the image is in portrait orientation, the infant glows amber in contrast to the black background, its eyes are closed, and its head seems to rest on its hands.

I noticed this image, this portrait and scan, in advertisements for multiple clinics around the city. I mentioned its ubiquity in conversation with the director of global programs for GE and showed her a photograph on my camera. She looked at it closely and said, "That's *our* image!" She paused and then wondered aloud if it was worth pursuing as copyright infringement. She shook her head slightly and then continued on to another topic.

Whose image is this? One could pursue this question in different ways. In this book I have considered the image of the machine, the image of tissues in the interior of the body, the image of the infant. In the opening story, the young woman came to the hospital for imaging. She knew about ultrasound, that it was a technology that could possibly show the cause of her discomfort, one that was accessible, meaning relatively affordable and relatively available. I have suggested different forces that may help understand why she was there, in that moment. Historical forces shape both the hospital as an institution and a site of technological care. Economic forces brought her to work in the suburban garment factory and put private ultrasound services out of reach. Instability and expertise are involved in seeing,

146

FIGURE E.1. The sign for Banteay Srey General and Maternity Clinic stands amid a traffic of electric wires. It lists clinic services: maternity–gynecology; cosmetic surgery; general medicine–pediatrics; X-ray imaging; color ultrasound imaging: see the face of the infant inside the belly; 24-hour service. The picture of an ultrasound monitor shows what you might see during a prenatal exam: the amber face and arm of a fetus inside the belly. Many different clinics across the city use this same image in their advertisements, its ubiquity somewhat uncanny. Photo by author, 2009.

and the seeing with ultrasound is powerful and authoritative but does not preclude other agents and experts.

This book is concerned with the appeal of technologies that make images of the body's interior. I have explored care with technological images in exam rooms, waiting areas of public hospitals, and personal and public spaces outside the clinic and through religious, aesthetic, and secularized practices to present a diversity of actors who participate in the production and circulation of medical images. Using a central image of fixing—fixing the image and an image that fixes—I show how ultrasound produces stabilizing authoritative knowledge, nudges unfolding beings toward desired futures, and elicits desire and pleasure linked to improvement, particularly for pregnant women. I argue that the force and appeal of ultrasound imaging—indeed, in some cases, its excess—have to do with the potential of repair and stability, offerings peculiar to the mechanized image. This fixing is set against a history of turbulent social and political economic history and genealogies of vision and skilled diagnosis grounded in Buddhist practice and in French colonial medicine, in which advanced technologies were associated with white colonizers.

The successive chapters of *Fixing the Image* move closer and closer to its object, beginning with imaging technology as instrument and symbol in Cambodian postcolonial modernity; to analysis of the distinctive mix of postconflict and postsocialist capitalism that structures ultrasound services; to ultrasound practices and patients' expectations of care; to skilled seeing with ultrasound and in Buddhist healing as managing interference; and ending with an intimate engagement with the prenatal ultrasound image, the interior body, and material desire and anxiety. This technology of imaging the body's interior is "newness that enters the world," to paraphrase Mrázek (2002), but the world is not smooth, and technology is not necessarily another rupture but rather, potentially, a source of stability.

In this book, I used images of thought as a loose organizing mechanism for thinking the way that ultrasound imaging operates in Phnom Penh. These images are not static—flickering histories, the mother-child relationship that must continuously be worked out, the echo. Together they convey the unfixity of life in Phnom Penh and the possibility of the technological image to intervene in this flux. We can understand technological practices as interventions through which bodies are made and also how these practices cluster and repeat in formations that are not random but not always designed.

Fixing the Image questions the value of disruption and unsettling as conceptual tools for deriving liberatory potential in social theory. Concepts such as instability, fluidity, improvisation, unsettling, plasticity, and indeterminacy are crucial theoretical interventions into debates about technology and the body that further feminist and critical race commitments to denaturalize categories that asymmetrically structure social and biological life. The challenge I have taken up in this book is how to think the relations of humans and technologies across different liberatory projections, especially when unsettling is not a radical intervention; when instability is what people are trying to get away from; and when people seek the stabilization, even if temporary, of symptoms into a diagnosis and the predictability, though often erratic, of a machine yet do not have naive expectations that the machine has the one and only answer. If unsettlement is historical experience and a prevalent condition of economic, political, and spiritual life, the scholarly desire for "disruption" might not serve liberatory ends. This is important for understanding the social life of health technologies in the majority of the world. Technology brings not just improvement but some stabilization of things in flux.

At the time of my research, ultrasound sales had declined in North America and Europe and increased in Asia Pacific (Freiherr 2010). As new visual diagnostic technologies and visual data become normalized in pregnancy (see, e.g., Reed, Kochetkova, and Whitby 2016 on fetal MRI), it remains important to be suspicious, to study their use in political economic, aesthetic, and ontological frames. We must continually question the unequal life-promoting and life-limiting effects of our imbrication in technoscience.

Fixing the Image explores what ultrasound can teach us about the politics of post-political health care, in which the ideologies of the old order have been reshaped by the demands of the market. Market transition from socialism over the past few decades presses the government to transfer the cost of and responsibility for health programs and infrastructures to private entities, smaller municipalities, and perhaps to development partners. In the 2010s, the relationship between private and government health care was being worked out, far from settled. I have argued that ultrasound services played a part in shaping this relationship. In Cambodia, as in many formerly socialist countries, diagnostic imaging services were the first green shoots of private practice. Ultrasound continues to be an easy entry into the health care market because it does not require much capital and infrastructure and labor costs are low. Ultrasound machines produce a tangible product for patients, something to show for your money, and thus are more like a pill than just words on a piece of paper. And in the case of prenatal ultrasound, the image serves interests beyond diagnosis or screening as the scan depicts kin as well as tissue. It is the specificity of *both* ultrasound technology and the structure and imagination of the political economy in health care that are the subjects of this book.

The tensions between legibility and illegibility in public and private health care create an openness for maneuvering for some actors—what some call freedom—that leaves open to question what good care can be with ultrasound. Though the private sector may obscure the workings of class—because the wealthy, middle class, and poor all go to private clinics—the benefits and harms of private care fall along lines of class. Ultrasound amplifies forms of care that are respectful and neglectful, in ways that are patterned along social hierarchies but also unscripted. This uncertainty and worry haunts health care. The fact that indebtedness is strongly related to health care expenses cannot be ignored or downplayed. The over-care that ultrasound facilitates through its diagnostic promise, its material form in the doctor-patient exchange of money and image, begs the important question: What does it mean to invest money and energy in technologies when good prenatal and medical care may still be wanting? *Fixing the Image* suggests that political economic analysis of technology is enriched by questions of affect, the senses, aesthetics, and ontology in the search for good care.

Fixing the Image advances a way of thinking about skilled seeing that is informed by the mode of seeing in ultrasound and in Buddhist healing, in which translation of interference is the crux of the practice. When a metaphysics of seeing includes interference, it is necessarily partial. Partiality admits other ways of doing, not for the purpose of romantic equality, but for empirical fidelity and pragmatic understanding of the multiplicity of visual practices in medicine.

One aim of this book is to unsettle notions of Cambodian health care as characterized by lack. Phnom Penh has laboratories, ethics review committees, and scientific expertise to conduct cutting-edge global health science. Phnom Penh is becoming a sentinel site (Keck 2013) of sorts for global health problems such as malaria drug resistance, antibiotic resistance, and, more recently, COVID-19 (Mallapaty 2020). Southeast Asia's historical reputation as a crossroads between India and China ("*Indochine*"), and as an area with diverse human and non-human beings and ways of living together, makes it a site of uncanny surplus (Ong 2016), a region with populations and environmental conditions that make it a crucial location for bioscientific research.

To mention just a few recent examples, in April 2020, WHO named the Institut Pasteur du Cambodge (IPC) in Phnom Penh an international reference laboratory for COVID-19, one of seventeen globally. This means IPC will receive and confirm COVID-19 samples from around the world and play a role in the development of new assays (IPC 2020). A collaboration of French, US, and Cambodian scientists in Phnom Penh sequenced the SARS-CoV-2 virus in April 2020 (Molteni 2020; Zeeberg 2021), the first group outside of China to do so. An international collaboration led by parasitologists at IPC identified a molecular marker for artemisinin resistance in *Plasmodium falciparum* (Ariey et al. 2014).

In the face of new kinds of drug resistance and new zoonoses, the crucial questions persist: What is the work of the technological fix? What forms will semi-privatization and underfunding of the public health system take? How will new biomedical technologies intertwine with long histories of scientific medicine, in Cambodia and in global health, to shape understandings of life, its instabilities and vulnerabilities?

I believe new diseases, parasites, and science will bring new questions about the directionality of knowledge production and transfer and how histories of colonial and post-Independence scientific practice animate contemporary forms of experimentation and policy. In this book, I have explored different ways to tell these stories. The goal is not fixing Cambodia, not saving it. Studying ordinary technologies provokes conversation about modernity, freedom, and kin, as it does about a cyst or the cost of a scan. The future project will be to hold the everyday practices and concerns of people together with theoretical questions about how particular diseases configure novel understandings of how humans, microbes, medicines, and environments live, transform, and die together.

Appendix

Medico-Political Timeline, Cambodia, 1863–2021

1863	Cambodia becomes a French Protectorate
1885	first extended biomedical institution (later, Mixed Hospital, then Preah Ket Mealea)
1907	Assistance Médicale, the civilian medical service, established
1946	Medical school opened in Phnom Penh
1953	Institute Pasteur opened in Phnom Penh
1953	Independence from France (9 November)
1955	Sihanouk abdicates, wins election, and becomes prime minister; beginning of Sangkum period (1955–70)
1959	Calmette Hospital built
1960	Khmer-Soviet Friendship Hospital (Russian Hospital) built; *Annals* published, 1960–71
1960	national chain begins manufacturing medical products
1965	Sihanouk severs diplomatic relations with the United States
1969	Operation Menu; heavy US bombing in NE; refugees come to Phnom Penh
1970	Lon Nol coup; establishment of Khmer Republic; Sihanouk in exile in China; open civil war; refugees settle in and around Phnom Penh straining infrastructure, especially the health care system

1975	Khmer Rouge take Phnom Penh and establish Democratic Kampuchea; massive relocation of populations, evacuation of cities, and abolishment of private property, Buddhism, health care and education systems, and money
1979	Vietnamese troops take Phnom Penh and establish People's Republic of Kampuchea; Khmer Rouge and other resistance groups retreat to the border with Thailand, forming a coalition that is recognized internationally; armed struggle continues
1980	Faculty of Medicine reopened in Phnom Penh
1984	beginning of K5 plan to seal the border with Thailand, both sides mine the border
1985	Hun Sen becomes prime minister, a post he continues to hold
1989	Vietnamese troops leave Cambodia; country renamed State of Cambodia; private ownership reestablished and Buddhism made the official religion
1989	first ultrasound machine donated to Calmette Hospital by French
1989	humanitarian aid groups begin entering the country and refugee camps
1991	Paris Peace Agreements end civil war
1992–93	United Nations Transitional Authority in Cambodia (UNTAC) mandate
1993	elections: FUNCINPEC wins majority, but the Cambodian People's Party (CPP) does not step down, resulting in a power-sharing agreement; country renamed Kingdom of Cambodia
1993	first ultrasound machine donated to Russian Hospital by the Japan International Cooperation Agency (JICA)
1996	Health Financing Charter introduces user fees at public health facilities
1997	fighting between FUNCINPEC and CPP supporters
1997	Cambodian Law on Abortion legalizes abortion until 14 weeks gestation
1998	elections: CPP wins but still must share power with FUNCINPEC; the parties divide up ministries, with FUNCINPEC heading the Ministry of Health

1998	Pol Pot dies; large chunk of Khmer Rouge leadership surrender or are arrested; considered the beginning of a period of political stability
1999	Cambodia joins Association of Southeast Asian Nations (ASEAN)
2000	law regulating private and paramedical services passed by National Assembly
2002	first multi-party local elections; CPP wins decisive majority
2002	International University (private), the second medical school in country, opens
2002	Ministry of Health establishes the National Ethics Committee for Health Research
2003	elections: CPP wins majority
2004	Cambodia's first clinical trial, an HIV pre-exposure prophylaxis (PrEP) trial, canceled due to controversy
2004	Sihamoni crowned King of Cambodia
2007	General Electric (GE) opens Cambodia office
2008	elections: CPP holds vast majority
2009	GE launches Developing Health Globally program
2011	Russian Hospital obtains its first CT machine
2012	Sihanouk dies
2012	ASEAN medical schools network holds first meeting
2013	elections: CPP wins 68 seats in the National Assembly (loss of 22 seats); Cambodian National Rescue Party wins 55 seats (gain of 26 seats)
2015	Law on Associations and Non-Governmental Organizations brings NGOs under more government control
2015	Telecommunications Law allows authorities to monitor any private speech
2016	Health Insurance Scheme introduced, part of the National Social Security Fund (BSS)

2016	Cambodia is classified as a "lower-middle income" economy by the World Bank (previously it was a "low income" economy)
2017	Supreme Court outlaws the Cambodian National Rescue Party; the *Cambodia Daily* newspaper closed on a tax charge
2018	Inter-Ministerial Prakas on Website and Social Media Control requires all internet service providers to install surveillance software to monitor content
2018	elections: CPP wins 100 percent of seats in the National Assembly
2020	Cambodia reports its first COVID-19 case on 27 January; government enacts state of emergency laws that extend government surveillance and control of media
2021	government sub-decree requires internet service providers to reroute services through the National Internet Gateway, which monitors online activity before it reaches users, by February 2022

Khmer Glossary

Prepared with Andrew Hollister

achar អាចារ្យ lay officiant

aekchon ឯកជន private, as in a private medical clinic

aoey doeng chbas ឱ្យដឹងច្បាស់ to make (someone) understand clearly

aoey trauv ឱ្យត្រូវ to be right, correct

Angkar អង្គការ organization; the Khmer Rouge

âphibal អភិបាល to take care of; to govern; to manage

âphivadd អភិវឌ្ឍន៍ development

ât brakad, anhchoeng that moel អត់ប្រាកដ អញ្ចឹងថតមើល to not be certain,
   so take a look (in this case, with ultrasound)

ât che moel អត់ចេះមើល to not know how to see or look at something

ât khoenh អត់ឃើញ to be unable to see (something)

ât mean chumngeua ey អត់មានជំនឿអី does not have any illness

ât tuk chett អត់ទុកចិត្ត to not trust, to lack confidence in

âyuttethoa អយុត្តិធម៌ injustice

barang បារាំង French; foreigner, specifically white/European

chbas ច្បាស់ clear

chbas haoey s'at cheang ច្បាស់ហើយស្អាតជាង clearer and prettier, better
   looking

chea phnaek moel khoenh ke cheua ជាផ្នែកមើលឃើញគេជឿ it is an eye for
   seeing, people believe

chenhchoem ចិញ្ចឹម to care for, raise (a child)

cheuan leuan រៀនលឿន to develop, advance, progress

chloh ឆ្លុះ to make an X-ray; to shine, reflect

chlong tonlé ឆ្លងទន្លេ to give birth (literally: to cross the river)

choh mouldthan ចុះមូលដ្ឋាន to go out down to the base (to the countryside,
   voting base)

chor chmouh ឈររឈ្មោះ   to stand behind the name (to register with someone else's name)

chumneanh ជំនាញ   ability, skill; skilled, expert

chumngeu toutov ជំងឺទូទៅ   general illness

daun chi ដូនជី   Buddhist nun

doeng ដឹង   to know, understand

doeng ât? ដឹងអត់?   do you understand, or not?

dom ដុំ   tumor, mass

echo អេកូ   ultrasound

Echo pouah haoey, âs pir moeun. Thât kbal, free. អេកូពោះហើយ អស់ពីរមុឺន។ ថតក្បាល «free»។   Scan the abdomen, 20,000 riel. Take a(nother) picture of your head, free.

echo khoenh knong អេកូឃើញក្នុង   with ultrasound, (one can) see inside

echosasrt អេកូសាស្ត្រ   ultrasonography

het âvey? ហេតុអ្វី?   why, how come?

kar bakbrae ការបកប្រែ   translation

kaun កូន   child

ke chumneanh, mean obakar krup kroan គេជំនាញ មានឧបករណ៍គ្រប់គ្រាន់   they are experts and have adequate equipment

khmae ខ្មែរ   Khmer

khmaoch ខ្មោច   ghost, spirit

khoenh ឃើញ   see

khsaoy ខ្សោយ   weak

kmeng ក្មេង   young; child

kmeng steav ក្មេងស្ទាវ   teenage hooligans

koat phey khmaoch, chong moel. គាត់ភ័យខ្មោច ចង់មើល។   they are afraid of ghosts/spirits, so they want to look (with ultrasound)

koat poukae moel គាត់ពូកែមើល   they are skilled at looking (said of traditional healers who are good at their job)

krama ក្រមា   type of traditional Cambodian scarf

kranat ក្រណាត់   cloth, fabric (in this case, a piece of red fabric for drawing yantra or writing Buddhist chants)

krou គ្រូ   teacher; expert; healer

krou boran គ្រូបូរាណ   traditional healer

krou khmae គ្រូខ្មែរ   Khmer healer

krou thmup គ្រូធ្មប់   sorcerer

kroupet គ្រូពេទ្យ   medical doctor

kuor aoy chngual គួរឱ្យឆ្ងល់   that is interesting, surprising

me មែ   mother
mephoum មេភូមិ   village leader
mechao មេចៅ   boss
mean omnach មានអំណាច   to have power, authority
moel មើល   to look, examine
moel chbas មើលច្បាស់   to see clearly
moel chheam មើលឈាម   to check the blood
moel khoenh មើលឃើញ   to look and see
moel chett manuss មើលចិត្តមនុស្ស   to look at a person's heart, spirit
moel kaun មើលកូន   watch or look after children
moel pi krov មើលពីក្រៅ   to see from the outside (perspective)
moel tov? មើលទៅ?   see? (can you see it is so?)
montirpety មន្ទីរពេទ្យ   hospital, clinic

nih chea santanchett knhum នេះជាសន្ដានចិត្តខ្ញុំ   this is my kindness, gratitude

obakar ឧបករណ៍   equipment

paritta បរិត្ត   Buddhist/Pali prayers, chants
pikroeah chumngeu ពិគ្រោះជំងឺ   to consult about an illness (phrase used to
   describe the clinic)
pit brakad ពិតប្រាកដ   to be certain, sure
poukae kasang ពូកែកសាង   to be good at building/creating
proleung ព្រលឹង   spirit, soul
pyeabal ព្យាបាល   care, treatment

Rasmei Kampuchea រស្មីកម្ពុជា   Light of Cambodia
rien moel រៀនមើល   to learn how to see
rodth រដ្ឋ   government/state
rouppheap phseng phseng knea រូបភាពផ្សេងៗគ្នា   different images

sabbay សប្បាយ   happy
samakki សាមគ្គី   solidarity, cooperation
s'at ស្អាត   good looking, nice appearance
sauth Pali សូធ្យបាលី   to chant Pali
sokhpeap សុខភាព   health
sompeah សំពះ   Cambodian gesture of respect, greeting
sraoch teuk ស្រោចទឹក   to sprinkle water, as in Buddhist practice

teang âs ទៀងអស់   having everything; being complete
tearok ទារក   infant
thae ថែ   to take care of

thae toam ថែទាំ   to take care of

thae roksa ថែរក្សា   to take care of

thât ថត   to photograph, record, take a picture (used with medical imaging)

thlai thlai l'a l'a thmey thmey ថ្លៃៗល្អៗថ្មីៗ   expensive, good, new

thleak chheam ធ្លាក់ឈាម   hemorrhage

thmey thmey kunpheap l'a ថ្មីៗគុណភាពល្អ   new and good quality

thnam phlauv chett ថ្នាំផ្លូវចិត្ត   psychological medicine

thnam ru veah kat ថ្នាំឬវះកាត់   medication or surgery?

tuk ទុក   to put; keep

thommota ru veah kat? ធម្មតាឬវះកាត់?   normal (vaginal birth) or C-section?

troem trauv ត្រឹមត្រូវ   honest, correct

tuk chett ទុកចិត្ត   to trust, have confidence

vay thomlae trauv វាយតម្លៃត្រូវ   to be good value

Vea neung haoey! Vea som mok nov vinh! វានឹងហើយ! វាសុំមកនៅវិញ!   It is him
     again! He asked to come back!

vityea វិទ្យា   science of, body of knowledge

yok chett tuk dak យកចិត្តទុកដាក់   to take care

yual យល់   to understand

yual sap យល់សប្ដិ   to dream

Notes

INTRODUCTION

1 I use the Franco-Khmer transcription system developed by Franklin Huffman in 1983 and modified by Ebihara, Mortland, and Ledgerwood (1994).

2 To be clear, no one thought a ghost could be seen by ultrasound. Furthermore, a ghost did not dwell in tissue in a Foucauldian sense of locating disease in bodily space. Whether ultrasound could see maladies caused by spirits, however, was uncertain.

3 The tragedy of the 2010 Water Festival brought forward ghost talk in the hospital. Hundreds of young people attending a concert on Diamond Island died in a stampede caused by overcrowding and a rumor that the bridge was collapsing. The corpses were brought to government hospitals around the city, their images displayed to help families identify loved ones. Patients and many staff stayed away from the hospital, including the imaging ward. So much death, bad death that came violently and too soon, meant there would be ghosts on the grounds, lingering in anger at being rent from the bodies now in the morgue. Neary, my research assistant and a fourth-year medical student, refused to join me at work that week. Her mother, a midwife at a different government hospital, and her father, a professor and researcher, backed her up. So many young and beautiful bodies, bruised, missing shoes. Ghosts will surely be there; they were not ready to leave the world and hunger for new bodies to materialize their return.

4 From the colonial period through the 1990s, public hospitals rather than private ones had the most advanced medical technologies in Cambodia, as they had the networks and resources to buy, lease, or receive donations and training. Private hospitals now have expensive and infrastructurally complex imaging, such as CT scanning and MRI.

5 For example, rapid diagnostic tests for malaria can be useful, as long as they do not substitute for a health care system with medical expertise, organizational capacity, and sufficient funding. See Beisel et al. (2016) and Street (2014b).

6 Note how *fixing* is co-defined with practices of making a mechanized image, using an optical technology, and preparing material for scientific study or display.

7 See Marston (2008) on building wats. See Nam (2017b) on urban development.

8 Many artists and filmmakers in the contemporary vanguard explore Phnom Penh as a character and as a scene of desire, exclusion, and alienation. Exemplary is the work of Sao Sreymao ("Untitled" series on Phnom Penh); Neak Sophal ("Green Net," "Behind" series); Kim Hak ("Stampede," "Left Behind," "On" series); Kavich Neang (*White Building, New Land Broken Road*); Danech San (*Sunrise in My Mind*); and Davy Chou (*Diamond Island, Cambodia 2099*), among others. See artists' websites and the website of the Anti-Archive film collective, www .antiarchive.com.

9 This hospital is referred to by slightly different names and acronyms by development and aid organizations, including National Maternal and Child Health Center, or NMCHC. I use the Ministry of Health's designation in its 2009 and 2010 organizational charts: National Center for Maternal and Child Health, or NCMCH, and Maternal Hospital for short. Taxi drivers and many Phnom Penh residents refer to it as Maternal Hospital or Japanese Hospital because it was built and jointly administered by JICA.

10 Kaing Guek Eav, alias Duch, was the former chairman of S-21, the Khmer Rouge detention center in Phnom Penh where 12,000 people perished. He was the defendant in Case 001 before the Extraordinary Chambers in the Courts of Cambodia (ECCC), also known as the Khmer Rouge Tribunal. Duch's trial ran from 2009 to 2010, with appeals decided in 2012. This was a major event in Cambodia and in international jurisprudence. The ECCC states that 36,493 people attended Duch's trial and appeal hearings, including students and everyday citizens, some who were bused in from the provinces. Phnom Penh, its newspapers and radio stations, its restaurants and bars, were filled with foreign experts doing work related to the trial—translators, judges, lawyers, law students, journalists, researchers (some having come from the Special Court for Sierra Leone, which, like the ECCC, was an independent tribunal established jointly with the UN and the government). Duch was convicted for crimes against humanity and grave breaches of the 1949 Geneva Conventions. He died in 2020 (at Russian Hospital) while serving his sentence. See "Case 001" on the ECCC

website (www.eccc.gov.kh/en/case/topic/90); Panh (2011); and Hinton (2016).

11 See Grant (2020) for additional writing about writing and care. Pertinent here is Klima's (2019, 19) question whether "serious realness and will-to-knowledge, performatively" are required to launch a theoretical claim or contestation.

12 See Padwe (2020, esp. 97–106) on the post-Independence government's "Khmerization" campaign of development in the northeast. For the Jarai and other Indigenous peoples, Khmerization involved hospitals, schools, and roads, as well as land dispossession and forced labor on rubber plantations, violence, and dehumanization.

13 The phrase *North Atlantic* is from Trouillot (2003). See Adas (1989) for a broad survey of colonial discourse about civilization, progress, technology, and modernity.

14 The Indochinese Union was a colonial territory of five very different political entities and kingdoms—Cambodia, Laos, Cochinchina, Annam, and Tonkin—that now comprise the countries of Cambodia, Lao PDR, and Viet Nam.

15 See Anderson (2006) on colonial medicine in the Philippines; Govindrajan (2018) on colonial forestry and wildlife conservation in India; Mavhunga (2018) on African knowledge of the tsetse fly and colonial efforts to control it in Southern Rhodesia, now Zimbabwe; Warren (2010) on medical and population sciences in colonial Peru; and Thongchai (1997) on geography in Siam, now Thailand.

16 About Cambodian responses to French colonial medicine, Au (2011, 62) writes, "Indigenous response was not always just resistance; it was often a considered reaction to particular experiences. Khmers did not simply refuse colonial medicine; they refused unknown, ineffective, or potentially dangerous treatments. Sometimes they were quite willing to embrace treatments with a clear medical value, but such treatments were rare in the early twentieth century." See also Au (2006) for a nuanced account of different forms of resistance to public health programs in the 1920s and 1930s and Grant (2016) for analysis of how some of these forms, such as petitioning the king, were used in protest against an HIV prevention trial in 2003–4. Padwe (2020, 90–108) describes tactics of Jarai refusal to submit to corvée labor for public works, such as construction of roads and bridges, in the 1920s and 1930s. This unfree labor supported private rubber plantations, and highland Indigenous groups were intensely dissatisfied with state-private collusion in the violent transformation of the land.

17 In Southeast Asia, Mrázek (2002), Rafael (2006), and Thongchai (1997) explore these colonial and anti-colonial entanglements of science and technology.

18 Some of the colonial logics about science and technology that persist, if mutated, in post-Independence governance are the association of modern technology with white supremacy and racial and caste hierarchy; technological progress as a rationale for the domination of Indigenous peoples and nature; and technoscientific expertise as justification for elite power. See Abraham (2006) and Subramaniam (2019) on science and technology in India; Geissler et al. (2017) on medical sciences in Africa; Kervran et al. (2018) on theorizing postcolonial science and technology studies (STS); Lowe (2006) on biodiversity conservation sciences in Indonesia; and Parreñas (2018) on orangutan rehabilitation in Malaysia.

19 Thanks to Andy Feenberg for pointing me to "Traditional Language and Technological Language."

20 The homogeneity of who the "we" are and what the "time" is unsatisfying, of course. For a start, who gets to be the human, and whose historical experience defines the human? This is not a simple politics of inclusion/ exclusion, but a politics of the grounds for theorization of the world. For Heidegger, the world was Europe defined by origination in ancient Greece and having gone through particular forms of industrial revolution and information revolution. Unthinkable in this world/Europe are the way in which understandings of nature, tools, and the human were made through imperialism, capitalism, racism, and violence. In other words, following Césaire ([1955] 1972), the demand that was peculiarly important to Heidegger, the treating of humans and nature as reserve that so horrified European thinkers following World War II, was long practiced in the colonies, yet this fact was not relevant to Heidegger's theorization of the who, how, and what of the human.

21 For analysis of prenatal ultrasound and consumption, see Bashour, Hafez, and Abdulsalam (2005); Gammeltoft and Nguyen (2007); Taylor (2008); and Morgan (2011). On prenatal ultrasound and a "modern" pregnancy, see Georges (1996) and Roberts (2012).

22 Fetal subjectivity, or fetality, constructed through ultrasound practices is explored in Barad (2007); Howes-Mischel (2016); Mitchell (2001); and Morgan (2000).

23 Ultrasound is just one in the (ever-growing) array of selective reproductive technologies. For interdisciplinary debate on the ethics of assisted reproductive technologies and genetic testing, see the Tarrytown Meetings, especially Asch (2010) and Roberts (2010): www.youtube.com /user/TarrytownMeetings. On prenatal ultrasound and selection for gender and perceived disability, see Bhatia (2018); Gammeltoft (2014); Ivry (2006, 2009); John (2011); and Unnithan-Kumar (2004).

24 For philosophical and historical study of imaging, see *Medical Imaging and Philosophy* (Fangerau et al. 2012). For cultural studies approaches, see Pauwels (2006) on the function of images in science communication.

See Myers (2015) for an ethnographic study of protein modeling in which scientists are reflective on their embodied role in producing visual representations of proteins. Studies of medical images in hospital settings focus on the role of medical imaging in the organization and ordering of diagnostic labor (Burri 2008; Saunders 2008), working conditions (Joyce 2008), and cultural economies of medicine (Prasad 2014).

25 In *The Birth of the Clinic*, particularly the chapter "Seeing and Knowing," Foucault ([1963] 1994) likens the medical gaze to a fire that isolates and purifies the "alphabetical" or finite elements and their relations in order to understand the disease at hand.

26 "In contrast to the European, the Negro-African does not draw a line between himself and the object, he does not hold it at a distance, nor does he merely look at it and analyze it. After holding it at a distance, after scanning it without analyzing it, he takes it vibrant in his hands, careful not to kill or fix it. He touches it, feels it, smells it" (Senghor 1964, 72, quoted in Mavhunga 2018, 18).

27 For analysis of scientific images in relation to the human, see van Dijck (2005); to posthumanism, Waldby (2000); or to radical humanism, Bailey (2016).

28 Internet saturation went from 6 percent of the population in 2013 to 84 percent in 2018. (Thanks to Maggie Jack, who presented these numbers in her oral paper at the 2019 AAS-in-Asia conference in Bangkok.) That digital and image technologies moved quickly into Cambodia is an understatement.

29 I thank one of the anonymous reviewers for emphasizing this point about anthropology of photography.

30 This is different from Deleuze's ([1968] 2001) project, in which "the image of thought" has to do with the nature and conditions of thought. My interest here is not in the nature of thought, nor in the relation of thought to morals or ethics.

1. FLICKERING HISTORIES

1 And GE was no stranger to Cold War Southeast Asia. In the late 1960s, a violent and turbulent time for the region, GE was operating in six Southeast Asian countries (US Embassy, Phnom Penh 2007).

2 Following Redfield and Bornstein (2010, 5–6), we can think of development as that which is oriented toward economic growth and poverty reduction and humanitarianism as "oriented towards the physical suffering of people in exceptional conditions of misfortune."

3 de Laet and Mol (2000) use the concept of a "fluid technology" to argue that for some technologies, in their case a water pump, the answer to the

question "Is the technology working?" cannot be answered with a yes or no. The answer depends on the capacities valued by particular users in particular contexts. For example, is the criterion volume of water, or cleanliness of water, or the ability for communities to maintain it?

4 I thank Claudia Castañeda for this image of the low flame, its potential for poisoning.

5 I use the term *biography* instead of *history* in imagination that the *bios* in *biography* (*bios* life + *graphia* writing) may refer to biological life, not narrowly to the life of a person. A biography of a hospital is the writing of life from the position of a hospital, an institution organized around the care of life.

6 On colonial medicine in Viet Nam, see Edington (2013); Monnais (2019); and Thompson (2003).

7 Le service de santé en Indochine 1945–1954, box 365, Archives de l'institut de médecine tropicale du service de santé des armées (AIMTSSA).

8 This is now called the Université des sciences de la santé, or the University of Health Sciences.

9 My Samedy, interview with author, 4 July 2011.

10 Anti-colonial struggles intensified in the 1940s and early 1950s in Madagascar, Algeria, and Cameroon. After defeat and departure from Indochina in 1954, France turned to Africa, where anti-colonial struggles grew into devastating wars of liberation. The majority of French colonies in Africa became independent in 1960, Algeria in 1962.

11 Grant Ross and Collins (2006) provide details on the design and construction process.

12 My, interview.

13 Remarks by Secretary of States at the Inauguration Ceremony of the Khmer-Soviet Friendship Hospital, 29 August, 1960, box 315, National Archives of Cambodia (hereafter cited as NAC) Collection of Cambodian Publications and Periodicals (hereafter cited as CPP).

14 Remarks by Secretary of States, 29 August 1960, box 315, NAC CPP.

15 Keo (2019, 1) follows Sophearith Siyonn's suggestion that the proper translation of Sangkum Reastr Niyum is "community favored by the people." For Sihanouk's unique merger of his persona with the Cambodian nation, see Chandler (1992, esp. 191–204) and Thompson (2004).

16 Slocomb's (2006) analysis of state publications of the 1960s illuminates how Sangkum policymakers rejected Marxism because of its universality; instead, they argued that Cambodia's socialism must be particular to Cambodian morality, tradition, and history.

17 See Grant (2018) for more on "friendship" and, later, "partnership."

18 See Skachkov (1960) for articulation of this policy; see Franke and Chasin (2005, 370) and Tsvetkova (n.d., 22) for analysis of non-capitalist development.

19 Sihanouk utilized the public face of neutrality to accept technical assistance and development aid from the United States ($350 million, from 1955–63), China ($25 million), France ($25 million, from 1955–62), the USSR ($15 million), and Japan ($4.28 million), as well as Czechoslovakia, Poland, and Yugoslavia (Guillou 2001, 109–11; see also Grant Ross and Collins 2006).

20 The Sangkum period saw a flourishing of cultural production, particularly in the domains of dance, music, film, art, architecture, literature, education, public works, and media, in addition to medicine (see Grant Ross and Collins 2006; Ly and Muan 2001).

21 "Ce que représente l'Hôpital de l'Amitié Khméro-Soviétique," *Cambodge d'Aujourd'hui*, August 1960, 35.

22 Remarks by Secretary of States, 29 August 1960, box 315, NAC CPP, 6, 9, 14–15.

23 "L'Hôpital de l'Amitié Khméro-Soviétique," *Cambodge d'Aujourd'hui*, August 1960, 30–40. The radiology piece appears on page 37. The 1960 Soviet film *Making a Gift to the People of Cambodia* depicts the packing and transport of the radiotherapy machine by ship from Odessa to Phnom Penh (Net-film.ru n.d.).

24 My, interview.

25 Training and professionalization were subject to postcolonial tensions with the metropole and to government manipulation. Sihanouk did not support French recognition of the Cambodian degree in medicine. Guillou (2009) suggests this was in order to prevent young graduates from emigrating, and because student groups abroad, particularly in Paris, were hotbeds of opposition to the Sangkum.

26 In the first decade of the 2000s, the relative political stability and relative bounty of work, services, and leisure for the urban middle class prompted some to liken that time to the Sangkum period.

27 Santé publique au Cambodge, 1962 and 1964, box 284, NAC CPP.

28 *Tossnavddey nei samakom bokkolik sokhaphibal phsay chenh roal* [Magazine of the Association for Health Workers], box 288, NAC CPP. The NAC has one publication from 1968 and one from 1969.

29 *Bulletin de la Société Royale de Médecine du Cambodge*, 1965, box 284, NAC CPP.

30 See Keo (2019) and Eat (2021) on the "modern woman" of the Sangkum.

31 *La femme Cambodgienne à l'heure du Sangkum*, 1960, NSI_VI_001568, Bophana Center.

32 Actualités no. 58, Sangkum, n.d., DDC_VI_001282, Bophana Center.

33 For studies of post-Independence medicine in Africa, see Chiffoleau (1997); Iliffe (1998); Geissler et al. (2017); Mika (2016); Prince (2013); and Tousignant (2018). For Southeast Asia and the Pacific, see Anderson and Pols (2012); Aso (2017); Aso and Guénel (2013); Neelakantan (2017); Street (2014a); and Sweet (2017).

34 Boxes 279, 281, 282, 283, and 287, NAC CPP.

35 In her work on disappearance as practice of the state, Gordon ([1997] 2008) is careful to situate her conceptualization of haunting as companion to the significant empirical work of journalists, lawyers, and human rights workers who document imprisonment and torture. If anything, the global blooming in the 2010s of government denials of violence, inequality, and environmental damage has provoked an insurgent empiricism, a creative reengagement with facts and digital archive structures (see the Drug Archive [https://drugarchive.ph], which examines Duterte's anti-drug campaign in the Philippines, and the Guerilla Archiving Project, which archives climate science data under threat from conservative governments of Canada and the United States).

36 For Khmer Republic newsreels depicting blood donation and military medicine, see newsreel no. 23, 1970, DDC_VI_001299; newsreel no. 55, 1970–1975 (n.d.), DDC_VI_001285; newsreel no. 58, 1971, DDC_VI_001308; newsreel no. 70, 1970–1975 (n.d.), DDC_VI_001281; newsreel no. 96 and no. 94, 1970–1975 (n.d.), DDC_VI_ 001290; all from Bophana Center.

37 Rethy Chhem, conversation with author, 15 May 2017.

38 After the Khmer Rouge, many people also tried to return to their home province, settle in a new province, or attempt the perilous crossing over the Thai border to reach the refugee camps. Most of the people in the camps would be repatriated in the early 1990s, another mass movement of people. Some refugees would settle in third countries.

39 Rethy, conversation.

40 *Scientific System of Instruction under the Khmer Rouge*, n.d., DDC_VI_001358, Bophana Center.

41 *The Visit of the Khmer Rouge in a Village*, n.d., DDC_VI_001735, Bophana Center. Guillou (2004) states that there was small-scale production of serum, penicillin, and vaccines in Phnom Penh during Democratic Kampuchea.

42 See also Panh (2012, 2013), in which he depicts his experience working in a Khmer Rouge hospital.

43 See Grant (2020) for analysis of My's repair of an X-ray machine for a Khmer Rouge clinic and its significance for theorizations of repair as a radical intervention in STS.

44 *The Role of Women in the Reconstruction of the Country*, n.d., DDC_VI_001738, Bophana Center.

45 *One Year After the Liberation*, 1980, DDC_VI_001296, Bophana Center.

46 *2nd General Assembly of the National Liberation Front*, n.d., DDC_ VI_001776, Bophana Center.

47 My, interview.

48 My, interview. One of Ovesen and Trankell's (2010, 97) informants said there were forty surviving doctors reunited in 1979 to organize the medical system.

49 *Rebirth of Kampuchea*, 1985, DDC_VI_001265, Bophana Center.

50 Hean Sokhom, personal communication with author, 2009.

51 Dr. Chhum, conversation with author, 16 December 2008.

52 Though four key actors (the State of Cambodia, the Khmer Rouge, the royalist party FUNCINPEC, and the KPNLF opposition faction) agreed to a ceasefire in 1990, instability and violence continued until 1998.

53 1989 per OW, interview with author, 15 October 2009; 1993 per VV, interview with author, 10 July 2009.

54 Lim, conversation with author, 16 November 2011.

55 In Khmer, indeed in Southeast Asia, many scientific, philosophical, or technical words derive from Sanskrit or Pali. The language politics of Pali and Sanskrit are explored by McDaniel (2008, 138) in Thailand and Thompson (2016) in Middle Period Cambodia.

56 See Pfeiffer and Chapman (2010) on structural adjustment and health care.

57 The authors continue: "However, the true value of these donations to recipients in developing countries might be less than the value that was recorded on US tax returns" (Ravishankar et al. 2009, 2121). This discrepancy is not explained further. Perhaps it is a case of "the cunning of data" (Lea and Torzillo 2016), in which the value of a particular item in the "donation" column depends on the document in which it appears. A US tax return, or a Cambodian Ministry of Health budget?

58 AusAID (Australia, now Australian Aid), DFID (UK, now Foreign, Commonwealth & Development Office or FCDO), Brunei, CIDA (Canada, now Global Affairs Canada, or GAC), China, Cuba, European Union, France, GTZ (Germany, now GIZ), India, Indonesia, JICA (Japan), KOICA (South Korea), North Korea, Malaysia, Lao PDR, Myanmar, Singapore, Sweden, Thailand, United States, and Viet Nam. Ministry of Health, Cambodia, http://moh.gov.kh, accessed 24 July 2012. That Australian, Canadian, and European development programs closed, merged, or were absorbed by general foreign affairs departments in the 2010s marks the diminished mood for development after the 2008 financial crisis.

59 ADB (Asian Development Bank), UNAIDS, UNFPA, UNICEF, UNDP, World Bank, and WHO. Ministry of Health, Cambodia, http://moh.gov.kh,

accessed 24 July 2012. See the 2018 special issue of *Medicine Anthropology Theory* for analyses of global health partnerships.

60 As of 2021, the ten ASEAN member states are Brunei Darussalam, Cambodia, Indonesia, Lao PDR, Malaysia, Myanmar, Philippines, Singapore, Thailand, and Viet Nam.

61 University of Toronto, Canada; Institute of Tropical Medicine, Antwerp, Belgium; and University of New South Wales, Sydney, Australia.

62 See Praspaliauskiene (2016) on postsocialist transparency practices in Lithuanian hospitals.

63 On laboratory work in hospitals, see Carsten (2019); Okeke (2011); and Street (2014a).

64 Leopard Capital opened its Cambodia fund in 2008.

65 Benny Widyono, conversation with author, 2 January 2010.

66 I first encountered this phrase in a talk by Heidi Dahles at SEA Update, 22 June 2012, Radboud University, Nijmegen, the Netherlands.

67 Franklin Huffman's observations in a State Department debriefing interview are interesting, if essentialist: "The State Department has never given credence to the excuse of 'Asian values' by dictators such as Lee Kuan Yew in Singapore to justify authoritarian rule, but in fact authoritarianism and patronage are seen as the proper way to run a government, not only in Cambodia but in Asia in general. The problem for US diplomacy in touting Western-style democracy is that in Asia, harmony between the peasants and the power elite (who are after all powerful because of good deeds in past lives) is more important than the right of individuals to challenge the power structure; in fact, to do so is considered somewhat improper in Asian cultures." Huffman was public affairs officer in Cambodia in the 1990s and again in 2002 and wrote the Khmer-English dictionary that was used in my Khmer classes. See Huffman's 2006 interview with Charles Stuart Kennedy, published in the Association for Diplomatic Studies and Training (n.d.), *Cambodia Reader*.

68 Why resource extraction and labor exploitation, and the "special economic zones" that enable them, are not considered "strings attached" indicates the boundaries of the comfortable within Hun Sen's political ideology. Free press chafes but unfree labor does not.

69 See Rasmei Kampuchea (2009b). Hun Sen's comparison of Western conditions to Vietnamese conditions addressed two audiences simultaneously. For Cambodian audiences: those with concerns about Viet Nam violating Cambodia's sovereignty, those who call Hun Sen a "Vietnamese puppet," should refocus on the real threat, the West. For Western audiences: Viet Nam's violation of Cambodia's sovereignty was justification for a decade of crippling international isolation in 1980s, but more severe violations of sovereignty perpetrated by development agents today

are fine? Your imperialist hypocrisy is patent. Hun Sen's words around the 2009 donor meeting came a few years prior to the full-on mobilization of the Cambodian People's Party, following their near win, or many would say, near loss, in the 2013 elections. The government has since enacted laws that intimidate or force closure of key civil institutions. The 2015 Law on Associations and Non-Governmental Organizations (NGO Law) requires domestic and foreign NGOs to register with the government and report on their activities and finances quarterly. The government may disband organizations for activities that jeopardize public order or harm Cambodian culture and tradition (Johnson 2015). Vocal members of environment, land, and labor rights groups have been threatened, exiled, and in some cases assassinated. In 2017, the Supreme Court outlawed the main opposition party for "fostering dissent with the help of foreign countries" (Al Jazeera 2017), an act many inside and outside the country saw as the end of multi-party democracy. Leaders have been imprisoned, forced into exile, and, in some cases, murdered. Also in 2017, the government pressured the English and Khmer language paper the *Cambodia Daily* to close as a result of a tax charge (Cambodia Daily 2018). The other English and Khmer daily, the *Phnom Penh Post*, was bought by a Malaysian public relations firm with ties to Hun Sen (BBC 2018). The COVID-19 pandemic was the justification for State of Emergency laws that extend the powers of the prime minister and allow the government to conduct widespread surveillance and assume total control of media (Aun, Narin, and Vicheika 2020; Human Rights Watch 2021). In sum, the ambivalence toward democratization that characterized the 1990s and 2000s is gone. Cambodia is now, legally and practically, a one-party authoritarian state.

70 See Schwenkel (2013) for analysis of postsocialism in Viet Nam as a disenchantment with socialist optimism and hopes for solidarity.

2. MOTHER AND CHILD

1 The date was 17 June 2010.
2 Metronidazole is an antibiotic used to treat conditions caused by certain bacteria and parasites. In this context, it may have been intended to treat *Trichomonas vaginalis*, a vaginal parasite.
3 Roberts (2012, 98) describes similar promotional activities at a private clinic in Quito; in that case, it was a raffle, and the prize was a free in-vitro fertilization cycle. Both the Phnom Penh and Quito scenes convey the entanglement of medicine and commerce. The appeal is getting something for free that is not usually free.
4 Names in this chapter are pseudonyms unless stated otherwise.

5 Nam (2011, 2017a) argues that upward expansion in Phnom Penh, the vertical trend of building high-rise condominiums and offices in a city known for its low-rise French colonial charm, derives from the desire to build the future on a distinctly Asian model—Seoul, Bangkok, Ho Chi Minh City—using primarily Asian circuits of capital, investment, and design. Over six hundred high-rises (greater than five stories) were built in Phnom Penh between 2006 and 2016 (Nam 2017a; citing Kang 2016).

6 Conversation on 2 September 2010.

7 In his stories about doctoring in the early 1970s, Haing Ngor deplores proscriptions for female modesty for their effects on health. According to Ngor (1988), women knew little about their anatomy; women were disinclined to be physically examined by male doctors (and sometimes, their male partners prohibited it); the common practice of showering wearing a *krama* (cloth) made it difficult to thoroughly clean the vagina.

8 I thank Rima Praspaliauskiene for conversations about postsocialist health care in Lithuania and Cambodia, which were generative for my thinking here.

9 Prenatal ultrasound is the subject of chapter 5. See Gammeltoft (2014) and Gammeltoft and Nguyen (2007) on prenatal ultrasound in market reform Viet Nam; see Taylor (2008) on ultrasound's role in the commercialization of pregnancy in the United States.

10 Interview with author, 27 September 2010.

11 See Davis's (2008) beautifully titled essay, "Imaginary Conversations with Mothers about Death," which explores linguistic and symbolic uses of the mother. *Me*, "mother," is a prefix in titles of prestige and relative status in Cambodian hierarchy, such as *mephoum*, the village chief, and even *mechao*, the master thief. In folktales, killing off the mother is a path to success. "The hero with a dead mother appears as a fantasy of authentic power, unburdened by dependence or debts, by social dependence and hierarchy" (Davis 2008, 230).

12 Dr. My Samedy's (2000) memoir, *Survivor for the Surviving*, details this reconstruction period, both in the country and abroad as he traveled with the Red Cross to request aid.

13 Quoted in Slocomb (2006, 390).

14 In 1994, the National Assembly passed the Law on Investment, which opened up all sectors of the economy, including state-owned enterprises, to private initiatives (Nam 2017b, 655).

15 Desired outcomes include "Enhanced trust in public health services" and "Spending from the private/informal sector redirected to the public health sector." The means to achieve these objectives include "Develop financial incentives for rational health seeking behaviors (e.g., maternity grants)"; "Implement financial incentives for delivery of client-oriented services at public health facilities"; and "Support community

participation in local decision making and policies that will affect their access to health services, and in monitoring and evaluation of demand-side financing schemes" (Ministry of Health 2008, 11).

16 Cambodia is rarely included in postsocialism literatures, but it should be. Indeed, the World Bank and WHO categorize Cambodia as a transition economy (in Asia, along with China, Lao PDR, Mongolia, and Viet Nam; see WHO—Regional Office for the Western Pacific 2018).

17 See debates on user fees and equity funds in Cambodia within health policy and economics literatures, e.g., Bigdeli and Annear (2009); Brikci and Philips (2007); Meessen et al. (2006); and Van Leemput et al. (2007). Authors from Médecins Sans Frontières put it pragmatically: "From an implementation perspective, the question is how large the proportion of people unable to afford the existing fees should be before it becomes more sensible to abolish fees for all" (Van Leemput et al. 2007, 638).

18 In 2016, the government introduced a health insurance scheme as part of its National Social Security Fund. Formal sector workers and their employers are required to contribute to the scheme, which covers inpatient, outpatient, pre- and postnatal, and other care. As of 2018, employers are responsible for the entire contribution, equivalent to 2.6 percent of a worker's gross annual wage (Ministry of Labor and Vocational Training 2017). The goal of the Ministry of Health and the Ministry of Labor is to provide universal health care by 2025. Inpatient and outpatient imaging services are covered under the scheme that people refer to as the BSS, which are the social security fund's initials in Khmer. Those with a BSS card receive services at participating health facilities, which include most health facilities in the country, at a reduced cost. This may mean a shared room as opposed to a private room and, for some, different quality of care. In other words, it continues a two-tier system. Prior to the 2018 election, the CPP government encouraged those with a BSS card to use the autonomous government hospitals and receive the same quality of services as those paying out of pocket for "VIP" services. A colleague whose father was ill at the time said that the crowds at Calmette Hospital were unbearable. She was there for more than twelve hours to get imaging and lab work.

19 In 2015, government health expenditure as a share of GDP was 1.5 percent; out-of-pocket expenditure was 62 percent of health expenditure (WHO—Regional Office for the Western Pacific 2016, 19).

20 Data from the Ministry of Health (2012) and the Organizational Chart on its website, http://moh.gov.kh, accessed 22 April 2013.

21 They are Calmette, Preah Kossamak, Khmer-Soviet Friendship Hospital (Russian Hospital), Ang Duong, National Pediatric Hospital, Kantha Bopha, Norodom Sihanouk Hospital, and Phnom Penh Municipal Referral Hospital.

22 Figures are from the World Bank (2011, 41). These numbers are lower than the number of private clinics in operation. It has always been difficult to account for the totality of the private sector. At the time of research, there were three large private hospitals in the country: Royal Rattanak and Sen Sok in Phnom Penh and Royal Angkor in Siem Reap, Cambodia's primary tourist destination. Sen Sok was associated with International University, the private university and Cambodia's second medical school. Rattanak and Royal Angkor were run by the same Thai company.

23 Interview with author, 27 September 2010.

24 Cambodians, even those with modest means, travel outside of the country for medical care, most commonly to neighboring Viet Nam and Thailand but also to Singapore and Malaysia. The autonomy movement is sometimes articulated as a strategy to improve accountability and quality in health care so that people will pay for services in Cambodia rather than go abroad (see also Ros 2009).

25 The autumn moon festival is a traditional Chinese holiday celebrated across Asia and in Asian diaspora. It originated as a festival of gratitude after harvest. In Cambodia, it includes exchanging small gifts, eating moon cakes, and carrying lanterns.

26 See Bourdier (2016) for analysis of neoliberal reform in the case of malaria control policy. See Prince (2013) for resonance with public health "reform" in Africa.

27 "Liberalization" of the economy redirected resources and responsibility for the public good to nongovernment entities, such as NGOs, corporations, and international bodies in Africa too. See Eaton (2006); Ombongi (2011); and Rottenburg (2009).

28 *Asian Biotech* (Ong and Chen 2010) explores biotechnology endeavors across Asia.

29 The date was 22 September 2009.

30 As Rao (2014, 19) notes, "speculation's classical Latin roots, *specere* and *speculari*, suggest that looking, observing, and anticipating are the active components of the act of speculating." *Speculum*, mirror, is its other root. It would be interesting to consider further the visuality of speculation: How central are imagination, production, and circulation of images to speculative practices?

31 The billboard also illustrates the indexical relationship between English language and good health care.

32 For example, Kimsay and Retka (2016): "Private Clinic Shuttered after Man's Death."

33 Though the 2007 Civil Code of Cambodia stated that interest rates should be 5 percent per year, there is no cap on interest rates charged by microfinance institutions and unregistered money lenders,

and interest rates may range from 24 percent to 60 percent (SAC/D 2016).

34 CPA categorization is based on WHO guidelines concerning the range of services and trained staff at a given site. In Cambodia, CPA 3 are generally national or provincial hospitals, also called referral hospitals; CPA 2 are district hospitals that have surgical services; and CPA 1 are also district hospitals that do not have surgical but do have maternity services.

35 The development partner varies depending on the item. For example, WHO was the main partner of the Ministry of Health, JICA was the key advisor for medical equipment management and for developing guidelines, UNICEF supplied vaccines, and the World Bank also gave money for materials.

36 See Hall, Massey, and Rustin (2013) on common sense in neoliberalism; see Mol (2008) for this specifically in terms of how neoliberalism and logics of choice operate in health care.

37 For example, see Mouffe (2005); Rancière (1999); and Žižek (2008).

38 The scene is changing markedly. Leaders in Southeast Asia have brushed aside democracy discourse and practice, either through military force, as in Thailand and Myanmar; election, as in the Philippines; or a combination of force, law, and pseudo-election, as in Cambodia.

39 Bourdier, Man, and Res (2014) have traced circulations of antimalarials, showing how they are siphoned out of public health centers, causing stockouts, and sold in the private sector. For Cambodians, voicing criticism of this elite theft can put their jobs, and even their families, at risk.

3. OVER-CARE AND UNDER-CARE

1 Portable and handheld ultrasound, some of which connect to a mobile phone, were not available when I was doing my research but are now a global business that involves established companies such as Philips, GE, and Mindray and startups such as Butterfly and Clarius. "Experts compare this development to the advent of tablets or smartphones in the computing world" (Schmitt 2019). Butterfly, one of the brands of portable ultrasound scanners that work with a phone, declares its mission "is to democratize medical imaging and contribute to the aspiration of global health equity" (www.butterflynetwork.com).

2 The focus of this book is on cosmopolitan medicine, but it is important to state that ultrasound services are situated within a health care field that involves a diversity of practitioners and practices. Langwick (2008, 427) observes that the category "traditional medicine" emerged with the spread of colonial medicine to refer to all that is not "modern" medicine,

or biomedicine: "It ['traditional medicine'] has served as a catchall category indexing forms of healing, kinds of affliction, and types of experts that were not officially included in missionary or colonial health care." In Cambodia, there is heterogeneity beneath the misleadingly uniform label "traditional medicine." I only deal with Buddhist healing here, and in a limited way (in chapter 4), but key actors in the health care scene are nurses, midwives, and doctors; *krou khmae* (traditional healers); healing monks; spirit mediums; "neo-traditional" and "official (*fonctionnaire*) *krou*" (Guillou 2009); herbalists; and *krou thmup*, or "sorcerers" (Ovesen and Trankell 2010). In Cambodia, people go to pharmacists and medicine-sellers in the markets for health problems as well as masseuses, who use techniques such as coining (*kah khyal*), cupping, and massage of muscles and nerves (Guillou 2009; Ovesen and Trankell 2010). There has been no sustained promotion or regulation of "traditional" medicine by the state, except for a brief and disingenuous embrace during the Khmer Rouge (Guillou 2004).

3 MSF stands for Médecins Sans Frontières (Doctors Without Borders), the international humanitarian medical organization.

4 At Russian Hospital, ultrasound reports were Microsoft Word documents. A doctor or nurse typed the exam report over the report of the previous patient. Information fields such as name, age, and scan details were highlighted, deleted, and then filled in with data for the next patient.

5 See Howes-Mischel (2016) on hearing the heartbeat and the social presence of the fetus. I could find little else written about the richness and complexity of "hearing the baby," unfortunately. See Harris (2016) on listening and sound in medical practice.

6 Field notes, 2 September 2010.

7 There is no commonly used equivalent Khmer term for "fetus." *Tearok*, infant; *kaun*, child, a relative term (i.e., a child of someone, child in relation to someone, person under control or subordinate to someone else); *kmeng*, child, young person, to be young. See http://sealang.net /khmer/.

8 For other accounts of care in Thailand, see Funahashi (2016) on moral governance; Seo (2017) on circuits of infrastructure; and Stonington (2012) on ethical location.

9 Field notes, 4 October 2010.

10 Interview with author, 9 November 2010.

11 See Taylor (2008); Gammeltoft and Nguyen (2007a); and Bashour, Hafez, and Abdulsalam (2005).

12 Low salaries have been the object of reform in the education sector.

13 Rima Praspaliauskiene, conversation with author, 29–30 June 2018.

14 This was on 20 September 2010.

15 Davis (2013) situates garment workers, Cambodia's first mass waged labor force, within a broader sketch of accumulation by dispossession. According to the ILO (2018), based on data from 2016, 80 percent of garment workers are women, 80 percent are under thirty-five years old, and 90 percent are literate. Women earn 13 percent less than men. Garment manufacturing has been a significant part of the export economy for the past decade—77 percent of exports in 2013, 75 percent in 2018—the majority to the European Union and the United States.

16 In their study of women's perspectives of giving birth in rural public and private facilities, Ith et al. (2013) found that women attributed the disrespect and rudeness they experienced from midwives to bias against the poor and low educated.

17 There is a correlation between fetal size and malnourishment, though fetuses can be small for reasons other than maternal malnourishment, and maternal malnourishment does not necessarily mean a small fetus. In children, malnourishment is commonly measured through the indicators "stunting" (falling two standard deviations or more below the median height-for-age of the reference population) and "wasting" (falling two standard deviations or more below the median weight-for-height of the reference population). According to the United Nations Development Program, 39.5 percent of the Cambodian population under five experience stunting, and 28.8 percent experience wasting. Despite progress on other Millennium Development Goals, these two indicators remain stubbornly and worryingly low. For comparison, the figures for neighboring countries are the following: Lao PDR, 47.6 percent and 31.6 percent; Viet Nam 30.5 percent and 20.2 percent; Thailand 15.7 percent and 7 percent; and Singapore 4.4 percent and 3.3 percent (Klugman 2011, 150–53).

18 Chan Dara, conversation with author, 16 December 2008.

19 How technology shifts authority and control over women's bodies is a central concern in feminist scholarship on prenatal ultrasound and the medicalization of pregnancy. For perspectives from history, gender studies, and anthropology, see Davis-Floyd, Sargent, and Rapp (1997); Duden (1993); Jordan (1997); Mitchell (2001); Morgan (2000); Saetnan, Oudshoorn, and Kirejczyk (2000); and Taylor (2008).

20 Conversation with author, 18 March 2009.

4. ULTRASOUND IS AN EYE FOR SEEING

1 Conversation with author, August 2010.

2 See also Castañeda (2001, 227) on how vision and touch are rematerialized in AI projects.

3 SEAlang Library Khmer Dictionary (www.sealang.net/khmer/) is composed of a corpus of two different editions of the *Cambodian-English*

Dictionary (1977, 1997) and the definitive *Khmer Dictionary* (1966) by Chuon Nath.

4 Siti Keo, personal communication with author, 13 March 2011.

5 Emiko Stock, personal communication with author, 27 October 2009.

6 Trent Walker, personal communication with author, 10 July 2012.

7 Eve Zucker, personal communication with author, 28 September 2010.

8 This was on 20 September 2010.

9 Sambath (and I) did not have a smartphone with a camera. Nine years later, tuk-tuk drivers use phones to pick up passengers, listen to music, video chat while driving, not to mention, of course, take pictures.

10 Training fees and machine sales covered most of UDC's operating costs, though they received donations—for example, one foreign organization donated 1,000 Euros—and Dr. Uch asked me to help prepare a grant proposal to support the clinic. UDC also received periodic donations of medicine and eyeglasses that Dr. Uch distributed to patients for free.

11 AusAID ceased to be an independent agency in 2013 and was integrated into the Department of Foreign Affairs and Trade. PSI began a condom use program in Cambodia in 1993 and has since expanded to other health programs. Mith Samlanh, founded in Phnom Penh in 1994, is an NGO that works with marginalized youth and their families. Khana, originally a project of the International HIV/AIDS Alliance but independent since 1997, is an NGO that provides integrated HIV prevention, care, and support. Nyemo, founded in 1998, is an NGO focused on economic and social reintegration of vulnerable women and children.

12 There are now twenty-five provinces in Cambodia. The government created Tboung Khmum on 31 December 2013.

13 Conversation with author, 11 September 2010.

14 Changes in digital imaging and picture archiving and communication systems (PACS) enable another form of distributed seeing. Radiologists learn to see with others, remotely. Dr. Vesselle, a radiologist at the University of Washington, ran a regular Tuesday Skype session with radiology residents in Phnom Penh. Together they discussed cases, looked at images, and talked through diagnoses. The sociality of diagnostic labor, about which Saunders (2008) writes in *CT Suite*, is partially achieved online for these residents. The spatial distribution of imaging labor enabled by PACS systems, in which a radiologist or a technologist takes the image and a different radiologist reads it, is indeed a global phenomenon that is configuring new spaces and practices of medical training and care. See, for example, Duclos (2015) on how the Pan-African e-Network divides diagnostic labor between health centers in Africa and tertiary hospitals in India.

15 Toshiba Medical Systems Corporation, marketing brochure for Nemio XG Premium Compact Ultrasound, 2006–8; Shenzhen Mindray

Bio-Medical Electronics Co., Ltd., marketing brochure for Mindray DC-3 Diagnostic Ultrasound System, 2008; and Shenzhen Mindray Bio-Medical Electronics Co., Ltd., marketing brochure for Mindray DC-6 Expert Diagnostic Ultrasound System, 2008.

16 Mindray DC-6 Expert brochure, page 2.

17 In Toshiba's words, "3D/4D Imaging creates volumes and surface renderings of structures such as the fetal face" (Nemio brochure, page 7).

18 This resonates with the practices of herbalists and evangelical healers in Chile, described by Cristóbal Bonelli (2015), who see inside the body through noticing gesture, for example, as a key to the heart.

19 Loak Suon used the common terms for monk, *loak song* and *preah song*, and included himself in this category despite having recently retired.

20 Dark red as in *poar chheam chrouk*, the color of pig's blood.

21 Bertrand (2004, 161) continues: "The word of the Buddha is used for protection against evil spells (*ampoe*). Buddhist morality or psychology is employed in particular in order to give counsel to persons suffering from troubles that we would call depressive."

22 The therapeutic practices Suon described are standard ones. See de Bernon (1998) and Ovesen and Trankell (2010, 159–64).

23 Pre-assembled gift baskets for monks may contain a tin of sweetened condensed milk, salt, soda, water, candles, ramen, fruit, sometimes toiletries.

24 A monk's building projects make merit while also demonstrating that "he already has a font of merit that empowers him" (Marston 2008, 187).

25 See Dhamma Aid (2010).

26 Because of their religious legitimacy, healing monks have wider networks, including connections to officials, and higher social status than *krou* (Guillou 2009, 156–57).

27 Kampuchea Krom ("lower Cambodia") is the Mekong Delta region that was part of the Khmer empire and is currently a part of Viet Nam. It has long been subject and symbol of debate—geopolitical, religious, nationalist, and ethnic. It was "arbitrarily included" as part of French Cochinchina in 1873 (Edwards 2007, 188). After the Vietnamese ousted the Khmer Rouge in 1979, the PRK brought monks from Kampuchea Krom to reestablish Buddhism, albeit in restricted form (Ledgerwood 2008, 205). To some, notably politician Sam Rainsy and his followers, Kampuchea Krom is a symbol of the present government's submission to Vietnamese imperialism and its persecution of ethnic Khmers, especially monks, and is a rallying cry for ethno-nationalist aspirations. Perhaps more generally, Kampuchea Krom represents lost territory and troubled minoritarian politics. And clever monks.

28 "The Buddha is a source of power transferred to his relics, the consecrated images or statues as well as the Buddhist holy texts, and the Pali

chants that are used in rituals, with some appropriated to deal with supernatural beings. This same sacred language is inscribed on the square pieces of cloth called yantra (pronounced 'yuan') and the magical plaques distributed as amulets of protection" (Bertrand 2004, 161). Monks chanting *keatha*, verses, imbues the plaques with protective power. Coderey (2019, 321) notes that laypeople stress the importance of attentive listening, which is aided by knowledge of the purpose of the chant and the monk's skill in chanting—the sound of his voice, taking correct pauses, using correct rhythm and tone: "The power of recitation comes from the nature and origin of the text itself as well as from the way in which it is recited by the monks and approached by the audience."

29 *Cham* is a multivalent term. For some it is synonymous with "Muslim," but for others it is a stateless ethnic group tracing their origins to the ancient kingdom of Champa, which spanned parts of present-day Viet Nam, Laos, and Cambodia between the seventh and fifteenth centuries. For an overview of Muslim communities in Cambodia and Southeast Asia, see Stock (2010). For a short essay on the cultural politics of a contemporary Cham identity movement, see Pérez-Pereiro (2014).

30 Conversation with author, 22 May 2009. He said, "Oh! So many children! It's not good . . . there's no money."

31 On impermanence as everyday philosophy, see Cassaniti (2015); on impermanence and practices of making and relating to images, see Fuhrmann (2016) and Klima (2002).

32 This was on 15 October 2010.

33 Schantz (2015, 53) argues that the question asked by the consciousness of a previous life to a pregnant woman—"Mother, can I live in your womb?"—constitutes the social recognition of the fetus. In Bruno's (1989) film *Samsara*, which follows returnees after the defeat of the Khmer Rouge, there is a similar story to Saroun's of untimely death, dream, and rebirth. A woman's dead brother visits her in a dream and asks to be reborn into the family. The next child born in the family resembles this brother.

5. PORTRAIT AND SCAN

1 The optimal time to get care at public hospitals is in the morning, between 7 a.m. and noon. It is more difficult to get services in the afternoon, when most staff are at other jobs, typically in private practice.

2 Gammeltoft (2014), working in Hanoi, found an average of nine per pregnancy, but some of the middle- and working-class women she talked to got upwards of fifteen.

3 Conversation with author, 13 September 2010.

4 Bashour, Hafez, and Abdulsalam (2005), Mitchell (2001), and Taylor (2008) describe how pregnant women may use ultrasound exams and images to involve a partner or other family members in pregnancy and invest in the coming child.

5 Whereas doctors often have to deal with patient expectations they cannot fulfill, prenatal ultrasound's multiplicity of genre muddles what some patients expect the doctor is able to see. On one of the evenings I joined him at his second job at the private clinic Sorphea VIP, Dr. Sophal described a tricky case, when a female patient, a wealthy elite, came for a prenatal scan and asked him, "What color is the baby's skin?" Dr. Sophal did not want to disappoint or displease this particular patient, but he had to tell her that ultrasound cannot show skin color. The cultural politics of skin color in Cambodia are complex, involving changing ideologies of beauty, status, purity, labor, and foreignness. People value light skin—the skin-whitening industry thrives, despite media stories about serious harms from whitening creams—though the rhetoric of the Khmer Rouge valued dark skin as the color of the true Khmer, the peasant who worked outside.

6 See also Street (2014a) on these comparative evaluations of medicine.

7 Berlin and Kay (1969) proposed that there is a limited stable of basic color terms. The most elemental are black and white. Ethnolinguistic groups add additional terms in a predictable pattern. Berlin and Kay claim that all natural languages have between two and eleven basic color terms. English has eleven. The progression looks like this: "If a language has two terms, they are black and white. If three: black, white, and red. Four: black, white, red, and green or yellow. Five: black, white, red, and green and yellow." And so on, adding blue, then brown, and then purple, pink, orange, and gray in no consistent hierarchy.

8 Their approach resonates with that of Sahlins (1976, 11–12): color terms (and perceptions) differentiate social categories; they do not just correspond to natural differences in the world.

9 Taussig (2009) cautions that color in clothing is its own special field, a projection of the subject's subjectivity. Certainly, subjectivity had to be redone by *Angkar*, the subject de-individuated. About 1975, Rithy Panh (2012, 23) writes, "The history of my childhood is abolished. Forbidden. From that day on, I, Rithy Panh, thirteen years old, have no more history, no more emotions, no more thoughts, no more unconscious. Was there a name? Was there an individual? There's nothing anymore."

10 "*La femme est plus que femme, mais pas encore pleinement mère*" (Ang 1982, 90).

11 See Casper (1994); Gammeltoft (2014); Georges (1996); Nishizaka (2011); and Taylor (2008). In this scholarship, the ways of doing subjectivity are

diverse across cultures and contexts rather than within, let alone within a single imaging practice.

12 By *iconophobia* I mean a suspicion of the image that is too pretty, too pictorial (Beaulieu 2002), "too imagistic for its own good" (Galt 2011, 4).

13 Ultrasound uses non-ionizing radiation, which does not have the same safety risk as X-ray, for example, but does produce bioeffects. Ultrasound heats tissue, and hyperthermia is teratogenic in pregnancy. WHO (2016) recommends one scan per pregnancy, before twenty-four weeks gestation, and the US FDA (2014) discourages non-medical use. Acoustic exposure is comparable in 2D and 3D/4D ultrasound (Sheiner et al. 2007); however, scanning time in 3D/4D may increase, which can lead to an increase in exposure.

14 Conversation with author, 20 September 2010.

15 Barad (2007, 220) writes that 3D prenatal ultrasound images "seduce the viewer into thinking that the representation of the object is isomorphic with the object itself; the image seems to be just like what we would see with our own eyes, but even better (if only our visual faculties had a zoom feature, the ability to rotate images without physically moving around an object, and the ability to slice away with a virtual scalpel any opaque section of the object that is obstructing our view!)."

16 See Yates-Doerr (2015) on fatness as good, as richness, in contrast to obesity.

17 Calmette Hospital is an autonomous (semi-private) teaching hospital, which has the largest and most well-regarded maternity center of the public hospitals in Phnom Penh. Schantz et al. (2016, 112) report that there were 11,080 deliveries at Calmette in 2015, and the cost for an overnight stay ranged from US$10 to US$250, depending on the kind of room. For all patients, a vaginal birth cost US$60 and a C-section US$278.

18 Art historian Barbara Stafford (1991, 311) describes active debates in eighteenth-century European painting and philosophy concerning the nature and mechanism of "action at a distance." A pregnant woman looking at an image, person, or scene experiences mental states that can affect the developing fetus. Taylor (2008, 103) notes links between these ideas of "maternal impressions" and contemporary US discourse on "bonding." Both assume that visual images powerfully influence the maternal imagination and therefore offer a means of intervention. The problem is that the well-being of fetuses calls for surveillance of thoughts, emotions, and actions of pregnant women. The backdrops are quite different: for Taylor, the politics of life and abortion in the United States; for Stafford, philosophers and doctors were working through the implications of mind-body dualism for conception.

19 There is resonance with Dorrestijn's (2012, 239) proposal for an ethics of technology, elaborated through Foucault's aesthetics of existence, as "a will to give style to the way one is transformed through engagement with new technologies."

20 Conversations with Leslie Grant were, as always, so thought provoking.

21 The 2018 exhibit *Double Exposure: Edward S. Curtis, Marianne Nicolson, Tracy Rector, Will Wilson* at the Seattle Art Museum, part of a year-long reappraisal of Curtis by more than twenty organizations in the Pacific Northwest, was interesting in regard to the politics of fixing people "on the verge of disappearance." Hanging Curtis's portraits adjacent to work by Nicolson, Rector, and Wilson (Diné) was provocative, intentionally so. This was the caption for Curtis's *Lummi Type* (1912): "Following anthropological practices that categorized groups of people by their physical traits, he [Curtis] sometimes took frontal and profile views and labeled the sitters as 'types.' Applying a fixed set of definitions to a culture can foster stereotypes that are long lived." And this was the caption for *We Are Still Here* by Asia Tail (Cherokee): "We are still here. Against all odds and despite attempted genocide, Native peoples not only have survived but continue to thrive in the present . . . Let's use this moment, 150 years after Curtis's birth, as a turning point." Tail's call must be answered again and again and again.

References

Abraham, Itty. 2006. "The Contradictory Spaces of Postcolonial Techno-Science." *Economic and Political Weekly* 41 (3): 210–17.

Abrahamsson, Sebastian, Filippo Bertoni, Annemarie Mol, and Rebeca Ibáñez Martín. 2015. "Living with Omega-3: New Materialism and Enduring Concerns." *Environment and Planning D: Society and Space* 33 (1): 4–19.

Adas, Michael. 1989. *Machines as the Measure of Men: Science, Technology, and Ideologies of Western Dominance*. Ithaca, NY: Cornell University Press.

After Globalism Writing Group. 2018. "Visuality as a Site of Struggle." *Social Text* 36 (1): 35–36.

Agard-Jones, Vanessa. 2013. "Bodies in the System." *Small Axe* 17 (3): 182–92.

Akrich, Madeleine. 1992. "The De-scription of Technical Objects." In *Shaping Technology/Building Society: Studies in Sociotechnical Change*, edited by Wiebe E. Bijker and John Law, 205–24. Cambridge, MA: MIT Press.

Alam, Shahidul. 2008. "Majority World: Challenging the West's Rhetoric of Democracy." *Amerasia Journal* 34 (1): 88–98.

Al Jazeera. 2017. "Cambodia Supreme Court Dissolves Opposition CNRP Party." *Al Jazeera*, 16 November. www.aljazeera.com/news/2017/11/16/cambodia-supreme-court-dissolves-opposition-cnrp-party.

Amaro, Yesenia. 2018. "Cancer Facility Inaugurated." *Phnom Penh Post*, 16 January.

Anderson, Warwick. 2006. *Colonial Pathologies: American Tropical Medicine, Race, and Hygiene in the Philippines*. Durham, NC: Duke University Press.

———. 2012. "Asia as Method in Science and Technology Studies." *East Asian Science, Technology and Society* 6 (4): 445–51.

Anderson, Warwick, and Hans Pols. 2012. "Scientific Patriotism: Medical Science and National Self-Fashioning in Southeast Asia." *Comparative Studies in Society and History* 54 (1): 93–113.

Ang Chouléan. 1982. "Grossesse et accouchement au Cambodge: Aspects rituels." *ASEMI* 13:87–109.

———. 2004. *Brah Ling*. Phnom Penh: Reyum Publishing.

Apichatpong Weerasethakul. 2010. *Loong Boonmee raleuk chat [Uncle Boonmee Who Can Recall His Past Lives]*. 113 min. Kick the Machine and Illuminations Films. Thailand/UK.

Ariey, Frédéric, Benoit Witkowski, Chanaki Amaratunga, Johann Beghain, Anne-Claire Langlois, Nimol Khim, Saorin Kim, et al. 2014. "A Molecular Marker of Artemisinin-Resistant *Plasmodium falciparum* Malaria." *Nature* 505:50–55.

Åsberg, Cecilia, and Jennifer Lum. 2009. "PharmAD-ventures: A Feminist Analysis of the Pharmacological Imaginary of Alzheimer's Disease." *Body & Society* 15 (4): 95–117.

———. 2010. "Picturizing the Scattered Ontologies of Alzheimer's Disease: Towards a Materialist Feminist Approach to Visual Technoscience Studies." *European Journal of Women's Studies* 17 (4): 323–45.

Asch, Adrienne. 2010. "Selection, Markets and 'Symbolic Harms.'" Tarrytown Meetings, Center for Genetics and Society. https://youtu.be/-eNq_25Tk5Y.

Aso, Michitake. 2017. "Learning to Heal the People: Socialist Medicine and Education in Vietnam, 1945–54." In *Translating the Body: Medical Education in Southeast Asia*, edited by Hans Pols, C. Michele Thompson, and John Harley Warner, 146–72. Singapore: National University of Singapore Press.

Aso, Michitake, and Annick Guénel. 2013. "The Itinerary of a North Vietnamese Surgeon: Medical Science and Politics during the Cold War." *Science, Technology and Society* 18 (3): 291–306.

Association for Diplomatic Studies and Training (ADST). n.d. *Cambodia Reader*. www.adst.org/Readers/Cambodia.pdf.

Au, Sokhieng. 2006. "Indigenous Politics, Public Health and the Cambodian Colonial State." *South East Asia Research* 14 (1): 33–86.

———. 2011. *Mixed Medicines: Health and Culture in French Colonial Cambodia*. Chicago: University of Chicago Press.

Aulino, Felicity. 2016. "Rituals of Care for the Elderly in Northern Thailand: Merit, Morality, and the Everyday of Long-Term Care." *American Ethnologist* 43 (1): 91–102.

———. 2019. *Rituals of Care: Karmic Politics in an Aging Thailand*. Ithaca, NY: Cornell University Press.

Aun Chhengpor, Sun Narin, and Kann Vicheika. 2020. "'State of Emergency' Draft Law Gives Gov't Sweeping Powers; Permits Human Rights Restrictions." *VOA Cambodia*, 31 March. www.voacambodia.com/a/state-of-emergency-draft-law-gives-gov-t-sweeping-powers-permits-human-rights-restrictions-/5353728.html.

Badano, Aldo, Craig Revie, Andrew Casertano, Wei-Chung Chen, Phil Green, Tom Kimpe, Elizabeth Krupinski, et al. 2015. "Consistency and Standardization of Color in Medical Imaging: A Consensus Report." *Journal of Digital Imaging* 28 (1): 41–52.

Bailey, Moya. 2016. "Misogynoir in Medical Media: On Caster Semenya and R. Kelly." *Catalyst: Feminism, Theory, Technoscience* 2 (2). https://catalystjournal.org/index.php/catalyst/article/view/28800/21401.

Barad, Karen. 2007. *Meeting the Universe Halfway: Quantum Physics and the Entanglement of Matter and Meaning.* Durham, NC: Duke University Press.

Bashour, Hyam, Raghda Hafez, and Asmaa Abdulsalam. 2005. "Syrian Women's Perceptions and Experiences of Ultrasound Screening in Pregnancy: Implications for Antenatal Policy." *Reproductive Health Matters* 13 (25): 147–54.

Batchen, Geoffrey. 1997. *Burning with Desire: The Conception of Photography.* Cambridge, MA: MIT Press.

BBC. 2018. "Phnom Penh Post: Firing and Resignations after Sale of Cambodia Daily." *BBC News*, 7 May. www.bbc.com/news/world-asia-44027032.

Beaulieu, Anne. 2002. "Images Are Not the (Only) Truth: Brain Mapping, Visual Knowledge, and Iconoclasm." *Science, Technology, & Human Values* 27 (1): 53–86.

Beban, Alice. 2021. *Unwritten Rule: State-Making through Land Reform in Cambodia.* Ithaca, NY: Cornell University Press.

Beisel, Uli, René Umlauf, Eleanor Hutchinson, and Clare I. R. Chandler. 2016. "The Complexities of Simple Technologies: Re-imagining the Role of Rapid Diagnostic Tests in Malaria Control Efforts." *Malaria Journal* 15: Article 64.

Benjamin, Ruha. 2019. *Race after Technology: Abolitionist Tools for the New Jim Code.* Cambridge: Polity.

Benjamin, Walter. 2006. *Berlin Childhood around 1900.* Translated by Howard Eiland. Cambridge, MA: Belknap Press.

Berger, John. (1972) 1990. *Ways of Seeing.* London: Penguin Books.

Berlin, Brent, and Paul Kay. 1969. *Basic Color Terms: Their Universality and Evolution.* Berkeley: University of California.

Bertrand, Didier. 2004. "A Medium Possession Practice and Its Relationship with Cambodian Buddhism." In *History, Buddhism, and New Religious Movements in Cambodia*, edited by John Marston and Elizabeth Guthrie, 150–69. Honolulu: University of Hawai'i Press.

Bhatia, Rajani. 2018. *Gender before Birth: Sex Selection in a Transnational Context.* Seattle: University of Washington Press.

Bigdeli, Maryam, and Peter Leslie Annear. 2009. "Barriers to Access and the Purchasing Function of Health Equity Funds: Lessons from Cambodia." *Bulletin of the World Health Organization* 87 (7): 560–64.

Blume, Stuart. 1992. *Insight and Industry: On the Dynamics of Technological Change in Medicine.* Cambridge, MA: MIT Press.

Bonelli, Cristóbal. 2015. "To See That Which Cannot Be Seen: Ontological Differences and Public Health Policies in Southern Chile." *JRAI: Journal of the Royal Anthropological Institute*, n.s., 21 (4): 872–91.

Bourdier, Frédéric. 2016. "Health Inequalities, Public Sector Involvement and Malaria Control in Cambodia." *Sojourn: Journal of Social Issues in Southeast Asia* 31 (1): 81–115.

Bourdier, Frédéric, Boravann Man, and Phasy Res. 2014. "La circulation non contrôlée des médicaments en Asie du Sud-Est et au Cambodge." *L'Espace politique [en ligne]* 24. http://espacepolitique.revues.org/3220.

Boxer, Charles Ralph. 1969. "Portuguese and Spanish Projects for the Conquest of Southeast Asia, 1580–1600." *Journal of Asian History* 3 (2): 118–36.

Braun, Lundy. 2014. *Breathing Race into the Machine: The Surprising Career of the Spirometer from Plantation to Genetics*. Minneapolis: University of Minnesota Press.

Brikci, Nouria, and Mit Philips. 2007. "User Fees of Equity Funds in Low-Income Countries." *Lancet* 369:10–11.

Bruno, Ellen. 1989. *Samsara: Survival and Recovery in Cambodia*. 29 minutes. Transit Media.

Burri, Regula Valérie. 2008. "Doing Distinctions: Boundary Work and Symbolic Capital in Radiology." *Social Studies of Science* 38 (1): 35–62.

Burri, Regula Valérie, and Joseph Dumit. 2008. "Social Studies of Scientific Imaging and Visualization." In *The Handbook of Science and Technology Studies*, 3rd ed., edited by Edward J. Hackett, Olga Amsterdamska, Michael E. Lynch, and Judy Wajcman, 297–317. Cambridge, MA: MIT Press.

Cambodia Daily. 2018. "About Us." www.cambodiadaily.com/about-us/.

Campt, Tina M. 2012. *Image Matters: Archive, Photography, and the African Diaspora in Europe*. Durham, NC: Duke University Press.

———. 2017. *Listening to Images*. Durham, NC: Duke University Press.

Carsten, Janet. 2019. *Blood Work: Life and Laboratories in Penang*. Durham, NC: Duke University Press.

Cartwright, Lisa. 1995. *Screening the Body: Tracing Medicine's Visual Culture*. Minneapolis: University of Minnesota Press.

Casper, Monica J. 1994. "At the Margins of Humanity: Fetal Positions in Science and Medicine." *Science, Technology & Human Values* 19 (3): 307–23.

Cassaniti, Julia. 2015. *Living Buddhism: Mind, Self, and Emotion in a Thai Community*. Ithaca, NY: Cornell University Press.

Castañeda, Claudia. 2001. "Robotic Skin: The Future of Touch?" In *Thinking through the Skin*, edited by Sara Ahmed and Jackie Stacey, 223–36. London: Routledge.

Césaire, Aimé. (1955) 1972. *Discourse on Colonialism*. Translated by Joan Pinkham. New York: Monthly Review Press.

Chandler, David P. 1992. *A History of Cambodia*. 2nd ed. Boulder: Westview Press.

Chen, Kuan-Hsing. 2010. *Asia as Method: Toward Deimperialization*. Durham, NC: Duke University Press.

Chhem, Rethy. 2018. "Cobalt Diplomacy in Cambodia." *Medicine Anthropology Theory* 5 (2): 73–78.

Chiffoleau, Sylvia. 1997. *Médecines et médecins en Égypte: Construction d'une identité professionnelle et projet médical*. Paris: L'Harmattan/Maison de l'Orient Méditerranée.

Cipolla, Cyd, Kristina Gupta, David A. Rubin, and Angela Willey, eds. 2017. *Queer Feminist Science Studies: A Reader*. Seattle: University of Washington Press.

Cock, Andrew Robert. 2010. "External Actors and the Relative Autonomy of the Ruling Elite in Post-UNTAC Cambodia." *Journal of Southeast Asia Studies* 41 (2): 241–65.

Coderey, Céline. 2019. "Healing Sounds in Rakhine (Myanmar): Auspicious and Apotropaic Recitations in a Theravada Buddhist Context." In *Hearing Southeast Asia: Sounds of Hierarchy and Power in Context*, edited by Nathan Porath, 308–40. Copenhagen: NIAS Press.

Collins, Erin. 2016. "Postsocialist Informality: The Making of Owners, Squatters and State Rule in Phnom Penh, Cambodia (1989–1993)." *Environment and Planning A: Economy and Space* 48 (12): 2367–82.

Coopmans, Catelijne, and Karen M. McNamara. 2020. "Care in Translation: Care-ful Research in Medical Settings." *East Asian Science, Technology and Society* 14 (1): 1–14.

Crochet, Soizick. 2008. "La santé au Cambodge: Histoire et défis." In *Cambodge contemporain*, edited by Alain Forest, 363–418. Paris: Irasec/Les Indes savantes.

Dahles, Heidi. 2012. "Cambodia Research Group." Oral presentation at SEA Update, 22 June 2012, Radbound University Nijmegen, the Netherlands.

Daston, Lorraine, and Peter Galison. 1992. "The Image of Objectivity." *Representations* 40:81–128.

Datuin, Flaudette May V. 2012. "Uncommon Sense: 'Empty the Visual from Eyes of Flesh.'" In *Modern and Contemporary Southeast Asian Art: An Anthology*, edited by Nora A. Taylor and Boreth Ly, 211–23. Ithaca, NY: Cornell Southeast Asia Program Publications.

Davis, Erik W. 2008. "Imaginary Conversations with Mothers about Death." In *At the Edge of the Forest: Essays on Cambodia, History, and Narrative in Honor of David Chandler*, edited by Anne Ruth Hansen and Judy Ledgerwood, 221–48. Ithaca, NY: Cornell Southeast Asia Program Publications.

———. 2013. "Beginning a Sketch of Accumulation by Dispossession in Contemporary Cambodia." *Fieldsights*, 20 June. https://culanth.org /fieldsights/beginning-a-sketch-of-accumulation-by-dispossession-in -contemporary-cambodia.

Davis-Floyd, Robbie E., and Carolyn F. Sargent, eds. 1997. *Childbirth and Authoritative Knowledge: Cross-Cultural Perspectives*. Berkeley: University of California Press.

de Bernon, Olivier. 1998. *Yantra et Mantra*. Phnom Penh: Centre culturel français de Phnom Penh.

Dedet, Jean-Pierre. 2008. "The Overseas Pasteur Institutes, with Special Reference to Their Role in the Diffusion of Microbiological Knowledge: 1887–1975." *Research in Microbiology* 159 (1): 31–35.

de Laet, Marianne, and Annemarie Mol. 2000. "The Zimbabwe Bush Pump: Mechanics of a Fluid Technology." *Social Studies of Science* 30 (2): 225–63.

Deleuze, Gilles. (1968) 2001. *Difference and Repetition*. Translated by Paul Patton. London: Continuum.

Dhamma Aid. 2010. Updates. www.parami.org.

Dorrestijn, Steven. 2012. "Technical Mediation and Subjectivation: Tracing and Extending Foucault's Philosophy of Technology." *Philosophy & Technology* 25:221–41.

Duclos, Vincent. 2015. "Global eHealth: Designing Spaces of Care in the Era of Global Connectivity." *Medicine Anthropology Theory* 2 (1): 154–64.

Duden, Barbara. 1993. *Disembodying Women: Perspectives on Pregnancy and the Unborn*. Cambridge, MA: Harvard University Press.

Dumit, Joseph. 2004. *Picturing Personhood: Brain Scans and Biomedical Identity*. Princeton, NJ: Princeton University Press.

———. 2012. *Drugs for Life: How Pharmaceutical Companies Define Our Health*. Durham, NC: Duke University Press.

Dussauge, Isabelle. 2008. "Technomedical Visions: Magnetic Resonance Imaging in 1980s Sweden." Stockholm Papers in the History and Philosophy of Technology.

Dyer, Michael. 1997. *White*. London: Routledge.

Eat, Sambath. 2021. "'Paste-up Modernity': Images of Modern Cambodia in the Sangkum Reastr Niyum." MA thesis, University of Washington.

Eaton, David. 2006. "Diagnosing the Crisis in the Republic of Congo." *Africa: Journal of the International African Institute* 76 (1): 44–69.

Ebihara, May M., Carol A. Mortland, and Judy Ledgerwood, eds. 1994. *Cambodian Culture since 1975: Homeland and Exile*. Ithaca, NY: Cornell University Press.

Edington, Claire. 2013. "Going in and Getting out of the Colonial Asylum: Families and Psychiatric Care in French Indochina." *Comparative Studies in Society and History* 55 (3): 725–55.

Edwards, Elizabeth, ed. 1992. *Anthropology and Photography, 1860–1920*. New Haven, CT: Yale University Press.

Edwards, Penny. 2007. *Cambodge: The Cultivation of a Nation, 1860–1945*. Honolulu: University of Hawai'i Press.

———. 2008. "The Moral Geology of the Present: Structuring Morality, Menace and Merit." In *People of Virtue: Reconfiguring Religion, Power and Moral Order in Cambodia Today*, edited by Alexandra Kent and David Chandler, 213–40. Copenhagen: NIAS Press.

Epstein, Steven. 2007. *Inclusion: The Politics of Difference in Medical Research.* Chicago: University of Chicago Press.

Erikson, Susan L. 2012. "Social Embodiments: Prenatal Risk in Postsocialist Germany." *Anthropologica* 54 (1): 83–94.

Ewing, Cindy. 2019. "The Colombo Powers: Crafting Diplomacy in the Third World and Launching Afro-Asia at Bandung." *Cold War History* 19 (1): 1–19.

Fangerau, Heiner, Rethy K. Chhem, Irmgard Müller, and Shih-Chang Wang, eds. 2012. *Medical Imaging and Philosophy: Challenges, Reflections and Actions.* Stuttgart: Franz Steiner Verlag.

Fehérváry, Krisztina. 2013. *Politics in Color and Concrete: Socialist Materialities and the Middle Class in Hungary.* Bloomington: Indiana University Press.

Food and Drug Administration (FDA). 2014. "Avoid Fetal 'Keepsake' Images, Heartbeat Monitors." 16 December. www.fda.gov/consumers/consumer -updates/avoid-fetal-keepsake-images-heartbeat-monitors.

Fortun, Kim. 2014. "From Latour to Late Industrialism." *HAU: Journal of Ethnographic Theory* 4 (1): 309–29.

Foucault, Michel. (1963) 1994. *The Birth of the Clinic: An Archaeology of Medical Perception.* Translated by A. M. Sheridan Smith. New York: Vintage.

Franke, Richard W., and Barbara H. Chasin. 2005. "Kerala: Radical Reform as Development in an Indian State." In *The Anthropology of Development and Globalization: From Classical Political Economy to Contemporary Neoliberalism*, edited by Marc Edelman and Angelique Haugerud, 368–72. Malden, MA: Blackwell.

Franklin, Sarah. 1995. "Postmodern Procreation: A Cultural Account of Assisted Reproduction." In *Conceiving the New World Order: The Global Politics of Reproduction*, edited by Faye D. Ginsburg and Rayna Rapp, 323–45. Berkeley: University of California Press.

Freiherr, Greg. 2010. "Ultrasound Hurt by Global Recession, but Asia Softens the Blow." Diagnostic Imaging, 4 August. www.diagnosticimaging.com /view/ultrasound-hurt-global-recession-asia-softens-blow.

French, Lindsay. 2002. "Exhibiting Terror." In *Truth Claims: Representation and Human Rights*, edited by Mark Philip Bradley and Patrice Petro, 131–55. New Brunswick, NJ: Rutgers University Press.

Frost, Erin A., and Angela M. Haas. 2017. "Seeing and Knowing the Womb: A Technofeminist Reframing of Fetal Ultrasound toward a Decolonization of Our Bodies." *Computers and Composition* 43:88–105.

Fuhrmann, Arnika. 2016. *Ghostly Desires: Queer Sexuality and Vernacular Buddhism in Contemporary Thai Cinema*. Durham, NC: Duke University Press.

Funahashi, Daena Aki. 2016. "Rule by Good People: Health Governance and the Violence of Moral Authority in Thailand." *Cultural Anthropology* 31 (1): 107–30.

Galt, Rosalind. 2011. *Pretty: Film and the Decorative Image*. New York: Columbia University Press.

Gammeltoft, Tine M. 2014. *Haunting Images: A Cultural Account of Selective Reproduction in Vietnam*. Berkeley: University of California Press.

Gammeltoft, Tine M., and Hanh Thi Thuý Nguyen. 2007. "The Commodification of Obstetric Ultrasound Scanning in Hanoi, Viet Nam." *Reproductive Health Matters* 15 (29): 163–71.

Geissler, Paul Wenzel, Guillaume Lachenal, John Manton, and Noémi Tousignant, eds. 2017. *Traces of the Future: An Archaeology of Medical Science in Africa*. Chicago: University of Chicago Press.

GE Medical Systems. 2000. *LOGIQ 200 PRO Series Advanced Reference Manual*. Technical Publications 2233222–100, Revision 1. Milwaukee: General Electric Co.

Georges, Eugenia. 1996. "Fetal Ultrasound Imaging and the Production of Authoritative Knowledge in Greece." *Medical Anthropology Quarterly* 10 (2): 157–75.

Glissant, Édouard. 1997. *Poetics of Relation*. Ann Arbor: University of Michigan Press.

Gordon, Avery F. (1997) 2008. *Ghostly Matters: Haunting and the Sociological Imagination*. Minneapolis: University of Minnesota Press.

Govindrajan, Radhika. 2018. *Animal Intimacies: Interspecies Relatedness in India's Central Himalayas*. Chicago: University of Chicago Press.

Grant, Jenna. 2014. "Government Official" [Montrey reachka]. In *Figures of Southeast Asian Modernity*, edited by Joshua Barker, Erik Harms, and Johan Lindquist, 89–90. Honolulu: University of Hawai'i Press.

———. 2016. "From Subjects to Relations: Bioethics and the Articulation of Postcolonial Politics in the Cambodia Pre-exposure Prophylaxis Trial." *Social Studies of Science* 46 (2): 236–58.

———. 2017a. "'Cambodian Pathology': Imagining Modern Biomedicine in the Cambodian-Soviet Medical Journal, *Revue Médico-Chirurgicale de l'Hôpital de l'Amitié Khméro-Soviétique* (1961–71)." In *Translating the Body: Medical Education in Southeast Asia*, edited by Hans Pols, C. Michele Thompson, and John Harley Warner, 194–229. Singapore: National University of Singapore Press.

———. 2017b. "How to Rename a Hospital: Biomedical Technologies and New Combinations of Business and Charity in Cambodian Public Health." *Anthropological Quarterly* 90 (3): 605–36.

———. 2018. "Friends, Partners, and Orphans: Relations that Make and Unmake a Hospital." *Medicine Anthropology Theory* 5 (2): 56–72.

———. 2020. "Repair in Translation." *East Asian Science, Technology and Society* 14 (1): 15–33.

———. Forthcoming. "Portrait and Scan." *Public Culture*.

Grant Ross, Helen, and Darryl Collins. 2006. *Building Cambodia: "New Khmer Architecture," 1953–1970*. Bangkok: Key Publisher.

Groslier, Bernard Philippe. 2006. *Angkor and Cambodia in the Sixteenth Century: According to Portuguese and Spanish Sources*. Translated by Michael Smithies. Bangkok: Orchid Press.

Guillou, Anne Yvonne. 2001. "Les médecins au Cambodge: Entre élite sociale traditionnelle et groupe professionnel moderne sous influence étrangère." École des hautes études en sciences sociales, Paris. www.theses.fr /2001EHES0215.

———. 2004. "Medicine in Cambodia during the Pol Pot Regime (1975–1979): Foreign and Cambodian Influences." East Asian Medicine under Communism: A Symposium, Graduate Center, City University of New York.

———. 2009. *Cambodge, soigner dans les fracas de l'histoire* [Cambodia, healing in the clamor of history]. Paris: Les Indes savantes.

Hall, Stuart, Doreen Massey, and Michael Rustin. 2013. "After Neoliberalism: Analysing the Present." *Soundings: A Journal of Politics and Culture* 53:8–22.

Haraway, Donna J. 1991. "Situated Knowledges: The Science Question in Feminism and the Privilege of Partial Perspective." In *Simians, Cyborgs, and Women: The Reinvention of Nature*, 183–201. New York: Routledge.

———. (1992) 2004. "The Promises of Monsters: A Regenerative Politics for Inappropriate/d Others." In *The Haraway Reader*, 63–124. New York: Routledge.

Hardeman, Wim, Wim Van Damme, Maurits Van Pelt, Por Ir, Kimvan Heng, and Bruno Meessen. 2004. "Access to Health Care for All? User Fees Plus a Health Equity Fund in Sotnikum, Cambodia." *Health Policy and Planning* 19 (1): 22–32.

Harris, Anna. 2016. "Listening-Touch: Affect and the Crafting of Medical Bodies through Percussion." *Body & Society* 22 (1): 31–61.

Hausken, Liv, Bettina Papenburg, and Sigrid Schmitz. 2018. "Introduction: The Processes of Imaging / The Imaging of Processes." *Catalyst: Feminism, Theory, Technoscience* 4 (2): 1–23.

Heidegger, Martin. (1962) 1998. "Traditional Language and Technological Language." Translated by Wanda Torres Gregory. *Journal of Philosophical Research* 23:129–45.

———. (1977) 2013. *The Question Concerning Technology and Other Essays*. Translated by William Lovitt. New York: Harper Perennial Modern Thought.

Hien, Nina Mai. 2012. "Ho Chi Minh City's Beauty Regime: Haptic Technologies of the Self in the New Millennium." *positions* 20 (2): 471–93.

———. 2014. "Photo Retoucher." In *Figures of Southeast Asian Modernity*, edited by Joshua Barker, Erik Harms, and Johan Lindquist, 67–69. Honolulu: University of Hawaiʻi Press.

Hinton, Alexander Laban. 2004. *Why Did They Kill? Cambodia in the Shadow of Genocide*. Berkeley: University of California Press.

———. 2016. *Man or Monster? The Trial of a Khmer Rouge Torturer*. Durham, NC: Duke University Press.

Hinton, Peta, Tara Mehrabi, and Josef Barla. 2015. "New Materialisms/New Colonialisms." Proceedings of ISCH COST Action IS1307 New Materialism Working Group Two: New Materialism on the Crossroads of the Natural and Human Sciences. https://newmaterialism.eu/content/5 -working-groups/2-working-group-2/position-papers/subgroup-position -paper-_-new-materialisms_new-colonialisms.pdf.

Hobart, Hiʻilei Julia Kawehipuaakahaopulani, and Tamara Kneese. 2020. "Radical Care: Survival Strategies for Uncertain Times." *Social Text* 38 (1): 1–16.

Howes-Mischel, Rebecca. 2016. "'With This You Can Meet Your Baby': Fetal Personhood and Audible Heartbeats in Oaxacan Public Health." *Medical Anthropology Quarterly* 30 (2): 186–202.

Human Rights Watch. 2021. "Cambodia: Escalating Crackdown amid Pandemic." 13 January. www.hrw.org/node/377409.

Iliffe, John. 1998. *East African Doctors: A History of the Modern Profession*. Cambridge: Cambridge University Press.

Institut Pasteur du Cambodge (IPC). 2020. "Institut Pasteur du Cambodge Receives Designation as WHO International Reference Laboratory for COVID-19." 10 April. www.pasteur-kh.org/2020/04/10/institut-pasteur-du -cambodge-receives-designation-as-who-international-reference -laboratory-for-covid-19/.

International Labour Organization (ILO). 2018. Cambodia Garment and Footwear Sector Bulletin, 8 (December). www.ilo.org/wcmsp5/groups /public/—-asia/—-ro-bangkok/documents/publication/wcms_663043.pdf.

Ith, Ponndara, Angela Dawson, and Caroline S. E. Homer. 2013. "Women's Perspective of Maternity Care in Cambodia." *Women and Birth* 26 (1): 71–75.

Ivry, Tsipy. 2006. "At the Back Stage of Prenatal Care: Japanese Ob-Gyns Negotiating Prenatal Diagnosis." *Medical Anthropology Quarterly* 20 (4): 441–68.

———. 2009. "The Ultrasonic Picture Show and the Politics of Threatened Life." *Medical Anthropology Quarterly* 23 (3): 189–211.

Japan International Cooperation Agency (JICA). 2010. "For Better Medical Services: Project for Strengthening Medical Equipment Management."

Visit to JICA Project no. 14. *NyoNyum*, 2–3. www.jica.go.jp/cambodia
/english/office/others/pdf/visit_14.pdf.

Jensen, Casper Bruun. 2017. "Pipe Dreams: Sewage Infrastructure and Activity
Trails in Phnom Penh." *Ethnos* 82 (4): 627–47.

John, Mary E. 2011. "Sexing the Fetus: Feminist Politics and Method across
Cultures." *positions* 19 (1): 7–29.

Johnson, Constance. 2015. "Cambodia: Law on NGOs Passed." Law Library of
Congress, 15 July. www.loc.gov/item/global-legal-monitor/2015-07-15
/cambodia-law-on-ngos-passed/.

Jordan, Brigitte. 1997. "Authoritative Knowledge and Its Construction." In
Childbirth and Authoritative Knowledge: Cross-Cultural Perspectives,
edited by Robbie E. Davis-Floyd and Carolyn F. Sargent, 55–88. Berkeley:
University of California Press.

Joyce, Kelly A. 2008. *Magnetic Appeal: MRI and the Myth of Transparency*.
Ithaca, NY: Cornell University Press.

Kamat, Sangeeta. 2014. "The New Development Architecture and the Post-
Political in the Global South." In *The Post-Political and Its Discontents:
Spaces of Depoliticisation, Spectres of Radical Politics*, edited by Japhy
Wilson and Erik Swyngedouw, 67–85. Edinburgh: Edinburgh University
Press.

Kammen, Michael. 1991. *Mystic Chords of Memory: The Transformation of
Tradition in American Culture*. New York: Knopf.

Kang Sothear. 2016. "133-Story Twin Towers Get Initial Approval." *Cambodia
Daily*, 18 February.

Kann, Vicheika. 2019. "Hun Sen Says Gov't Will Not Regulate Rice Prices as
Farmers Decry Lowering Profits." *VOA Cambodia*, 26 December. www
.voacambodia.com/a/hun-sen-says-gov-t-will-not-regulate-rice-prices-as
-farmers-decry-lowering-profits-/5220877.html.

Kazimierczak, Karolina Agata. 2018. "Medical Imaging and the 'Borderline
Gaze of Touch and Hearing': The Politics of Knowledge beyond 'Sense
Atomism.'" *Catalyst: Feminism, Theory, Technoscience* 4 (2): 1–29.

Keck, Frédéric. 2013. "Hong Kong as a Sentinel Post." *Limn*, 3. https://limn.it
/articles/hong-kong-as-a-sentinel-post/.

Kem, Bora, Jolyda Sou, Zoë Ng, and Penhleak Chan. 2019. *Startup Kingdom:
Cambodia's Vibrant Tech Startup Ecosystem in 2018*. Phnom Penh: Mekong
Strategic Partners and Raintree Development.

Keo, Siti. 2019. "Writing the Postcolonial City: Phnom Penh and Modernity
during Sangkum Reastr Niyum, 1955–1970." PhD diss., University of
California, Berkeley.

Keown, Damien. 2001. *Buddhism and Bioethics*. Basingstoke: Palgrave.

Kervran, David Dumoulin, Mina Kleiche-Dray, and Mathieu Quet. 2018.
"Going South: How STS Could Think Science in and with the South?"
Tapuya: Latin American Science, Technology and Society 1 (1): 280–305.

Khoun, Leakhana. 2011. "Hospital Director Denies Staff Mistreatment." *Phnom Penh Post*, 16 August.

Kimsay, Buth, and Janelle Retka. 2016. "Private Clinic Shuttered after Man's Death." *Cambodia Daily*, 24 May.

Klima, Alan. 2002. *The Funeral Casino: Meditation, Massacre, and Exchange with the Dead in Thailand*. Princeton, NJ: Princeton University Press.

———. 2019. *Ethnography #9*. Durham, NC: Duke University Press.

Klugman, Jeni. 2011. *UNDP Human Development Report 2011: Sustainability and Equity: A Better Future for All*. New York: United Nations Development Programme.

Kong, Sophea. 2014. "Malaria Intervention in Cambodia: Who Benefits from International Aid?" *International Research Journal of Arts and Sciences* 3 (2): 26–46.

Kong, Sothanarith. 2003. "Le secteur privé poursuit son implantation dans l'enseignement supérieur." *Cambodge Soir*, 25 June.

Langwick, Stacey A. 2008. "Articulate(d) Bodies: Traditional Medicine in a Tanzanian Hospital." *American Ethnologist* 35 (3): 428–39.

Latour, Bruno. 1986. "Visualization and Cognition: Thinking with Eyes and Hands." *Knowledge and Society: Studies in the Sociology of Culture Past and Present* 6:1–40.

Law, John, and Kevin Hetherington. 2003. "Allegory and Interference: Representation in Sociology." Department of Sociology, Lancaster University. www.lancaster.ac.uk/fass/resources/sociology-online-papers/papers/law-hetherington-allegory-interference.pdf.

Lea, Tess, and Paul Pholeros. 2010. "This Is Not a Pipe: The Treacheries of Indigenous Housing." *Public Culture* 22 (1): 187–209.

Lea, Tess, and Paul Torzillo. 2016. "The Cunning of Data in Indigenous Housing and Health." *Journal of Prevention & Intervention in the Community* 44 (4): 272–82.

Ledgerwood, Judy. 2008. "Ritual in 1990 Cambodian Political Theatre: New Songs at the Edge of the Forest." In *At the Edge of the Forest: Essays on Cambodia, History, and Narrative in Honor of David Chandler*, edited by Anne Ruth Hansen and Judy Ledgerwood, 195–220. Ithaca, NY: Cornell Southeast Asia Program Publications.

Lewitz, Saveros (Pou). 1974. "Recherches sur le vocabulaire cambodgien VIII: Du vieux Khmer au khmer moderne. IV Les noms de couleur." *Journal Asiatique* 262 (1–2): 152–58.

Liamdee, Khathaleeya. 2020. "On the Move across Phnom Dangrek: Mobilities and Silences in the Thai-Cambodian Borderland." PhD diss., University of Washington.

Lock, Margaret, and Vinh-Kim Nguyen. 2010. *An Anthropology of Biomedicine*. Malden, MA: Wiley-Blackwell.

Lowe, Celia. 2006. *Wild Profusion: Biodiversity Conservation in an Indonesian Archipelago*. Princeton, NJ: Princeton University Press.

Lu, Chunling, Matthew T. Schneider, Paul Gubbins, Katherine Leach-Kemon, Dean Jamison, and Christopher J. L. Murray. 2010. "Public Financing of Health in Developing Countries: A Cross-National Systematic Analysis." *Lancet* 375 (9723): 1375–87.

Ly, Boreth. 2003. "Devastated Vision(s): The Khmer Rouge Scopic Regime in Cambodia." *Art Journal* 62 (1): 66–81.

Ly, Daravuth, and Ingrid Muan. 2001. *Cultures of Independence: An Introduction to Cambodian Arts and Culture in the 1950s and 1960s*. Phnom Penh: Reyum Institute of Arts and Culture.

MacDougall, David. 2006. *The Corporeal Image: Film, Ethnography, and the Senses*. Princeton, NJ: Princeton University Press.

Mallapaty, Smriti. 2020. "Coronaviruses Closely Related to the Pandemic Virus Discovered in Japan and Cambodia." *Nature* 588:15–16.

Mallarmé, Stéphane. (1897) 2015. *A Roll of the Dice*. Translated by Robert Bononno and Jeff Clark. Seattle: Wave Books.

Marks, Laura U. 2000. *The Skin of the Film: Intercultural Cinema, Embodiment, and the Senses*. Durham, NC: Duke University Press.

Marston, John. 2008. "Constructing Narratives of Order: Religious-Building Projects and Moral Chaos." In *At the Edge of the Forest: Essays on Cambodia, History, and Narrative in Honor of David Chandler*, edited by Anne Ruth Hansen and Judy Ledgerwood, 163–93. Ithaca, NY: Cornell Southeast Asia Program Publications.

Martin, Aryn, Natasha Myers, and Ana Viseu. 2015. "The Politics of Care in Technoscience." *Social Studies of Science* 45 (5): 625–41.

Martin, Emily. 1995. *Flexible Bodies: Tracking Immunity in American Culture from the Days of Polio to the Age of AIDS*. Boston: Beacon Press.

Mavhunga, Clapperton Chakanetsa. 2018. *The Mobile Workshop: The Tsetse Fly and African Knowledge Production*. Cambridge, MA: MIT Press.

McArthur, Meher. 2002. *Reading Buddhist Art: An Illustrated Guide to Buddhist Signs and Symbols*. London: Thames & Hudson.

McDaniel, Justin Thomas. 2008. *Gathering Leaves & Lifting Words: Histories of Buddhist Monastic Education in Laos and Thailand*. Seattle: University of Washington Press.

M'charek, Amade. 2013. "Beyond Fact or Fiction: On the Materiality of Race in Practice." *Cultural Anthropology* 28 (3): 420–42.

Meessen, Bruno, Wim Van Damme, Christine Kirunga Tashobya, and Abdelmajid Tibouti. 2006. "Poverty and User Fees for Public Health Care in Low-Income Countries: Lessons from Uganda and Cambodia." *Lancet* 368:2253–57.

Michaels, Meredith W. 1999. "Fetal Galaxies: Some Questions about What We See." In *Fetal Subjects, Feminist Positions*, edited by Lynn M. Morgan and

Meredith W. Michaels, 113–32. Philadelphia: University of Pennsylvania Press.

Mika, Marissa. 2016. "Fifty Years of Creativity, Crisis, and Cancer in Uganda." *Canadian Journal of African Studies / Revue canadienne des études africaines* 50 (3): 395–413. https://doi.org/10.1080/00083968.2016 .1272061.

Ministry of Health, Royal Government of Cambodia. 2006. *National Guidelines on Complementary Package of Activities for Referral Hospital Development from 2006 to 2010.* Phnom Penh: Ministry of Health.

———. 2008. *Strategic Framework for Health Financing 2008–2015.* Phnom Penh: Bureau of Health Economics and Financing, Department of Planning and Health Information.

———. 2012. *Annual Health Financing Report 2012.* Phnom Penh: Ministry of Health.

Ministry of Health, Royal Government of Cambodia—TWGH Secretariat. 2011. Minutes of Technical Working Group for Health Meeting, 14 July.

Ministry of Labor and Vocational Training, Royal Government of Cambodia. 2017. "Prakas 449 (Determination of Contribution Rate and Formalities and Procedures of Contribution Payment for Social Security Schemes . . .)." Translated by National Social Security Fund. www.nssf.gov.kh/default/wp -content/uploads/2017/11/Prakas-449.pdf.

Mitchell, Lisa M. 2001. *Baby's First Picture: Ultrasound and the Politics of Fetal Subjects.* Toronto: University of Toronto Press.

Mol, Annemarie. 2002. *The Body Multiple: Ontology in Medical Practice.* Durham, NC: Duke University Press.

———. 2008. *The Logic of Care: Health and the Problem of Patient Choice.* London: Routledge.

———. 2017. "Exemplary: The Case of the Farmer and the Turpentine." In *The Ethnographic Case,* edited by Emily Yates-Doerr and Christine Labuski. www.matteringpress.org/books/the-ethnographic-case.

Molteni, Megan. 2020. "A Disease Tracker Backed by Gates and Zuckerberg Tackles Covid-19." Wired.com, 10 March. www.wired.com/story/a-disease -tracker-backed-by-gates-and-zuckerberg-tackles-covid-19/.

Monnais, Laurence. 2019. *The Colonial Life of Pharmaceuticals: Medicines and Modernity in Vietnam.* Cambridge: Cambridge University Press.

Moore, Elaine. 2010. "Catching Cambodia on the Cusp of Development." *Financial Times,* 14 February.

Morgan, Lynn M. 2000. "Magic and a Little Bit of Science: Technoscience, Ethnoscience, and the Social Construction of the Fetus." In *Bodies of Technology: Women's Involvement with Reproductive Medicine,* edited by Ann Rudinow Saetnan, Nelly Oudshoorn, and Marta Kirejczyk, 355–67. Columbus: Ohio State University Press.

———. 2011. "Mediated Bodies: Fetal Bodies, Undone." In *A Companion to the Anthropology of the Body and Embodiment*, edited by Frances E. Mascia-Lees, 320–37. Chichester: Wiley-Blackwell.

Morita, Atsuro. 2017. "Encounters, Trajectories, and the Ethnographic Moment: Why 'Asia as Method' Still Matters." *East Asian Science, Technology and Society* 11 (2): 239–50.

Mouffe, Chantal. 2005. *On the Political*. London: Routledge.

Mrázek, Rudolf. 2002. *Engineers of Happy Land: Technology and Nationalism in a Colony*. Princeton, NJ: Princeton University Press.

Muan, Ingrid. 2001. "Citing Angkor: Cambodian Arts in the Age of Restoration, 1918–2000." PhD diss., Columbia University.

Mukhopadhyay, Baijayanta. 2016. *A Labour of Liberation*. Regina, SK, Canada: Changing Suns Press.

Müller-Rockstroh, Babette. 2007. "Ultrasound Travels: The Politics of a Medical Technology in Ghana and Tanzania." PhD diss., Universitaire Pers Maastricht.

Murphy, Michelle. 2015. "Unsettling Care: Troubling Transnational Itineraries of Care in Feminist Health Practices." *Social Studies of Science* 45 (5): 717–37.

———. 2017. "What Can't a Body Do?" *Catalyst: Feminism, Theory, Technoscience* 3 (1): 1–15.

My Samedy. 2000. *Survivor for the Surviving*. Translated by David Oliveira and Thong Vichheka. Phnom Penh: Author.

Myers, Natasha. 2015. *Rendering Life Molecular: Models, Modelers, and Excitable Matter*. Durham, NC: Duke University Press.

Nam, Sylvia. 2011. "Phnom Penh: From the Politics of Ruin to the Possibilities of Return." *Traditional Dwellings and Settlements Review* 23 (1): 55–68.

———. 2017a. "Phnom Penh's Vertical Turn." *City* 21 (5): 622–31.

———. 2017b. "Urban Speculation, Economic Openness, and Market Experiments in Phnom Penh." *positions* 25 (4): 645–31.

Neelakantan, Vivek. 2017. "The Expansion and Transformation of Medical Education in Indonesia during the 1950s in Jakarta and Surabaya." In *Translating the Body: Medical Education in Southeast Asia*, edited by Hans Pols, C. Michele Thompson, and John Harley Warner, 173–93. Singapore: National University of Singapore Press.

Népote, Jacques, and Hoc Dy Khing. 1978. "L'organisation du champ de la couleur en cambodgien, et son évolution." In *Voir et nommer les couleurs*, edited by Serge Tornay, 83–107. Nanterre: Labethno Nanterre.

Ngor, Haing, with Roger Warner. 1988. *A Cambodian Odyssey*. New York: Macmillan Publishing Company.

Nishizaka, Aug. 2011. "The Embodied Organization of a Real-Time Fetus: The Visible and the Invisible in Prenatal Ultrasound Examinations." *Social Studies of Science* 41 (3): 309–36.

Norén-Nilsson, Astrid. 2016. *Cambodia's Second Kingdom: Nation, Imagination, and Democracy*. Ithaca, NY: Cornell Southeast Asia Program Publications.

Norindr Panivong. 1996. *Phantasmatic Indochina: French Colonial Ideology in Architecture, Film, and Literature*. Durham, NC: Duke University Press.

Norodom Sihanouk. 1968. "Cher Sahachivin." *Annales Médico-Chirurgicales de l'Hôpital de l'Amitié Khméro-Soviétique*, v.

Oguibe, Olu. 1996. "Photography and the Substance of the Image." In *In/sight: African Photographers, 1940 to the Present*, edited by Clare Bell, Okwui Enwezor, Danielle Tilkin, and Octavio Zaya, 231–50. New York: Guggenheim Museum.

Okeke, Iruka N. 2011. *Divining without Seeds: The Case for Strengthening Laboratory Medicine in Africa*. Ithaca, NY: Cornell University Press.

Ombongi, Kenneth S. 2011. "The Historical Interface between the State and Medical Science in Africa: Kenya's Case." In *Evidence, Ethos and Experiment: The Anthropology and History of Medical Research in Africa*, edited by P. Wenzel Geissler and Catherine Molyneux, 353–71. New York: Berghahn Books.

Ong, Aihwa. 2016. *Fungible Life: Experiment in the Asian City of Life*. Durham, NC: Duke University Press.

Ong, Aihwa, and Nancy N. Chen, eds. 2010. *Asian Biotech: Ethics and Communities of Fate*. Durham, NC: Duke University Press.

Ovesen, Jan, and Ing-Britt Trankell. 2010. *Cambodians and Their Doctors: A Medical Anthropology of Colonial and Postcolonial Cambodia*. Copenhagen: NIAS Press.

Padwe, Jonathan. 2020. *Disturbed Forests, Fragmented Memories: Jarai and Other Lives in the Cambodian Highlands*. Seattle: University of Washington Press.

Panh Rithy. 2011. *Duch: Master of the Forges of Hell*. 103 minutes. First Run Features.

Panh Rithy. 2012. *The Elimination: A Survivor of the Khmer Rouge Confronts His Past and the Commandant of the Killing Fields*. Translated by John Cullen. New York: Other Press.

———. 2013. *The Missing Picture* (English voice-over text). Translated by Letitia Farris Toussaint. Editions Grasset, Catherine Dussart Productions, and Bophana. *Cambodia Law and Policy Journal*, 85–118.

Parreñas, Juno Salazar. 2018. *Decolonizing Extinction: The Work of Care in Orangutan Rehabilitation*. Durham, NC: Duke University Press.

Pauwels, Luc, ed. 2006. *Visual Cultures of Science: Rethinking Representational Practices in Knowledge Building and Science Communication*. Hanover, NH: Dartmouth College Press.

Pérez-Pereiro, Alberto. 2014. "Cham Modernizer" [Neak sakammniyum Cham]. In *Figures of Southeast Asian Modernity*, edited by Joshua Barker,

Erik Harms, and Johan Lindquist 78–80. Honolulu: University of Hawai'i Press.

Pfeiffer, James, and Rachel Chapman. 2010. "Anthropological Perspectives on Structural Adjustment and Public Health." *Annual Review of Anthropology* 39:149–65.

Pinney, Christopher. 1997. *Camera Indica: The Social Life of Indian Photographs*. Chicago: University of Chicago Press.

———. 2003. "Notes from the Surface of the Image: Photography, Postcolonialism, and Vernacular Modernism." In *Photography's Other Histories*, edited by Christopher Pinney and Nicolas Peterson, 202–20. Durham, NC: Duke University Press.

Pols, Hans. 2018. *Nurturing Indonesia: Medicine and Decolonisation in the Dutch East Indies*. Cambridge: Cambridge University Press.

Poole, Deborah. 1997. *Vision, Race, and Modernity: A Visual Economy of the Andean Image World*. Princeton, NJ: Princeton University Press.

Pou Saveros and Ang Chouléan. 1987–90. "Le vocabulaire khmer relative au surnaturel." *Seksa Khmer* 10–13:59–129.

Prasad, Amit. 2005. "Making Images/Making Bodies: Visibilizing and Disciplining through Magnetic Resonance Imaging." *Science, Technology, & Human Values* 30 (2): 291–316.

———. 2014. *Imperial Technoscience: Transnational Histories of MRI in the United States, Britain, and India*. Cambridge, MA: MIT Press.

Praspaliauskiene, Rima. 2016. "Enveloped Lives: Practicing Health and Care in Lithuania." *Medical Anthropology Quarterly* 30 (4): 582–98.

Prince, Ruth J. 2013. "Introduction: Situating Health and the Public in Africa: Historical and Anthropological Perspectives." In *Making and Unmaking Public Health in Africa: Ethnographic and Historical Perspectives*, edited by Ruth J. Prince and Rebecca Marsland. Athens: Ohio University Press.

Puig de la Bellacasa, María. 2011. "Matters of Care in Technoscience: Assembling Neglected Things." *Social Studies of Science* 41 (1): 85–106.

———. 2017. *Matters of Care: Speculative Ethics in More Than Human Worlds*. Minneapolis: University of Minnesota Press.

Radosevich, Frank, and Prak Chan Thul. 2009. "Fees Put Hospital Care Out of Reach for Poor." *Cambodia Daily*, 1 June.

Rafael, Vicente L. 2006. *The Promise of the Foreign: Nationalism and the Technics of Translation in the Spanish Philippines*. Durham, NC: Duke University Press.

Ramalingam, Chitra. 2008. "Stopping Time: Henry Fox Talbot and the Origins of Freeze-Frame Photography." *Endeavour* 32 (3): 86–93.

Ramírez-i-Ollé, Meritxell. 2019. "Friendship as a Scientific Method." *Sociological Review* 67 (2): 299–317.

Rancière, Jacques. 1999. *Disagreement: Politics and Philosophy*. Minneapolis: University of Minnesota Press.

Rao, Vyjayanthi Venuturupalli. 2014. "Speculation, Now." In *Speculation, Now: Essays and Artwork*, edited by Vyjayanthi Venuturupalli Rao, with Prem Krishnamurthy and Carin Kuoni, 14–25. Durham, NC: Duke University Press, with Vera List Center for Art and Politics.

Rasmei Kampuchea. 2009a. "Not Only the Rich, but Also the Middle Class Go to Foreign Doctors." *Rasmei Kampuchea* 17 (4813), 5 February. Translated by *The Mirror* 13 (598). https://cambodiamirror.wordpress.com/2009/02/06/not-only-the-rich-but-also-middle-class-people-go-to-foreign-doctors-thursday-522009/.

———. 2009b. "The Head of the Royal Government Warned Donor Countries." *Rasmei Kampuchea* 17 (5016), 9 October. Translated by *The Mirror* 13 (633). https://cambodiamirror.wordpress.com/2009/10/10/.

Ravishankar, Nirmala, Paul Gubbins, Rebecca J. Cooley, Katherine Leach-Kemon, Catherine M. Michaud, Dean T. Jamison, and Christopher J. L. Murray. 2009. "Financing of Global Health: Tracking Development Assistance for Health from 1990–2007." *Lancet* 373:2113–24.

Redfield, Peter, and Erica Bornstein. 2010. "An Introduction to the Anthropology of Humanitarianism." In *Forces of Compassion: Humanitarianism between Ethics and Politics*, edited by Erica Bornstein and Peter Redfield, 3–30. Santa Fe: School for Advanced Research Press.

Reed, Kate, Inna Kochetkova, and Elspeth Whitby. 2016. "Visualising Uncertainty: Examining Women's Views on the Role of Magnetic Resonance Imaging (MRI) in Late Pregnancy." *Social Science & Medicine* 164:19–26.

Rivkin-Fish, Michele. 2005. *Women's Health in Post-Soviet Russia: The Politics of Intervention*. Bloomington: Indiana University Press.

Roberts, Dorothy. 2010. "Race and the New Biocitizen." Tarrytown Meetings, Center for Genetics and Society. https://youtu.be/d7GIU6XF3Dw.

Roberts, Elizabeth F. S. 2012. *God's Laboratory: Assisted Reproduction in the Andes*. Berkeley: University of California Press.

Rony, Fatimah Tobing. 1996. *The Third Eye: Race, Cinema, and Ethnographic Spectacle*. Durham, NC: Duke University Press.

Ros, Dina. 2009. "Public Health Reform in Cambodia: Hospitals Gain Autonomy." *Ka-Set*, Tuesday, 28 April. http://khmernz.blogspot.nl/2009/04/public-health-reform-in-cambodia.html.

Rottenburg, Richard. 2009. "Social and Public Experiments and New Figurations of Science and Politics in Postcolonial Africa." *Postcolonial Studies* 12 (4): 423–40.

Roy, Deboleena, and Banu Subramaniam. 2016. "Matter in the Shadows: Feminist New Materialism and the Practices of Colonialism." In *Mattering: Feminism, Science, and Materialism*, edited by Victoria Pitts-Taylor, 23–42. New York: New York University Press.

Sachs, Lisbeth. 1989. "Misunderstanding as Therapy: Doctors, Patients and Medicines in a Rural Clinic in Sri Lanka." *Culture, Medicine and Psychiatry* 13 (3): 335–49.

Saetnan, Ann Rudinow, Nelly Oudshoorn, and Marta Kirejczyk, eds. 2000. *Bodies of Technology: Women's Involvement with Reproductive Medicine.* Columbus: Ohio State University Press.

Sahlins, Marshall. 1976. "Colors and Cultures." *Semiotica* 16 (1): 1–22.

Said, Edward. (1978) 2003. *Orientalism.* 25th anniv. ed. New York: Vintage Books.

Sanabria, Emilia. 2016. *Plastic Bodies: Sex Hormones and Menstrual Suppression in Brazil.* Durham, NC: Duke University Press.

Saunders, Barry. 2008. *CT Suite: The Work of Diagnosis in the Age of Noninvasive Cutting.* Durham, NC: Duke University Press.

Schantz, Clémence. 2015. "'Maman, je peux habiter dans ton ventre?': Rêve et socialisation du fœtus au Cambodge." *Moussons: Recherche en sciences humaines sur l'Asie du Sud-Est* 25:39–56.

———. 2016. "'Cousue pour être belle': Quand l'institution médicale construit le corps féminin au Cambodge." *Cahiers du Genre* 2 (61): 131–50.

Schantz, Clémence, Kruy Leang Sim, Véronique Petit, Heng Rany, and Sophie Goyet. 2016. "Factors Associated with Caesarean Sections in Phnom Penh, Cambodia." *Reproductive Health Matters* 24 (48): 111–21.

Schmitt, Kellie. 2019. "The Mobile Ultrasound Revolution: How Technology Is Expanding This Medical Tool to New Frontiers." GeekWire Podcasts, 23 January. www.geekwire.com/2019/mobile-ultrasound-revolution -technology-expanding-medical-tool-new-frontiers/.

Schwenkel, Christina. 2013. "Post/Socialist Affect: Ruination and Reconstruction of the Nation in Urban Vietnam." *Cultural Anthropology* 28 (2): 252–77.

Senghor, Léopold Sédar. 1964. *On African Socialism.* Translated by Mercer Cook. New York: Praeger.

Seo, Bo Kyeong. 2017. "Locating Care within the Nascent Infrastructure: Renal Dialysis in Thailand." Allegra Lab. http://allegralaboratory.net /locating-care-within-the-nascent-infrastructure-renal-dialysis-in -thailand-medtech/.

Serres, Michel. (1980) 2007. *The Parasite.* Translated by Lawrence R. Schehr. Introduction by Cary Wolfe. Minneapolis: University of Minnesota Press.

Sharpe, Christina. 2016. *In the Wake: On Blackness and Being.* Durham, NC: Duke University Press.

Sheiner, Eyal, Rinat Hackmon, Ilana Shoham-Vardi, et al. 2007. "A Comparison between Acoustic Output Indices in 2D and 3D/4D Ultrasound in Obstetrics." *Ultrasound in Obstetrics & Gynecology* 29 (3): 326–28.

Simpson, Bob. 2010. "A 'Therapeutic Gap': Anthropological Perspectives on Prenatal Diagnostics and Termination in Sri Lanka." In *Frameworks of*

Choice: Predictive and Genetic Testing in Asia, edited by Margaret Sleeboom-Faulkner, 27–42. Amsterdam: International Institute for Asian Studies/Amsterdam University Press.

Skachkov, S. 1960. "USSR Economic Cooperation with Asian and African Countries." *Current Digest of the Russian Press* 6 (12): 19–20. Originally published in *Pravda*, 9 February 1960, 3–4.

Slocomb, Margaret. 2006. "The Nature and Role of Ideology in the Modern Cambodian State." *Journal of Southeast Asian Studies* 37 (3): 375–95.

———. 2010. *An Economic History of Cambodia in the Twentieth Century.* Singapore: National University of Singapore Press.

Social Action for Community and Development (SAC/D). 2016. "Summary of Health and Debt Report." https://sac.unitedsisterhood.org/index.php?page=detail&ctype=article&id=835&lg=en.

So Satta. 1970/71. "Préface." *Annales Médico-Chirurgicale de l'Hôpital de l'Amitié Khméro-Soviétique*, ii.

Stafford, Barbara Maria. 1991. *Body Criticism: Imaging the Unseen in Enlightenment Art and Medicine.* Cambridge, MA: MIT Press.

Stevenson, Lisa. 2014. *Life Beside Itself: Imagining Care in the Canadian Arctic.* Oakland: University of California Press.

Stock, Emiko. 2010. "Les communautés musulmanes du Cambodge: Un aperçu." In *Atlas des minorités musulmanes en Asie*, edited by M. Gilquin, 183–216. Bangkok/Paris: IRASEC/CNRS.

———. 2019. "Touching Image of History: Cham Practices of Looking across Cambodia and Iran." PhD diss., Cornell University.

Stonington, Scott D. 2012. "On Ethical Locations: The Good Death in Thailand, Where Ethics Sit in Places." *Social Science & Medicine* 75 (5): 836–44.

Strassler, Karen. 2010. *Refracted Visions: Popular Photography and National Modernity in Java.* Durham, NC: Duke University Press.

Street, Alice. 2014a. *Biomedicine in an Unstable Place: Infrastructure and Personhood in a Papua New Guinean Hospital.* Durham, NC: Duke University Press.

———. 2014b. "Rethinking Infrastructures for Global Health: A View from West Africa and Papua New Guinea." *Somatosphere*, December 11. http://somatosphere.net/2014/rethinking-infrastructures.html/.

Subramaniam, Banu. 2019. *Holy Science: The Biopolitics of Hindu Nationalism.* Seattle: University of Washington Press.

Sweet, Kathryn. 2017. "Women's Health in Laos: From Colonial Times to the Present." In *Translating the Body: Medical Education in Southeast Asia*, edited by Hans Pols, C. Michele Thompson, and John Harley Warner, 116–45. Singapore: National University of Singapore Press.

Swyngedouw, Erik. 2009. "The Antinomies of the Postpolitical City: In Search of a Democratic Politics of Environmental Production." *International Journal of Urban and Regional Research* 33 (3): 601–20.

Tadiar, Neferti X. 2009. *Things Fall Away: Philippine Historical Experience and the Makings of Globalization*. Durham, NC: Duke University Press.

Taussig, Michael. 2009. *What Color Is the Sacred?* Chicago: University of Chicago Press.

Taylor, Janelle S. 2005. "Surfacing the Body Interior." *Annual Review of Anthropology* 34:741–56.

———. 2008. *The Public Life of the Fetal Sonogram: Technology, Consumption, and the Politics of Reproduction*. New Brunswick, NJ: Rutgers University Press.

Thompson, Ashley. 2004. "The Suffering of Kings: Substitute Bodies, Healing, and Justice in Cambodia." In *History, Buddhism, and New Religious Movements in Cambodia*, edited by John Marston and Elizabeth Guthrie, 91–112. Honolulu: University of Hawai'i Press.

———. 2006. "Terrible but Unfinished: Stories of History." *New Literary History* 37 (1): 197–215.

———. 2016. *Engendering the Buddhist State: Territory, Sovereignty and Sexual Difference in the Inventions of Angkor*. London: Routledge.

Thompson, C. Michele. 2003. "Medicine, Nationalism, and Revolution in Vietnam: The Roots of a Medical Collaboration to 1945." *East Asian Science, Technology, and Medicine* 21:114–48.

Thongchai Winichakul. 1997. *Siam Mapped: A History of the Geo-Body of a Nation*. Honolulu: University of Hawai'i Press.

Tousignant, Noémi. 2018. *Edges of Exposure: Toxicology and the Problem of Capacity in Postcolonial Senegal*. Durham, NC: Duke University Press.

Trinh T. Minh-ha. 1989. *Woman, Native, Other: Writing Postcoloniality and Feminism*. Bloomington: University of Indiana Press.

Trouillot, Michel-Rolph. 2003. *Global Transformations: Anthropology and the Modern World*. New York: Palgrave Macmillan.

Tsing, Anna Lowenhaupt. 2005. *Friction: An Ethnography of Global Connection*. Princeton, NJ: Princeton University Press.

———. 2015. *The Mushroom at the End of the World: On the Possibility of Life in Capitalist Ruins*. Princeton, NJ: Princeton University Press.

Tsvetkova, Natalia. 2008. "International Education during the Cold War: Soviet Social Transformation and American Social Reproduction." *Comparative Education Review* 52 (2): 199–217.

———. n.d. "Penetrated Societies in the Cold War, 1950–1990: Soviet Mode of Influence through Education." Unpublished manuscript, 22.

Tuck, Eve. 2009. "Suspending Damage: A Letter to Communities." *Harvard Educational Review* 79 (3): 409–27.

Un, Kheang, and Judy Ledgerwood. 2003. "Cambodia in 2002: Decentralization and Its Effects on Party Politics." *Asian Survey* 43 (1): 113–19.

Un, Kheang, and Sokbunthoeun So. 2011. "Land Rights in Cambodia: How Neopatrimonial Politics Restricts Land Policy Reform." *Pacific Affairs* 84 (2): 289–308.

Un, Leang. 2012. "A Comparative Study of Education and Development in Cambodia and Uganda from Their Civil Wars to the Present." PhD diss., University of Amsterdam.

Ung, Loung. (2000) 2006. *First They Killed My Father: A Daughter of Cambodia Remembers*. New York: Harper Perennial.

Unnithan-Kumar, Maya. 2004. "Conception Technologies, Local Healers, and Negotiations around Childbearing in Rajasthan." In *Reproductive Agency, Medicine and the State: Cultural Transformations in Childbearing*, edited by Maya Unnithan-Kumar, 59–81. New York: Berghahn Books.

US Embassy, Phnom Penh. 2007. "GE Establishes New Branch Office in Cambodia." Press release, July 23. http://cambodia.usembassy.gov.

van Dijck, José. 2005. *The Transparent Body: A Cultural Analysis of Medical Imaging*. Seattle: University of Washington Press.

Van Leemput, Luc, Frédérique Ponsar, Mit Philips, and Nouria Brikci. 2007. "Health Equity Funds in Cambodia (Correspondence)." *Lancet* 369 (9562): 638.

Vu, Kim. 2003. "Lettre ouverte sur la formation médicale au Cambodge, par le Pr Vu Kim Por." *Cambodge Soir*, 22 July.

Waldby, Catherine. 2000. *The Visible Human Project: Informatic Bodies and Posthuman Medicine*. London: Routledge.

Warren, Adam. 2010. *Medicine and Politics in Colonial Peru: Population Growth and the Bourbon Reforms*. Pittsburgh: University of Pittsburgh Press.

Winner, Langdon. 1993. "Upon Opening the Black Box and Finding It Empty: Social Constructivism and the Philosophy of Technology." *Science, Technology, & Human Values* 18 (3): 362–78.

World Bank. 2011. *Cambodia: More Efficient Government Spending for Strong and Inclusive Growth. Integrated Fiduciary Assessment and Public Expenditure Review (IFAPER)*. World Bank Report Number 61694-KH.

World Health Organization. 2016. "WHO Recommendations on Antenatal Care for a Positive Pregnancy Experience." 28 November. www.who.int /publications/i/item/9789241549912.

World Health Organization (WHO) and Ministry of Health, Cambodia. 2012. *Cambodia Health Services Delivery Profile, 2012*. https://time.com/wp -content/uploads/2015/05/service_delivery_profile_cambodia.pdf.

World Health Organization—Regional Office for the Western Pacific. 2016. *Cambodia-WHO Country Cooperation Strategy 2016–2020*. https://apps .who.int/iris/handle/10665/246102.

———. 2018. "Meeting on Health Professional Education Reforms in Transition Economy Countries." https://apps.who.int/iris/handle/10665/273161.

Wright, Christopher. 2008. "'A Devil's Engine': Photography and Spirits in the Western Solomon Islands." *Visual Anthropology* 21 (4): 364–80.

Yates-Doerr, Emily. 2015. *The Weight of Obesity: Hunger and Global Health in Postwar Guatemala*. Oakland: University of California Press.

Zeeberg, Amos. 2021. "Piecing Together the Next Pandemic." *New York Times*, 16 February.

Žižek, Slavoj. 2008. *The Ticklish Subject: The Absent Centre of Political Ontology*. 2nd ed. London: Verso.

Zucker, Eve Monique. 2013. *Forest of Struggle: Moralities of Remembrance in Upland Cambodia*. Honolulu: University of Hawai'i Press.

Index

color, 7*fig.*, 179n20, 181n7, 181n9;
Berlin and Kay system of, 133, 135,
181n7; and film, 38*fig.*, 42; and
photography, 18, 109–10, 141–42;
skin color, 181n5; and social
subjectivity, 132–34, 181n8; and
ultrasound, 4*fig.*, 6, 11, 57, 62*fig.*,
66, 68, 126–47, 147*fig.*
communism, 34, 40, 53, 75
complementary package of activities
(CPA), 27, 71–72, 175n34
computerized tomography (CT), 6,
46, 155, 161n4
corporate citizenship, 27, 36
corruption, 39, 41, 89, 133–34
cosmopolitanism, 38, 56, 175
cost recovery schemes, 76
COVID-19, 150, 156, 170n69
critical race studies, 8–9, 79, 148
critical visual studies, 9, 114, 132
Crochet, Soizick, 39
Cuba, 169n58
Czechoslovakia, 167n19

Dahles, Heidi, 170n66
Dalat, Viet Nam, 32
dark regime, 44
Daston, Lorraine, 18
daun chi (Buddhist nuns), 115
Davis, Erik W., 60, 172n11, 177n15
decentralization, 48, 52, 65
de–Cold War, 10, 52
decollectivization, 61
decoloniality, 37, 52–53, 79. *See also*
anti-colonialism; postcolonialism
de-imperialism, 52
de Laet, Marianne, 165n3
Deleuze, Gilles, 165n30
democracy, 52, 58, 73–76, 99, 170n67,
170n69, 175n1, 175n38
Democratic Kampuchea (1975–79),
10, 28, 38, 41, 43–44, 154, 158n41
dengue fever, 71

Department of Hospital Services,
59–60
development, 27–28, 37, 40, 75, 132,
162n7, 162n9, 167n19, 169n58,
170n69, 177n17; development
partners, 50–51, 69, 72, 149,
175n35; development reports, 5,
89; and Khmerization, 163n12; and
medical equipment, 29–30, 39, 69,
72; neocolonial, 85; non-capitalist,
34, 167n18; postconflict, 13, 48;
post-UNTAC, 46–52; resistance
to, 16. *See also* development
assistance for health (DAH);
donation; foreign aid; humanitarianism; nongovernmental
organizations (NGOs); underdevelopment; *individual organizations and agencies*
development assistance for health
(DAH), 49–51. *See also* development; donation; foreign aid;
humanitarianism
DFID (Department for International
Development, UK), 169n58
Dhammananda, K. Sri, 117
Diamond Island (Koh Pich), 84*fig.*,
161n3, 162n8
Din, Dr., 81–83, 99, 128
diplomacy, 39, 153, 170n67; diplomats,
51, 61; medical, 35
dirty materialism, 39–40
disability studies, 8
Disease Control Unit, 31*fig.*
distance, 10, 20, 22, 106, 165n26,
182n18
distributed seeing, 112, 178n14
distrust, 3, 58, 80. *See also* trust
Doctors Without Borders. *See*
Médecins Sans Frontières
donation, 69, 72, 161n4, 169n57,
170n69, 178n10; bilateral, 29,
50–51; donor reports, 29, 53, 71; of

equipment, 6, 12, 23–30, 35–36, 39, 46, 48–54, 66, 68, 96*fig.*, 154; and health-related development, 50–54, 63–64, 73, 75. *See also* development; development assistance for health (DAH); foreign aid; humanitarianism

Doppler scans, 82, 128, 130

Dorrestijn, Steven, 183n19

dreaming, 3, 16, 23, 86, 106, 116, 121–24, 180n33

Duch. *See* Kaing Guek Eav (Duch)

Dumit, Joe, 20, 134

Dussauge, Isabelle, 20, 114

Dyer, Michael, 95

Dynamic Pharma Co., Ltd., 66–69, 87, 113

Ebihara, May M., 161n1

echo (term), 3, 7–8

École des officiers de santé, 32

Edwards, Penny, 94

electrocardiogram (ECG), 4*fig.*

emergency rooms (ERs), 6

emerging markets, 30

empiricism, 14

enactment, 22. *See also* co-enactment

endoscopy, 6

end users, 68

English (language), 5, 26–27, 47, 85, 107, 131, 181n7; English-language media, 90, 170n69; in health settings, 56, 62, 70, 82, 111, 118, 174n31; and methodology of book, 13, 94, 170n67

entrepreneurship, 42, 52, 58–59, 61, 75–76

equipment, 32, 59, 67, 69, 71–72, 175n35; donation of, 6, 12, 23–30, 35–36, 39, 46, 48–54, 66, 68, 96*fig.*, 154. *See also individual machines*

ethics, 50, 95, 136, 154n30, 164n23, 176n8, 183n19; medical, 79–80, 150, 155; political, 80, 85. *See also* morality

ethnographic film, 19

ethnography, 18–20, 36, 144, 164n24; and methodology of book, 5, 9–14, 23, 53

ethnolinguistics, 181n7

etiology, 25, 118

Europe, 18, 95, 97, 106, 149, 164n20, 165n26, 182n18; and colonial medicine, 16; and development, 52, 66, 169n58; Eastern, 45; European colonialism, 15; and post-political theory, 75; post-Soviet, 11, 149. *See also individual countries*

European Union, 89, 169n58, 177n15

extractivism, 16, 58, 80, 88, 103, 172n68. *See also* over-care

Extraordinary Chambers in the Courts of Cambodia (ECCC), 13, 162n10

Facebook, 126

false consciousness, 39

Family Health International (FHI), 111

Fanon, Frantz, 19

fees-for-service, 88

Fehérváry, Krisztina, 134

femininity, 132

feminism, 8–9, 138, 144, 148, 177n19; feminist new materialism, 20, 114; feminist technoscience studies, 8, 19, 25, 58, 79, 85, 105, 113

fetal subjectivity, 136, 164n22

fetus size, 97

fieldwork, 12, 50, 70, 101

film, 5, 16, 47, 110, 132, 162n8, 167n23, 180n33; and colonial medicine, 31*fig.*; ethnographic, 19; under the Khmer Rouge, 38*fig.*, 42; and mechanical objectivity, 12–13, 18, 20, 23–24, 28–29, 108; medical images in, 20; and methodology of

film (*continued*)
book, 5, 53; under the PRK, 43–45; and race, 95; under Sangkum Reastr Niyum, 37, 43, 167n20; ultrasound, 130–31, 131*fig.*; X-ray, 101. *See also individual films*

Financial Times, 51

fixing, definition, 5–10

flickering, 23–24, 26–54, 148

fluidity, 9, 22, 118, 126, 128, 130–31, 148, 165n3

fonctionnaire-entrepreneur (civil servant–entrepreneur), 42, 58, 61, 76

foreign aid, 117, 154, 162n9, 167n19, 172n12; and democracy discourse, 52, 75; medical, 10, 29–30, 34, 45–47, 49, 53–54, 60, 66, 71–73; no-strings, 52. *See also* development; development assistance for health (DAH); donation; nongovernmental organizations (NGOs)

Foucault, Michel, 19, 23, 105–6, 161n2, 165n25, 183n19

4D ultrasounds, 128–29, 138, 139, 179n17, 182n13

France, 150; and colonialism, 15, 30, 60, 132, 153, 166n10, 172n5, 179n27; and colonial medicine, 30–32, 36, 60, 105, 148, 163n16; Paris, 41, 45–46, 95, 154, 167n25

Franklin, Sarah, 113–14

freedom, 52, 57–59, 73–77, 79, 149, 151

French (language), 32, 38, 111; French-language media, 12, 73, 132; in patient care, 98, 123*fig.*, 131*fig.*; terminology, 7, 64, 105, 110, 120, 130

French Cultural Institute, 109*fig.*

French protectorate (1863–1953), 15, 30, 60, 132, 153

French Revolution, 105

Galison, Peter, 18

Galt, Rosalind, 132

Gammeltoft, Tine M., 164n21, 164n23, 172n9, 180n2, 181n11

GAVI, 50

gaze: medical, 105–6, 165n25; white colonial, 19

gender, 4, 9, 22, 80, 85, 95, 102, 122, 172n7, 178n11; and images, 18, 20; and labor, 177n15; under the PRK, 37, 43–44; and technology, 8, 20, 95, 97, 177n19; and ultrasound, 17, 121, 164n23

genealogy, 8, 11, 17, 23, 52–53, 105, 148

General Electric (GE), 43, 53, 69, 72, 87, 146, 165n1, 175n1; Developing Health Globally, 27, 46, 96*fig.*, 155; equipment donation, 12, 26–27, 30, 35–36, 46, 49, 96*fig.*; GE Healthcare, 12, 95

general medicine, 4, 6, 35, 147

Geneva Conventions, 162n10

Germany, 26, 169n58; East (German Democratic Republic), 45

germ theory, 15

Geschichtsphilosophie, 14

ghosts, 2–3, 119, 136–37, 161nn2. *See also* haunting

global feeling, 16

the Global Fund, 50

Global South, 75

Gordon, Avery F., 168n35

government hospitals, 3, 6, 12, 43, 52–57, 61, 64, 66, 69, 74, 131, 161n3, 173n18

Great Britain, 122; and colonialism, 15

Groslier, George, 132

Guerilla Archiving Project, 168n35

Guillou, Anne, 32, 39, 42, 61, 167n25, 168n41

gynecology, 4, 6, 46, 91, 147

Haraway, Donna, 119

Hardeman, Wim, 71

Japan, 30, 45–46, 66–67, 111, 114, 167n19, 169n58; Osaka, 95, 97, 110

Japanese Hospital. *See* National Center for Maternal and Child Health

Japan International Cooperation Agency (JICA), 30, 48–49, 68, 71, 154, 162n9, 169n58, 175n35

Jarai People, 163n12, 163n16

Java Café, 12

Kaing Guek Eav (Duch), 13, 162n10

Kamat, Sangeeta, 75

Kampong Cham, 100, 122

Kampong Som, 34

Kampuchea Krom, 118, 179n27

Kandal, 91

Kanitha, 100–101

Kantha Bopha IV Hospital, 3, 173

Kay, Paul, 133, 135, 181n7

Kemhan, Hor, 117–18, 120

Keo, Siti, 107, 166n15

Keown, Damien, 136

K5 Plan, 154

Khana, 111, 178n11

Khing Hoc Dy, 133, 135

Khmer (language), 56, 94, 111, 117–19, 140, 169n55, 173n18, 176n7, 177n3; advertisements in, 4*fig.*, 62*fig.*; color in, 133–34; idioms of care, 9; Khmer-language media, 1, 12, 37, 44, 79, 90, 170n69; and methodology of book, 5, 12–13, 170n67; music in, 26; and patient care, 81–83, 85–86, 98; terminology, 7, 47, 60, 64, 85–86, 105–7, 125, 157–60; transcription system, 161n1

Khmer-American Friendship Highway, 34

Khmerization, 163n12

Khmer People's National Liberation Front (KPNLF), 169n52

Khmer Republic (1970–75), 28, 40, 153, 168n36

Khmer Rouge, 155, 168n38, 169n52; color under, 133–35; and medical language, 96–97; and medicine, 38*fig.*, 42, 59, 61, 76, 168nn42–43, 175n2; ousting of, 43, 61, 154, 179n27, 180n33; and race, 181n5; Tribunal (Extraordinary Chambers in the Courts of Cambodia), 13, 162n10; and violence, 10, 41, 137, 154. *See also* Democratic Kampuchea (1975–79)

Khmer Rouge Tribunal, 13, 162n10

Khmers (ethnic group), 119, 163n16, 179n27

Khmer-Soviet Friendship Hospital. *See* Russian Hospital (Khmer-Soviet Friendship Hospital)

khsae keatha (amulet chains), 17, 115, 119–20, 122

Kiev, Ukraine, 45

Kim Hak, 162n8

Kingdom of Cambodia, 56, 154; first decade (1993–2003), 28; second decade (2003–13), 28

Klima, Alan, 14, 163n11, 180n31

Koh Pich (Diamond Island), 84*fig.*, 161n3, 162n8

KOICA, 169n58

Kong Sovicha: *A Woman Is Birth Giver*, 137*fig.*

Korea, 52, 57; North, 169n58; Seoul, 172n5; South, 66, 169n58

krou (healer), 3, 100, 107, 115, 119, 122, 179n26

krou khmae (Khmer healer), 108, 175n2

krou thump (sorcerer), 175n2

Kyiv, Ukraine. *See* Kiev, Ukraine

laboratory science, 15

Lao People's Democratic Republic (PDF)/Laos, 30, 41, 163n14, 169n58, 170n60, 173n16, 177n17, 180n29

Latin America, 47. *See also individual countries*

Law on Associations and Non-Governmental Organizations (2015), 155, 170n69

Law on Investment (1994), 172n14

Lea, Tess, 29, 39

Ledgerwood, Judy, 161n1

Lee Kuan Yew, 170n67

Leopard Capital, 51–52, 170n64

Letracolor, 133, 135

Lewitz, Saveros (Pou), 133

Lim, 47

Lina, Nurse, 81, 121

linguistics, 45, 60, 172n11, 181n7; linguistic anthropology, 133

Lithuania, 89, 170n62, 172n8

Loak Suon, 115–17, 119–20, 179n19

LOGIQ, 91, 95; LOGIQ 200, 96*fig.*

Long Phirum, 66–69, 87–88, 113, 129

Lon Nol, 153

low feedback, 99

Lum, Jennifer, 144

Madagascar, 166n10

magnetic resonance imaging (MRI), 46, 113, 149, 161n4

maintenance, 29–30, 46, 48–49, 71

Makara, 93–94, 99, 131–32

Making a Gift to the People of Cambodia, 167n23

malaria, 150, 162n5, 174n26, 175n39

Malaysia, 52, 117, 164n18, 169n58, 170n60, 170n69, 174n24

Mallarmé, Stéphane, 143

mammography, 6, 91, 99–101, 107

Man Boravann, 175n39

Marston, John, 117, 162n7

Martin, Emily, 101

Marxism, 39, 166n16

Maternal Hospital. *See* National Center for Maternal and Child Health

Matsuo, Takeshi, 48–49

matter as process, 114

M'charek, Amade, 8

médecin, machine, malade, 130

les médecins fonctionnaires-entrepreneur, 42, 61

Médecins Sans Frontières (MSF, Doctors Without Borders), 81, 173n17, 176n3

medical records, 92–93, 93*fig.*, 101–2, 102*fig.*

Mekong River, 11, 15, 179n27

methodology of book, 5, 10–14, 23, 127. *See also* ethnography; fieldwork; genealogy

microscopy, 5, 8, 19, 37, 101

midwifery, 6, 12, 15, 31, 37, 57, 65, 90, 161n3, 175n2, 177n16

Mindray, 66–68, 114, 175n1; DC-3 Expert Diagnostic Ultrasound System, 113; DC-6 Expert Diagnostic Ultrasound System, 113; iTouch/iBeam/iScape, 113

Ming, 92, 140

Ministry of Economy and Finance, Cambodian, 51, 72

Ministry of Health, Cambodian, 44, 53, 56–57, 60, 64, 110, 154, 162n9, 173n18, 175n35; Department of Budgeting and Finance, 72; and medical equipment, 30, 48–51, 59, 68–69, 71–72, 169n57; National Ethics Committee for Health Research, 155; *National Guidelines*, 71; and regulation, 70–73, 111; *Strategic Framework for Health Financing 2008–2015*, 63, 65–66; Technical Working Group on Health (TWGH), 49

Mitchell, Lisa, 139, 181n4
Mith Ran, 90
Mith Samlanh (Friends), 111, 178n11
Mixed Hospital, 153
moel chbas (to see clearly), 107–8, 128
moel kaun (to watch/look after
    children), 82, 107
moel khoenh (to look and see), 104, 106
Mokchniouk, Dr., 38
Mol, Annemarie, 14, 85–86, 90,
    165n3, 175n36
Mongolia, 173n16
monks, 13, 23–24, 35, 132, 136, 179n19,
    179nn23–24, 179n27; as healers, 3,
    106, 115–23, 175n2, 179n26
Mony, Nurse, 66, 76, 99
morality, 8, 16, 18, 86, 94, 165n30,
    166n16; Buddhist, 179n21; Khmer
    Rouge, 43; moral governance,
    176n8. *See also* ethics
Mortland, Carol A., 161n1
Mrázek, Rudolf, 19, 148, 163n17
Muan, Ingrid, 134
Mukhopadhyay, Baijayanta, 94
Murphy, Michelle, 85
My, Samedy, 32, 44, 53, 168n43,
    172n12; *Survivor for the Surviving*,
    43, 172n12
Myanmar, 169n58, 170n60, 175n38

Nam, Sylvia, 70, 162n7, 172n5
National Archives of Cambodia, 12
National Assembly, Cambodian,
    69–70, 155–56, 172n14
National Center for Maternal and
    Child Health (NCMCH, Maternal
    Hospital), 56–57, 64–65, 68, 92,
    99, 121, 128–29; and methodology
    of book, 12; name, 162n9; nurses'
    station, 93*fig.*; waiting rooms at,
    66, 89
National Center for TB/Leprosy, 64
National Institute of Public Health, 74

National Internet Gateway, 156
nationalism, 94, 117, 179n27
National Maternal and Child Health
    Center (NMCHC). *See* National
    Center for Maternal and Child
    Health
National Pediatric Hospital,
    173n21
National Social Security Fund (BSS),
    155, 173n18
National United Front for an
    Independent, Neutral, Peaceful
    and Cooperative Cambodia Party
    (FUNCINPEC), 154, 169n52
nation-building, 37, 43, 47, 53
Neak Sophal, 162n8
Neang Kavich, 162n8
neglect, 5, 8, 106, 117; of people, 11, 28,
    80–84, 90–94, 102–3, 149; of
    technology, 24, 27, 53–54. *See also*
    under-care
neocolonialism, 16, 85
neoliberalism, 47, 58, 75, 174n26,
    175n36. *See also* privatization;
    structural adjustment policies
Népote, Jacques, 133, 135
Netherlands, 19, 85; Dutch colonial-
    ism, 15; Dutch Golden Age, 122
new materialism, 20, 114, 138
Ngaet, Sophy, 4*fig.*
Ngor, Haing, 172n7
Nigeria, 142
Nishizaka, Aug, 98
non-aligned countries, 33–34. *See*
    also Cold War
nongovernmental organizations
    (NGOs), 12, 63, 110–11, 174n27,
    178n11; and health-related
    development, 29, 47–51, 54; and
    refugee repatriation, 45; regula-
    tion of, 155, 170n69; as service
    providers, 68, 81, 125–26, 129.
    See also development;

development assistance for health (DAH); foreign aid; humanitarianism; Law on Associations and Non-Governmental Organizations (2015); *individual organizations*

Norindr Panivong, 132

Norodom Sihanouk, King, 15–16, 130, 153, 155, 166n15, 167n19; and health care development, 32, 34, 36–37, 39–41, 167n25

Norodom Sihanouk Hospital, 173n21

North America, 66, 75, 85, 149

North Atlantic, 15, 23, 85, 120, 124, 132, 163n13

Nov, Rattana, 56–57

NSC Clinic, 62*fig.*

Nyemo, 111, 178n11

objectivity, 142; mechanical, 18–20, 22

obstetrics, 6, 46, 57, 68, 82, 91, 95, 128, 139

Oguibe, Olu, 142

ontology, 8, 25, 138–39, 141, 149–50; and Buddhism, 120, 127; and care, 79; and Khmer traditional medicine, 107; and ultrasound, 5, 8, 17–19, 136

Operation Menu, 153

Orientalism, 132

O'Russei market, 7*fig.*, 146

Osaka table, 95, 97

over-care, 24, 88–90, 103, 149

Ovesen, Jan, 47, 169n48

Padwe, Jonathan, 163n12, 163n16

Pailin Referral Hospital, 90

Pali (language), 116, 118–19, 123, 169n55

Panh Rithy, 168n42, 181n9

Papua New Guinea, 124

Paris, France, 41, 95, 97, 167n25

Paris Peace Agreements (1991), 45–46, 154

partiality, 16, 24, 95, 114, 118–19, 150

patient referrals, 65–66, 68, 76, 88, 91–92, 99, 111–12, 125; referral hospitals, 64, 72, 90, 173n21, 175n34

pediatrics, 35, 147*fig.*, 173n21

Pen, Dr., 26

People's Republic of Kampuchea (1979–89), 28*fig.*

People's Republic of Kampuchea (PRK, 1979–89), 28, 61, 134, 154, 179n27; gender in, 43–44

Peru, 124, 163n15

Phalla, Dr., 87–88, 92, 94, 130–32

Phaptawan Suwannakudt, 106

Philippines, 163n15, 168n35, 170n60, 175n38

Philips, 175n1

Phnom Penh Municipal Referral Hospital, 173n21

Phnom Penh Post, 171n69

Pholeros, Paul, 29, 39

photography, 23, 25, 29, 53, 104, 118, 130, 143–45; in advertising, 4*fig.*, 62*fig.*, 146–47, 147*fig.*; in the *Annals of the Khmer-Soviet Friendship Hospital*, 38–39; and anthropology, 22, 134, 141, 165n29, 183n21; by author, 2*fig.*, 4*fig.*, 7*fig.*, 62*fig.*, 84*fig.*, 93*fig.*, 96*fig.*, 101–2, 102*fig.*, 109*fig.*, 123*fig.*, 131*fig.*, 137*fig.*, 147*fig.*; exhibits, 108–10; and fixing, 5, 8, 21; and mechanic objectivity, 18–20; and portraiture, 124, 134–35, 141–42; and race, 95; and spirituality, 21, 134–35, 142; *thât* (to photograph/ record), 125

Photo Phnom Penh, 108–9, 109*fig.*

Phuong Monich, 41

picture archiving and communication systems (PACS), 178n14

pikroeah chumngeu. See *cabinets*

Pinney, Christopher, 141

radiology, 6, 45–46, 95, 131, 178n14; radiologists, 12, 26, 32, 35, 40–41, 43, 53, 95, 99, 110, 128

Ramalingam, Chitra, 21

Rao, Vyjayanthi Venuturupalli, 174n30

Rasmei Kampuchea, 79–80

rebirth, 121, 136, 138, 180n33

Rebirth of Kampuchea, 44

reconstruction, 27–28, 117, 172n12; socialist, 43–45, 47, 58–59, 61, 76

Red Cross, 40, 125–26, 172n12

Redfield, Peter, 165n2

referral hospitals, 64, 72, 90, 173n21, 175n34

refugees, 10, 40–41, 45, 47, 153–54, 168n38

regulation, 6, 48, 59–60, 62, 69–77, 103, 126, 134, 155, 176n2

reincarnation, 122, 136

repair, 5–6, 8, 11, 47–49, 143, 147; of medical equipment, 27, 30, 39, 43, 46, 53, 168n43

representation, 6–7, 9, 18, 20, 25, 39, 116, 141–42, 164n24, 182n15

representationalism, 20, 22

Reproductive Health Association of Cambodia (RHAC), 68

Res, Phasy, 175n39

Revolutionary Children's Hospital, 42

Reyum, 12

rien moel (to learn how to see), 110

Rith, Dr., 86

Rivkin-Fish, Michele, 89

Roberts, Elizabeth F. S., 164n21, 171n3

The Role of Women in the Reconstruction of the Country, 43–44

Rony, Fatimah Tobing, 19

Rottenburg, Richard, 54

Rouen, 13, 91–92

Royal Angkor Hospital, 174n22

Royal Ballet Corps, 35

Royal Rattanak Hospital, 174n22

Royal School of Medicine, 36

Royal Society of Medicine, 37

Royal University of Phnom Penh, 12, 108

Russia, 33, 35, 61, 89. *See also* Soviet Union (USSR)

Russian (language), 32, 111

Russian Hospital (Khmer-Soviet Friendship Hospital), 43–44, 94, 105, 108, 121, 162n10, 173n21; *Annals of the Khmer-Soviet Friendship Hospital*, 37–38, 40–41, 53, 153; founding of, 32–34, 153; and Leopard Capital, 51–52; and medical equipment, 26–27, 29–30, 35–36, 39–40, 46, 49–51, 53, 68, 154–55; and methodology of book, 12; and race, 95; ultrasound reports at, 2–3, 82, 98–99, 123*fig.*, 176n4; waiting rooms at, 1–2, 2*fig.*, 26, 45, 84*fig.*, 87, 91, 100–102, 102*fig.*, 104, 107, 123*fig.*

Sahlins, Marshall, 181n8

Sambath, 108–10, 178

Samnang, 100–101

Sam Rainsy, 179n27

Sanabria, Emilia, 9

San Danech, 162n8

Sangkum Reastr Niyum (1955–70), 28, 34, 37, 39–40, 43, 61, 76, 153, 166nn15–16, 167n20, 167n25–26, 167n30

sanitariums, 32, 40

Sanskrit (language), 47, 169n55

Sao Sreymao, 162n8

Saroun, 121–22, 180n33

Sa Sa Gallery, 12

Saunders, Barry, 106, 178n14

Schantz, Clémence, 122, 180n33, 182n17

science and technology studies (STS), 17, 22, 114, 164n18, 168n43; feminist, 8, 19, 25, 58, 79, 85, 105, 113

United Nations Transitional Authority in Cambodia (UNTAC, 1991–93), 12, 28, 45, 47, 51, 59, 61, 63, 75, 117, 154

United States, 20, 86, 95, 101, 168n35, 177n15, 182n18; bombing of Cambodia, 10, 41, 153; and Cambodian health care, 36–37, 49, 56, 169n57; corporations, 26; and COVID-19, 150; and development, 49, 52, 167n19, 169n58, 170n67; diplomatic relations with Cambodia, 153; medical training in, 45; ultrasound in, 10, 88, 126, 130, 172n9

University of Health Sciences (UHS), 73; Faculty of Medicine, 36, 41, 154

Uon Sabo, Dr., 69

US Centers for Disease Control and Prevention (CDC), 13

user fees, 48, 63, 65, 77, 88, 154, 173n17

US Food and Drug Administration, 129, 182n13

vaccines, 15–16, 31, 37, 125, 168n41, 175n35

Vandy, Dr., 101, 119, 122

Vann Molyvann, 108

variolation, 16

Vesselle, Dr., 178n14

Vichet, Dr., 81, 83

Vietcong, 40

Viet Nam, 10, 33*fig.*, 61, 81, 163n14, 170n60, 173n16, 177n17, 179n27, 180n29; and development, 52, 169n58; economy, 47–48, 51; Hanoi, 31–32, 180n2; health care in, 32, 55–56, 64, 88, 166n6, 172n9, 174n24; Ho Chi Minh City (formerly Saigon), 32, 142; imperial courts in, 15; invasion of Cambodia, 40, 43, 154, 170n69, 179n27; medical training in, 32, 36, 45, 60; and

postsocialism, 171n70; pronatalism in, 44; withdrawal from Cambodia, 45, 154

Vietnamese (language), 4*fig.*, 111, 142

visual-discursive surrealism, 29

visual studies, 19, 105; critical, 9, 114, 132; postcolonial, 25

Vorn Yoeub, 90

Vu, Professor, 73, 76

vulnerability, 3, 34, 71, 102, 120, 127, 150, 178n11

waiting rooms: at Maternal Hospital, 66, 89; and methodology of book, 12, 23, 80, 147; at Russian Hospital, 1–2, 2*fig.*, 26, 45, 84*fig.*, 87, 91, 100–102, 102*fig.*, 104, 107, 123*fig.*; at Sorphea VIP, 56, 82

Walker, Trent, 107

Water Festival (2010). *See* Bon Um Tuk (Water Festival)

Wat Langka, 115

Wat Phnom, 3

Wat Saravantejo, 117–18

ways of seeing, 105, 114, 120, 122, 124

Wheel of Law, 118

whiteness, 33*fig.*, 45, 56, 95, 97, 181n5; and colonialism, 5, 14, 31*fig.*, 124, 148

white supremacy, 19–20, 97, 164n18

Widyono, Benny, 51–52

World Bank, 52, 72–73, 156, 169n59, 173n16, 175n35

World Health Organization (WHO), 13, 29, 37, 49, 63, 150, 169n59, 173n16, 175nn34–35, 182n13

World War II, 32, 164n20

X-rays, 6, 16, 32, 33*fig.*, 45, 48, 101, 117; advertisements for, 4*fig.*, 147*fig.*; in the *Annals of the Khmer-Soviet Friendship Hospital*, 38–39; in *Cambodian*

Women in the Time of the Sangkum, 37–38, 38*fig.*; donation of machines, 23, 27, 29–30; and radiation, 24, 30, 112, 182n13; repair of machines, 43, 53, 168n43; in *The Role of Women in the Reconstruction of the Country*, 44; at Russian Hospital, 35, 99; in *Scientific System of Instruction under the Khmer Rouge*, 42; and ultrasound, 46, 112, 125, 182n13

yantra, 116, 119, 179n28
Yin Luoth, 132
yok chett tuk dak (to take care), 80, 84–87, 90, 94, 99, 102, 107
Yugoslavia, 167n19

Zucker, Eve, 86

Printed in the USA
CPSIA information can be obtained
at www.ICGtesting.com
LVHW092034181223
766777LV00004B/419